CONFLICT
IN THE
CAUCASUS

Georgia, Abkhazia
and the
Russian Shadow

About Authentic Voices

AUTHENTIC VOICES is a new series designed specifically to give a voice in the West to those writers and commentators now emerging from the former Communist Bloc.

For too long we have only heard the opinions of western journalists and foreign correspondents on the political, intellectual and cultural lives of this massive mixture of nations, races and creeds. And yet we are perhaps not much closer to understanding their feelings, thoughts and attitudes. We continue to be surpised and shocked by the events taking place in the countries of the former Soviet dictatorship and are sometimes too keen to criticise or dismiss them.

AUTHENTIC VOICES aims to give us the understanding and insight which only the Insider's View can provide. In these books, 'insiders' will voice their concerns, their opinions, their hopes. And although their use of language and expression may differ considerably from our own, the intention of this series is to keep as closely as possible to the original style, emphasis, and use of words.

The titles in this AUTHENTIC VOICES series will be carefully chosen for their relevance to world affairs, or for the kind of unique observations only the insider can provide. These books may seriously challenge accepted views; certainly they will be thought-provoking. We hope that you, the reader, will find them of considerable interest.

CONFLICT
IN THE
CAUCASUS

Georgia, Abkhazia
and the
Russian Shadow

by Svetlana Chervonnaya

Translated by Ariane Chanturia

GOTHIC IMAGE
PUBLICATIONS

First English language edition 1994 by
Gothic Image Publications
7 High Street, Glastonbury, Somerset BA6 9DP

ISBN 0 906362 30 X

Russian Edition: *Abkhazia-1992: Post Communisticheskaya Vendeya*
(Mosgorpechat 1993, Moskva)

Cover illustration by Lucy Willis

A catalogue record for this book is available from
the British Library

Printed and bound in Great Britain by
Butler & Tanner Ltd, Frome and London

Contents

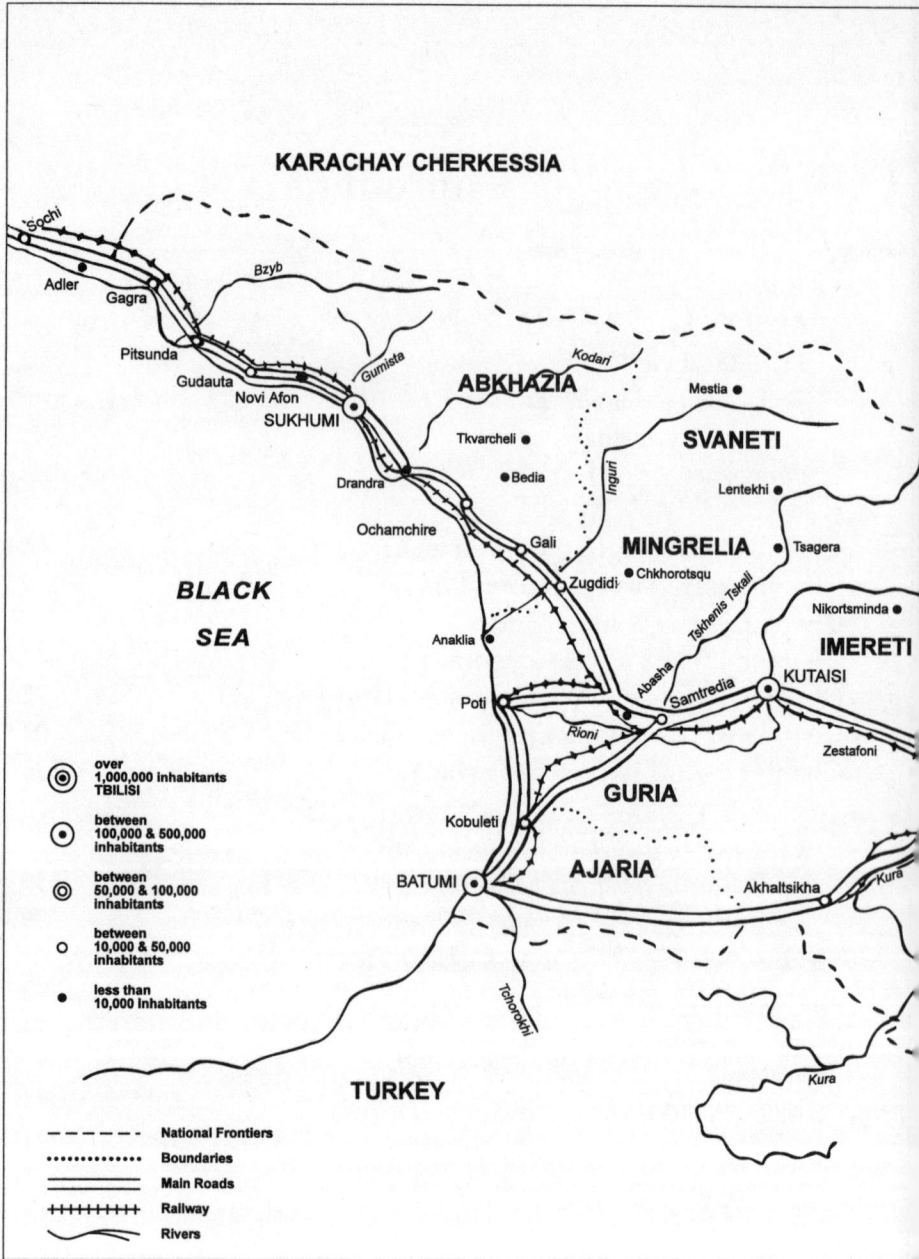

KARACHAY CHERKESSIA

Sochi

Adler

Gagra

Pitsunda

Gudauta

Novi Afon

SUKHUMI

Bzyb

Gumista

Kodari

ABKHAZIA

Mestia

Tkvarcheli

Bedia

SVANETI

Lentekhi

Drandra

Ochamchire

Gali

Inguri

MINGRELIA

Tsagera

Chkhorotsqu

Zugdidi

BLACK

SEA

Anaklia

Tskhenis Tskali

Nikortsminda

IMERETI

Abasha

Poti

Samtredia

KUTAISI

Rioni

Zestafoni

over
1,000,000 inhabitants
TBILISI

between
100,000 & 500,000
inhabitants

between
50,000 & 100,000
inhabitants

between
10,000 & 50,000
inhabitants

less than
10,000 inhabitants

GURIA

Kobuleti

BATUMI

AJARIA

Akhaltsikha

Kura

TURKEY

Tchorokhi

Kura

- - - - - National Frontiers

· · · · · · · · Boundaries

═══════ Main Roads

++++++++ Railway

〰〰〰 Rivers

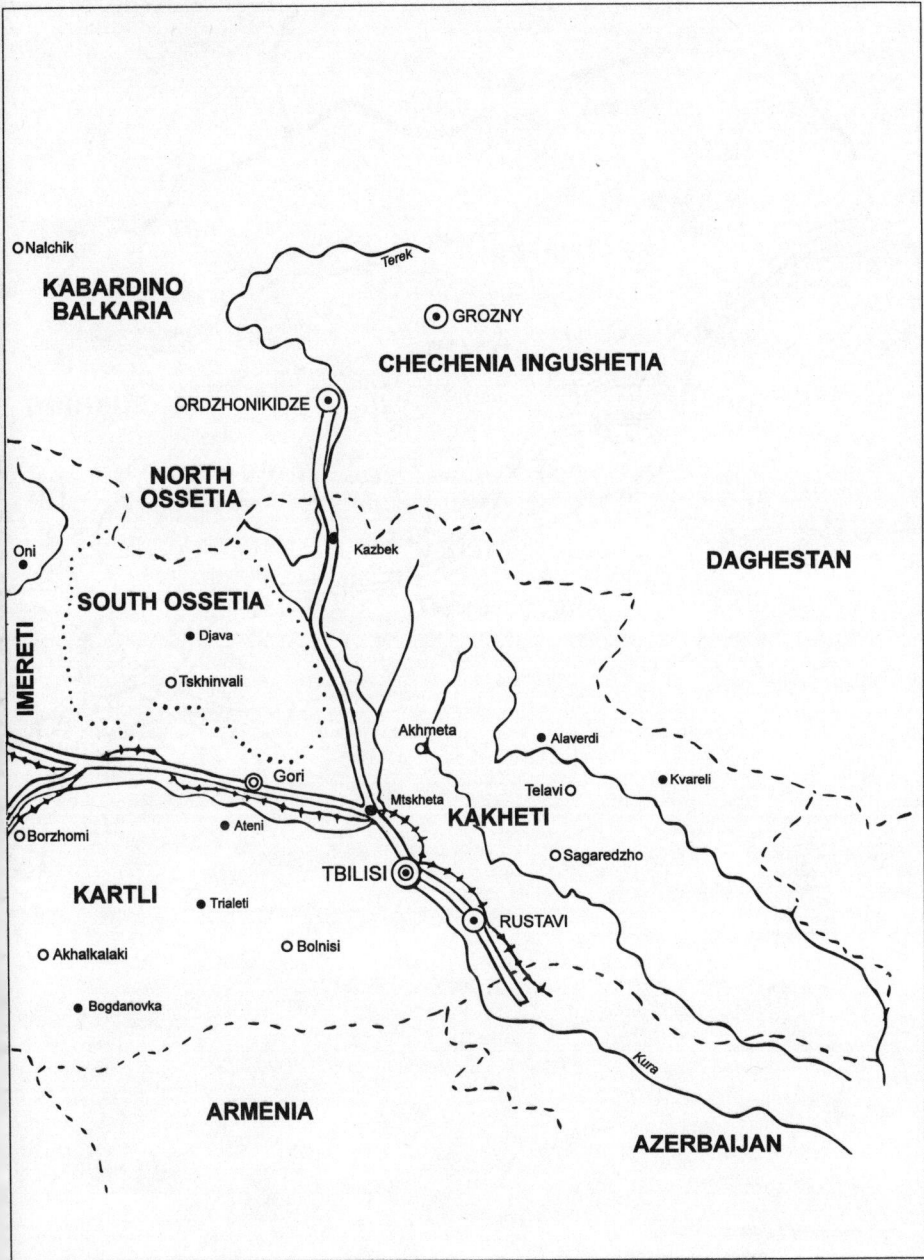

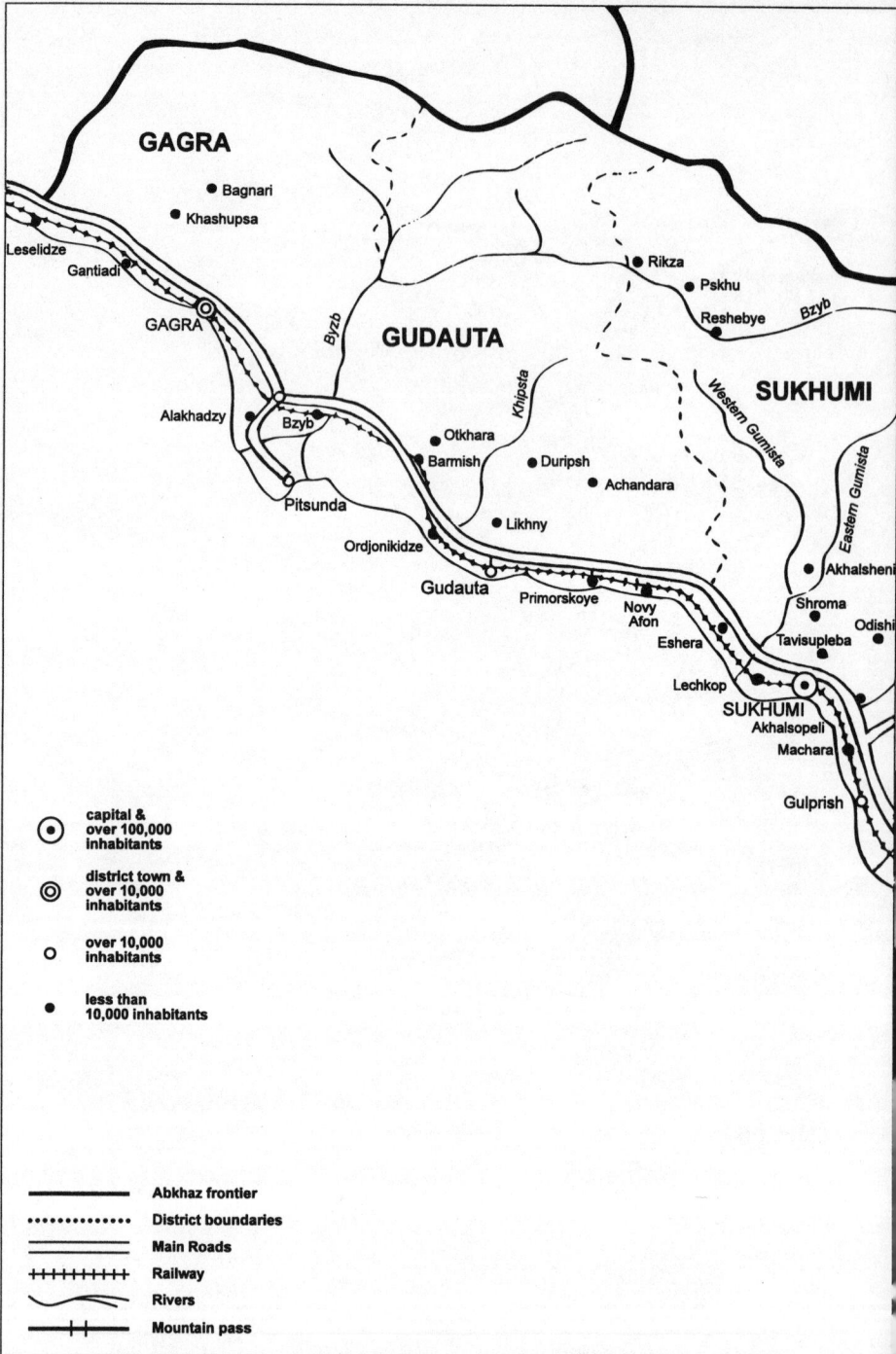

GAGRA

Bagnari

Khashupsa

Leselidze

Gantiadi

GAGRA

Rikza

Pskhu

Reshebye

Bzyb

Byzb

GUDAUTA

Khipsta

SUKHUMI

Western Gumista

Alakhadzy

Bzyb

Otkhara

Barmish

Duripsh

Achandara

Eastern Gumista

Pitsunda

Likhny

Ordjonikidze

Gudauta

Primorskoye

Novy Afon

Akhalsheni

Shroma

Odishi

Tavisupleba

Eshera

Lechkop

SUKHUMI

Akhalsopeli

Machara

Gulprish

capital &
over 100,000
inhabitants

district town &
over 10,000
inhabitants

over 10,000
inhabitants

less than
10,000 inhabitants

Abkhaz frontier

District boundaries

Main Roads

Railway

Rivers

Mountain pass

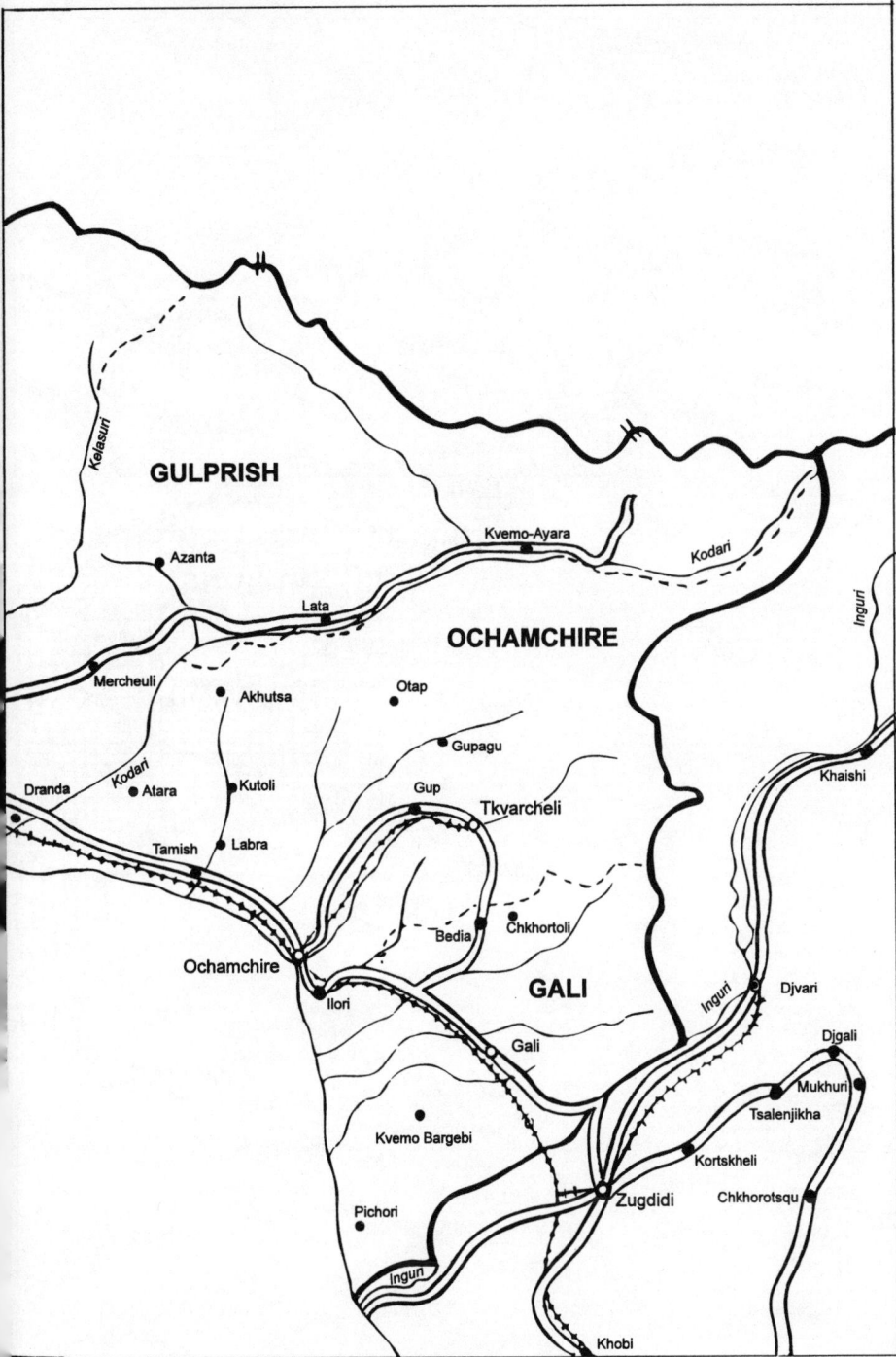

SKETCH MAP OF THE LANGUAGES

Kuban

Krasnodar

Stavropol

Belaia

Tchamlyk

Ouroup

Maikop

Laba

Cherkess

Touapse

KARACHAIS

KABARDIANS

Nalchik

Sotchi

BALKARS

OSSE

Gagra

Bzib

ABKHAZIANS

Inguri

SVANS

Sukhumi

Rioni

IMERULI

RATCHULI

OSSETI

BLACK SEA

MINGRELIANS

Koutaisk

KUTAISI

Tskhinvali

Gori

Poti

MTIULI

Batumi

AJARIA

Tchorokhi

Trabzon

T U R K E Y

Russian F.S.S.R.	■ Capital of S.S.R.
Armenian S.S.R.	▪ Capital of autonomous S.S.R.
Georgian S.S.R.	● Capital of autonomous Region
Azerbaijani S.S.R.	• Other towns

0   150 km

CASPIAN

SEA

Terek

● Grozny

CHECHENS

INGUSH

KUMYKS

Makhatchkala

Soulak

TIANS

Ordzhonikidze

DARGWA

DARGWA

● ANDI

Andi

BOLIKH

QARATA

Kolsou

GODOBERI

QUANADA

● KUNZAQ

TCHAMALA

● TINDI

KHEVSURULI

KHWARCHI

● AKHWAL

LAKS

QUBACI

ANS

TUSURI

AVARS

Kora Koisou

TABASSARANS

Derbent

PSAURI

QAPUCI

AVAR

● ARTCHI

AGULS

Alakhani

TCHAHURS

KURIS

KAKHURI

Samur

KHINALUG

● DJEK

Tbilisi ■

● BUDUKH

KARTLURI

Yora

INGILURI

OUDIS

Baku ■

AZERBAIJAN

A R M E N I A

Koura

Erevan ■

● Stepanakert

Araxes

■ Nakhichevan

IRAN

I R A N

SKETCH MAP OF THE CAUCASUS REPUBLICS 1989

CASPIAN SEA

Baku

AZERBAIJAN

Makhatchkala

Derbent

Samur

Koura

DAGHESTAN

Soulak

Kara Koïssou

Nagorny Karabakh AR

Stepanakert

Kirovabad

Lake Gotcha

Koïssou Avar

Koïssou Andi

Aladhani

Araxe

Terek

ARMENIA

NAKHICHEVAN

Grozny

Rustavi

Nakhichevan

NORTH OSSETIA

Ordzhonikidze

SOUTH OSSETIA AR

Tskhinvali

Tbilisi

Erevan

IRAN

KABARDINIA BALKARIA

Nalchik

GEORGIA

Kura

Karachai Cherkessia AR

Cherkess

AJARIA

Batumi

Ouroup

ABKHAZIA

Sukhumi

Ingouri

Rioni

Poti

TURKEY

Tchamlyk

Laba

Gagra

Kuban

Belaja

Sotchi

Adyghe AR

Maikop

Touapse

Krasnodar

BLACK SEA

Sea of Azov

150 km

0

xii

SKETCH MAP OF THE RUSSIAN CONQUEST OF THE CAUCASUS

CASPIAN SEA

BLACK SEA

Lake Van

Baku — 1806

AZERIS — 1805

AZERIS — 1813

KOUBAS — 1806

AZERIS — 1806

AND DAGHESTANIS

Derbent — 1806

KUMYKS — 1784

Makhatchkala — 1784

TATARS — 1723

DARGWA — 1830

LAKS

TABASSARANS — 1805

Samour

CHECHENS — 1859

INGUSH — 1801

Ordzhonikidze

KHAKASS

ARMENIANS OF KARABAKH

Stepanakert

Kirovabad — 1804

Kura

AZERIS — 1805

AZERIS — 1828

Nakhichevan

Araxes

OSSETIANS — 1806

KABARDIANS AND BALKARS — 1817

1825

Terek

1804

Rhioni

SVANS — 1858

1810

ABKHAZIANS

Sukhumi

1864

1829

ADYGHE

Kuban

Sochi

Novorossisk

GEORGIANS — 1801

Tbilisi

MINGRELIANS — 1803

GURIANS — 1804

Batumi

LAZ

Tchorokh

1878

ARMENIANS — 1828

Erevan

Kars

Russia in XVIII century

Expansion before 1806

Expansion between 1806-1929

Expansion between 1829-1878

Expansion between 1878-1914

Frontier of Russian Empire in 1878

Actual Frontiers of U.S.S.R.

0 — 150 km

List of Illustrations

From the Series Editor

This first book in the Series comes from the authentic inside voice of Svetlana Chervonnaya, a Russian academic and campaigner for minority ethnic rights in the former Soviet Union. As you will see, she is deeply concerned about the anti-democratic forces which are at work within the former Soviet Union. Her credentials could not be better, for she is neither Georgian nor Abkhazian and as an invited guest of the Slav Home in Abkhazia, she saw and heard at first hand how the conflict in the region developed.

This book was first published in booklet form in Moscow, 1993. It was circulated among politicians and parliamentarians in Moscow, but was never on sale in bookshops. The author is keen to point out that the book is not an academic treatise, but as the author told us 'a piece of journalism' written with emotion. But this is an academic's journalism and the book is also full of carefully researched fact and authoritative information.

Ariane Chanturia's skillful translation made this English edition possible. Clarifications and a certain amount of re-structuring have been necessary, but we have kept close to the original. We have also been fortunate to receive, at our request, Mr Shevardnadze's Foreword to this English edition.

Abkhazia is a particularly fascinating place among the rich variety of regions, races and languages of the Caucasus. It covers an area of 8600 square kilometres stretching from the Greater Caucasus range of mountains to the Black Sea coast where tea, tobacco and citrus fruits are grown in its subtropical climate. But it is an area full of contradititons with its deep roots in ancient history overlaid by a strong Russian presence. In a shifting alliance of Georgian states, Abkhazia has belonged to Colchis, Pontus, Rome and Byzantium, as well as to Turkey and Russia. In more recent times, it has become known as the Russian Riviera and its multitude of Soviet-style dachas, sanatoria and Trades Union holiday camps lining the coastal resorts, testify to its dominance by the Russians.

On my trips through the Caucasus, I had occasion to stay for periods of time in Georgia and Abkhazia just before the conflict erupted. Tremendous upheavals were afoot in Georgia itself, and in Abkhazia the tension was palpable. At last here is the book that explains to me what was really going on.

Frances Howard-Gordon

Preface to the English Edition

Georgia has a long, fascinating and often troubled history as a small country at the junction of neighbouring empires. Once again Georgia is in crisis: independence, longed for so desperately, greeted with such euphoria, has brought discord and war. Little illustrates better the complexity of the legacy left us by the collapse of the Soviet Union than the events of recent years in Georgia. In the West we talk of chaos and anarchy to describe a situation the causes of which we can only dimly perceive: a turmoil of warring factions with strange names jostling for control in a haze of accusation and counter-accusation. When the Abkhaz separatist movement flared into open conflict with Georgia, the war, in the very few reports that appeared in our media, was largely represented as the liberation struggle of one tiny nation against a larger and more powerful neighbour, a merely tribal affair, a local ethnic war.

In fact, matters were never so simple. After independence Georgia was beset by enormous internal problems, seriously compounded by the government under Zviad Gamsakhurdia, the first president in the post-communist era. Particularly, questions about the status of Abkhazia which had been festering for years, involving some deeply felt Abkhaz grievances and requiring considerable sensitivity, were mishandled, not to say wilfully inflamed. After 70 years of Soviet rule, bridges needed to be built but neither Georgians nor Abkhaz could manage this on their own with their institutions and infrastructure weakened and distorted as they were. Unhappily, the power struggles taking place within Russia herself reverberated here and the conflict deepened. For the post Soviet world is still one where the military needs and priorities of the old empire are being played out.

Dr Svetlana Chervonnaya demonstrates that whilst ethnic problems certainly existed, events which took place in Georgia were part of a deeply calculated and premeditated programme by certain elements within the Russian and Abkhazian political and military hierarchy. Her eye-witness account and unique access to documentary evidence show, for the first time, the depth of Russia's complicity in a programme of deliberate destabilisation. The hard-liners of the old regime are still at work within the lands of the former Soviet Union.

Abkhazia has always been important to Russia. The Caucasus were the scene of Tsarist Russia's longest colonial war and the whole area remains deeply engraved on the Russian psyche, in history and in literature. More particularly, Abkhazia became the playground of the communist elite. Here are the country cottages for the powerful, the dachas for the party faithful, the sanatoria, hotels and health resorts for the great and the good. And, of course, Abkhazia is strategically important with its ports on the Black Sea, especially now with the independence of Ukraine and difficulties in the Crimea. Could all this be left to the control of Abkhaz and of Georgians?

The conflict in Abkhazia was propelled by a Russian political agenda, a desire to maintain Russian influence against the perceived threat of an independent and democratic Georgia. The view that under Boris Yeltsin Russia has become a wholly benign force, ready to act as peace-keeper in troubled areas of the world, sits uneasily with evidence that shows Russia, or powerful elements within Russia, having a coherent strategy of intervention within the so-called independent countries of the former Soviet Union.

Though Chervonnaya's book stops before the outbreak of open war and the fall of Sukhumi to the separatists, it is important to put the preparations she describes into their present context. The result of the process of destabilisation which she anatomises was, quite simply, an act of 'ethnic cleansing' on a huge scale. Some 250,000 Georgians fled Abkhazia, many perished in the fighting in which there were acts of appalling barbarity, many died in the snows of the high mountain passes from hunger and cold during their flight. Such a huge transfer of people has not been seen since Stalin's time.

And how did 90,000 Abkhaz manage to force a quarter of a million Georgians from their homes? How did these 90,000 Abkhaz, or rather the militant group of separatists which claims to represent them, obtain the arsenal which enabled them to expel the Georgians and defeat their army? It is true that they had help from the North Caucasus, their forces joined by volunteers and mercenaries who identified with their cause. It is also true that internal Georgian feuding helped them too. But where did the fighter bombers come from and the gunships which enabled them to shell Sukhumi from the sea?

How do 90,000 get such resources and access to the necessary intelligence? Not from the export of oranges. There is only one great military power in the area.

Now the refugee problem in Georgia is acute and foreign aid agencies have set up offices in Tbilisi. The cost in human misery has been enormous. The situation is still tense, unresolved, with the Abkhazian separatists refusing to recognise the territorial integrity of Georgia, contrary to the demands of the UN Security Council, and Georgia refusing to recognise Abkhazia as a separate state. Russians, or rather troops of the CIS, are now acting as peace-keepers in the area with some 'observers' from the UN. They are also the sole suppliers of arms to both sides in the conflict. If it is to be at all possible to identify any long term solutions to the complex problems left by the break-up of the Soviet Union, with the inevitable future reliance of the world community on Russia's role as peace-keeper, then these events in Abkhazia need to be discussed, and are, indeed, of geo-political significance.

Eduard Shevardnadze has said that had Georgia not agreed, finally, to join the CIS, the country would have fallen apart, torn by civil war and separatist conflicts. But, of course, this means - to the despair of many Georgians - that the Russians are back. That was the price they had to pay for some of the weaponry promised them under the Tashkent agreement - the agreement on the distribution of military equipment after the break-up of the Soviet Union. With this they were able to quell the forces of the ex-President, Zviad Gamsakhurdia. And now Russia has, once more, large military bases throughout Georgia and, Russian troops still control the borders.

One major obstacle to any resolution of the problem is Russia's military involvement. Abkhazia is at present, de facto, a separate state, certainly no longer ruled from Tbilisi. We now know that Dr Chervonnaya's analysis of events leading up to the war has been substantiated by what has followed. The crucial peace agreement of 27 July 1993, which led to the withdrawal of Georgian forces and opened the way to the critical attack upon Sukhumi, was brokered by the Russians, and broken by the Abkhaz supported by elements of the Russian military. And the very people against whom Svetlana Chervonnaya has spoken out, are now in control of Abkhazia.

Tony Anderson
Editor

Acknowledgements

The publication of this book in England would not have been possible without the diligence and enthusiastic help of Nana Maraneli who first showed us the book. We would also like to thank: Zurab Revazishvili for his invaluable comments; Dr Tamara Dragadze for her advice and her good sense; Eliso for being such a helpful messenger; and particularly P.J. Hillery and his Georgian Chronicle for supplying much of the information for our Chronicle of Events, and also for his assistance with our many questions; and of course Oscar for his unstinting support.

Thanks are also due to Caryne Clark for her enthusiastic interest and encouragement and to the Network for Social Change for providing some of the funds to publish this book under the Caucasus Peace Project umbrella.

Foreword

According to an old definition, a good book is comprised of the best words arranged in the best order. I would add one more component to this: it must see the light of day at the best possible moment. Such is this book.

Over the last months I have had, unhappily, occasion to experience the feelings of a man under fire. Whoever follows the events which are taking place on the territory of the former Soviet Union, will understand that a multitude of armed conflicts have broken out after the collapse of the world's last empire. In this instance the conflict is in Abkhazia, one of the historic regions of my own country - Georgia.

The Georgians and Abkhazians have lived here since time immemorial. In this book, Svetlana Chervonnaya reveals the interwoven roots of this age-old common home. From time to time attempts have been made to separate us, and more often than not, this has happened at pivotal moments in Georgia's history.

I do not need to struggle to remember this. At the end of the seventies and the beginning of the eighties, I was leader of the Georgian Republic and there was considerable ethnic unrest at the time. Some highly placed politician in Moscow insisted that I should use force to solve the problem. I refused categorically. Instead, we started a peaceful dialogue, resulting in the expansion of Abkhazian autonomy with special consideration for the rights and interests of the Abkhazian minority. An Abkhazian University was opened, as were an Abkhazian TV channel and Abkhazian literary journals; measures were taken to develop the economy and culture. Abkhazians make up a little more than 17% of the population of the autonomous republic but were represented in the government - forming up to 80% of the political elite.

A new eruption of protest coincided with Georgia's independence and Abkhazia was used to light the fuse - just as it had been in 1918-

1921 after the collapse of the Russian Empire. Now, as the Soviet Union collapsed, the monster of separatism, of ethnic apartheid, reared its ugly head once more. However painful it is to admit, it began to devastate our country. But I believed and continue to believe that Georgians and Abkhazians have nothing to divide up, other than concerns about caring for this land. What has been destroyed by enmity can be resurrected by love. The time for this will come. And meanwhile we must pacify the monster and make quite clear who stands to gain in this war which is so ruinous for our people. Dr Chervonnaya, well-known for her academic works and her public defence of ethnic minorities, has written a book in which the real roots and causes of the Abkhazian conflict are laid bare.

From the very beginning the forces have been unequal. The army which backed the Abkhazian separatists, and then became involved in military action, is a lot more powerful than the army at my country's disposal. Svetlana Chervonnaya describes this collusion of forces in depth. She shows, too, that there was not only military collusion: the war was splashed across television and radio and across the pages of newspapers and magazines. It was a war of words, in which Georgia, with her humble means of disseminating information, suffered defeat after defeat. Why the conflict arose, what its origins were: all this was either kept secret from the public or was falsified. In Moscow, particularly, the cause of Abkhazian separatism received, to put it mildly, sympathetic propagandist support.

The circumstances in which the book was conceived will be revealed by the author. I would simply like to emphasise two points which are closely linked. First of all, the battleground was thoroughly prepared by an orchestrated stream of propaganda. It is said that when cannons are firing, the Muses fall silent, but here the Muse of History, Clio, has been deliberately perverted. Pseudo-historians with their pseudo-history have falsified the past and poisoned the present. The seeds of hatred have been intentionally sown. Dr Svetlana Chervonnaya, presenting an impressive amount of material, shows us how this was done.

Secondly, we now need to understand *why* this was done. Here again the author gives us an unambiguous answer and this is the major theme of her book. Her epilogue is dated 14 August 1992 - the day when the conflict in Abkhazia grew into an armed clash and then into the war which brought such incalculable suffering to our people. In this book neither the war itself, nor the many attempts to stop it, nor its dreadful consequences, are dwelt upon. These are not, here, the author's subject. But she has shown the danger which threatens not only the people of the former Soviet Union, but the whole world. The clear threat of the re-emergence of ultra-nationalism, of fascism, of neo-imperialist claims of right-wing forces in Russia, presents a grave danger to us all.

The author has dared to go where others have feared to tread and dared to write what others have been afraid to say. The publication of this book in English is without doubt both timely and essential.

Eduard Shevardnadze
February 1994

As for Abkhazian problems, I think, they have much in common with those faced by the whole country. A local twist - national colour - is present everywhere, but these problems are always deeply social and I do not see such a great national peculiarity...Unlawfulness, folly and venality have reigned in this country...and when a man is deprived of social dignity...it swells like a cancerous tumour...and a man begins to believe that if he is tried by a judge of his own nationality, he will try him more fairly.

Fazil Iskander
'Gulp of Oxygen'
Moskovsky Komsomolets, 21 May 1989

A totalitarian system leaves behind it a minefield built into both the country's social structure and the individual psychology of its citizens. And mines explode each time the system faces the danger of being dismantled and the country sees the prospect of genuine renewal.

Anatoly Sobchak
Mayor of St Petersburg

Chapter 1

'I thought they were mad'

The first pages of this book were formed in my mind and nurtured in my heart long before I was able to put them into their real context. Even after eleven months I cannot say that it has become completely clear how the Abkhazian conflict that started in August 1992 will end. I am afraid to look into the future for I cannot clearly see that end. Can anyone predict how many fates will be blighted, how many lives lost, human beings destroyed and fed into the furnace of this war to satisfy the ambitions of its perpetrators? And those führers in their comfortable mansions in Gudauta, what depth of ignominy will they finally heap upon the proud name of their tiny republic by their fatal decrees?

However, clarity has emerged and impels me to submit the evidence to public scrutiny. We can now draw some definite political and moral conclusions from the Abkhazian catastrophe. Indeed the scope of the crime that has been perpetrated, the aims and objectives of the ringleaders and their methods have all emerged into the light of day. It is this same clear light which now shines ruthlessly upon the tragic history of all our people.

I emphasise 'our people' and do not divide them according to their mother-tongues, nor blood, nor beliefs. For decades they shared a common grief together, be they Georgians, Abkhazians, Russians, Armenians, Greeks, Turks, Ossetians, or mountaineers of the Northern Caucasus. Many went through the rolling-mill of military conflict, others remained safe; but for all of them, for all the unfortunate Soviet peoples, the Abkhazian war is both tragic and shameful. Many made a truly heroic effort to escape from what I can only call the hell of Soviet Socialism; it cost lives, suffering, despair. But still the zealous *oprichniks* (*oprichina*: special administrative elite under Tsar Ivan the Terrible; also territory assigned to it.) of the Soviet regime make every effort to push the people back once more into the abyss.

The ethnic influences of my Russian, Tatar and Polish ancestors are deeply interwoven in my veins, but there is not a drop of Georgian nor of Abkhaz blood and not the thinnest thread that could connect me with any of the people of the Caucasus. Until 1992 I had never visited Georgia, I had never been before to Tbilisi, Batumi, Sukhumi or Tskhinvali. I have no distant relatives in any of these places. There is, therefore, no ground for any bias on my part. Perhaps it is difficult to judge current events in the Caucasus from the outside, but at the same time I feel that I can claim, as far as these things are possible, to be an impartial and objective observer. Traces of ancient Christian or Islamic culture in this land are of equal interest to me; the sounds of Abkhazian and Georgian speech equally melodious, though I lack knowledge of both. There was never any reason for me to predetermine my reaction to this conflict, no possible predisposition to favour one side or the other. Indeed one of the most important things I had to learn was that this was not merely a matter of two sides, a simple Georgian and Abkhazian interethnic problem; it was far more complex than that.

In the spring of 1992 the Abkhazian Society of Russian Culture - *the Slav Home* - asked for a specialist to be sent on an official mission to Sukhumi. They said that they wanted someone to study the existing situation in Abkhazia and to consult with them on various ethnic and cultural questions. They addressed their appeal to the institute in which I had just begun working, the Institute of Ethnology and Ethnic Anthropology of the Russian Academy of Sciences. The Slav Home had often looked to our institute for ideological allies and was always trying to broaden its sphere of influence. It had become, gradually, the idealogical headquarters of the powerful Abkhazian separatist movement.

Their immediate task was to provide ideological 'cover' for separatism by referring to the authority of Moscow scholars who had always evinced a special delicacy, interest and attention towards Abkhazian ethnic culture[1]. This may possibly have had something to do with the opportunity for pleasant holidays by the Black Sea that such interest gave rise to. Ethnographic expeditions were sent to Abkhazia annually and kind feelings for the Abkhazian national movement were openly declared. I had just written a book on the

Crimean Tatar National Movement[2] in which I had expressed considerable sympathy for the Tatar nationalists and, no doubt, my hosts at the Slav Home felt confident of a similar attitude towards their nationalist ambitions. Anyway, I gladly accepted the invitation though I then knew nothing of the situation in Abkhazia.

The dates were fixed and on 10 August 1992 I arrived at Adler airport where a government-run black Volga limousine was waiting for me. The Supreme Soviet of Abkhazia had sent a car to pick me up.

With a light and open heart, ready to support and understand the national movement of Abkhazia, which I was already picturing in a sort of heroic halo, I drove on along the memorable highway running between vineyards and orchards, by beaches so far not raked by fire. Houses were still intact, booths safely sold Georgian wines and Russian chocolate bars. Who could imagine that a few days later that very highway would become the first circle of hell for all those caught up in the war?

So when exactly did I begin to assemble the first lines and ideas for this book? What impelled me to write? It was when I found myself forced to flee from Abkhazia. I remember it started one scorching noon in Bombora, the Russian military airfield near Gudauta. The lieutenant on duty let me in after carefully studying my passport. Sure enough my Russian nationality and the right of permanent residence in Moscow, the so-called *propiska* (residence permit), were decisive as local residents and Georgian refugees from Abkhazia were refused entry by fraternal Russia. The lieutenant let me pass and waved me in the direction I should go: the two-kilometre walk to reach the take-off strip.

I was not the only one trying to escape. A launch from Sukhumi had brought a large group of holidaymakers from the Air Defence Sanatorium and other military health centres. Wounded were carefully lain on the ground and a major in command of evacuation ordered tarpaulin-covered corpses to be loaded into a military plane waiting for take-off to Moscow. The passengers who were already on board had to disembark and wait for the next flight. Though planes made shuttle flights - paratroopers to Gudauta in and refugees out - delays seemed poignantly long. One after another the planes landed and flew off to Taganrog, Klin, Ivanova, Adler and Moscow.

There was a huge crush of people trying to get out and by evening their number had increased. They came here on foot from the entire coast, carrying their children in their arms. There was no transport. Next to me an elderly Russian woman sobbed bitterly: she had failed to save her only daughter from a sniper's bullet, aimed from a multi-storey house next to the military sanatorium. This had happened in Sukhumi on August 15th. It now appears that by that time Boris Yeltsin had already intimated to Ardzinba, the leader of the Abkhaz separatist movement, that Russia would not intervene in any conflict on the territory of Georgia, especially as he then believed that Russian citizens living there were safe.

I do not know exactly who ordered the snipers to shoot at the holidaymakers at the Sukhumi military sanatorium. The only thing I saw with my own eyes was how they loaded the corpses onto those waiting planes on August 16th; and I heard with my own ears the sobbing of the old lady whose daughter had been killed.

And so I decided to write about this war, using nothing else but the facts as I could see them, the many documents I had access to and the eye-witness accounts of those caught up in the conflict. I had no idea where this tragic chain of events would lead me. I did not want to write a war chronicle, a journal of battles fought, a diary of death and destruction. What I wanted to discover was who had started this war, what were their objectives and against whom was it really directed.

I remember almost everything I was told in the spacious rooms of the Supreme Soviet of Abkhazia in those days immediately before the war. The rooms all had different door plates: Slav Home, Aidgylara, Human Rights Committee, names of other committees, departments, ministries. I met many different people; some were chary of words, others quite garrulous, some highly educated with courtly manners, others semi-literate. But Abkhazians were few among them. There were many Russians, mostly with the Muscovite or South Russian Cossack dialects. These leaders of Independent Abkhazia all spoke of one and the same thing. Their message was simple: the hour of action was drawing near; they would strike at Shevardnadze so hard that it would echo in Moscow; on the same aspen tree they would hang Shevardnadze, Yakovlev, Gorbachev and Yeltsin; before perestroika Abkhazia had been a communist paradise and they would fight to the end to restore the old order.

I did not assent, nor could I pretend to be sympathetic. I was terrified by them; I was indignant; I shouted at them. But they were not ashamed nor abashed, they were triumphant. They told me that everything was ready, that in half an hour the whole population could be under arms; that the depots were full of Russian weapons; that at any time they could double or treble their quantity; that as soon as war broke out the whole Caucasus and then all Russia would mobilise; that their emissaries abroad in Turkey and the Arab countries would help them; that the world would support them and those that did not would be treated accordingly. I thought they were mad.

An erudite doctor of History, the head of the Human Rights Committee, liked to discuss national topics with me: 'The goal of my life is to take Abkhazia away from Georgia. It is my scientific credo and I will never budge from it, the more so that it has never been so easily obtainable as it is now. There is only a thin Mingrelian line keeping us apart. Soon this will peter out and we shall have a head-on clash with our adversaries.'

'But this means that you are prepared to sacrifice other people's lives and the peace of this land in order to attain your ends', I said.

'You do not understand politics', said he. 'In the scheme of things this is of little importance. The main thing is to wrest Abkhazia from Georgia, annexe her to Russia and start a movement here which will only end with the revival of a great state. We cannot lose this historical chance.' (*Mingrelia, in the west of Georgia, was the home of Zviad Gamsakhurdia, the first President of post-communist Georgia, later deposed. His supporters continued to resist the new President, Eduard Shevardnadze, and thus Mingrelia became a buffer zone between Abkhazia and Georgia - Ed*).

That same evening, in Novy Afon, on the shore of the Black Sea, still calm and warm, a young Abkhazian and I were talking. His name was Alik and he worked as a life-guard at a boat station but had long since not been paid. He owned a pair of catamarans which he hired out. He had built himself a yacht in which he would sail to Turkey if war broke out. The story he told is well known to the residents of Novy Afon. He spoke thoughtfully and sadly: 'Those who hoisted the striped flag over the Supreme Soviet of Abkhazia never asked me about anything. I am an Abkhazian and, sure, I have my reasons for having a grudge against the Georgians, but I understand that today it is only possible to break out of the communist pen together with the new Georgia. All my hopes are pinned on Shevardnadze, but they have a savage hatred of him because he gave the Berlin Wall to the West and agreed to reductions in nuclear arms; because he defended the White House last year and presently wants to pull Georgia with its autonomies and peoples out of seventy years of filth.'

When I returned to Moscow, something happened that still seems to me incredible. All my endeavours to tell the truth about events in Abkhazia ran up against a brick wall. There was a total lack of understanding. People simply did not want to hear. They could not understand how the impression given out by the mass media corresponded to no reality, was so far from the truth. In the papers, on the radio and on TV, they constantly heard about Georgian imperialistic aggression against freedom-loving Abkhazia. I tried to explain that it was not Shevardnadze who started the war.

War was declared on the people of Georgia by Vladislav Ardzinba who, acting on his own separatist political agenda, was forcing the Abkhazian people into this terrible catastrophe. He had no legal or constitutional power to act as he did. His actions were quite plainly criminal: the illegal and forced total mobilization of all males aged between eighteen and forty-five; the unlawful arming of these recruits with weapons plundered from Russian armouries; the countless lawless actions of these armed units on the roads and in the towns and villages of Abkhazia with no enemy in sight and the resulting pogrom of searches, brazen marauding, plunder and bloody terror against a peaceful and unarmed Georgian population; the deliberate and provocative sniper fire against people holidaying at sanatoria in Sukhumi. For all these crimes responsibility must be taken and answers must be given. We now know the political aims of Ardzinba and his colleagues: the dismemberment of Georgia, the involvement of Russia in the war, the opportunity for Soviet-Communist revenge, with the eventual revival of the Soviet Union, extraordinary as this may seem.

But in Moscow no-one understood. A wise colleague, a man I respected, could only look at me thoughtfully and ask: 'But why are you against the Abkhazians? Are you perhaps a Georgian?' At the Scientific Council of the Institute where I, being agitated and confused, tried ardently to tell everyone what I had seen for myself in

Abkhazia, they condescendingly corrected me in the most extraordinary way: 'You are speaking of armed drunken men who, you allege, arranged checkpoints and then plundered those they stopped on the roads in Abkhazia. But for many years we took part in scholarly expeditions and we know that the Abkhazians cannot be drunk because they simply do not drink!' What could one say?

The bigwigs who assembled on 1 September 1992 for a round-table conference on the Abkhazian problem at the former Committee for the Defence of the Peace in Moscow, were indignant: 'For forty years Georgia has been oppressing Abkhazia'(G. Trapeznikov). 'Today the children of Abkhazia have not gone to school, their blood is on the hands of Shevardnadze' (V. Ivanov). 'When a brother sees that a brother is being killed, he does not ask a policeman for permission to go into another's premises. Fraternal people of the Northern Caucasus will come to the help of their Abkhazian brother' (M. Isaev). 'The time has come for great Russia to rise and take courageous Abkhazia to her bosom' (V. Kozhinov).

On the TV programme *Itogi*, Mikhail Chumalov talked of the 'fragile ethnic balance' in Abkhazia that had been 'violated' by the intervention of the State Council of Georgia. People in Russia have been the victims of rhetoric and disinformation. They have been misled. Let those who have ears hear, let those who have been deceived open their eyes!

I am not a novelist trying to create a great historical drama about the war in Abkhazia, nor am I a journalist trying to document every twist and turn in the tale. I cannot possibly cover all the vast historical, ethnocultural and political problems connected with Abkhaz-Georgian relations, nor even the general situation in the Caucasus. I must focus on what happened in Abkhazia and find out who is responsible for this war.

Obviously I can only give my version of events, but I have been scrupulous in trying to check and re-check every fact and all the sources of information I adduce. I want to express my gratitude to all those who gave me the courage to write this book, but also to express my ardent but probably vain hope for the tolerance of those of my friends and colleagues whose friendship and confidence I would not like to lose on account of political differences.

Chapter 2

History and Controversy

In this chapter I shall try to give a short review of the history of Abkhazia and Abkhazian-Georgian relations. No claims are made as to an in-depth study of the remote past nor as to any new discoveries.[3] However, I feel it necessary to express my own point of view about the cardinal issues of Abkhazian history over which fierce political controversies have been raging and, as far as possible, to dispel the mythology that surrounds it. So much contradictory nonsense has been touted as truth: the twenty five centuries of Abkhazian statehood; the dual aboriginality of the Abkhazians; Abkhazia is Russia; Abkhazians are Georgians[4]; Abkhazians came to Western Georgia in the 19th century; Abkhazians as bearers of Islamic fundamentalism; the wise Leninist national policy according to which Abkhazia should have been a union republic, and Stalin's pro-Georgian intrigues which turned the treaty-related Abkhazian republic into an autonomous one.

Early Times to 1917

The Abkhazian people (self-designation *Apsua*) constitute one of the most ancient autochthonous inhabitants of the eastern Black Sea littoral. According to the last All-Union census[5], within the Abkhazian ASSR, whose total population reached 537,000, the Abkhazians (93,267 in 1989) numbered just above 17% - an obvious ethnic minority.

With some difference in dialects (Abzhu - which forms the basis of the literary language, and Bzyb), and also in sub-ethnic groups (Abzhu; Gudauta, or Bzyb; Samurzaqano), ethnically, in social, cultural and psychological respects the Abkhazian people represent a historically formed stable community - a nation. The Abkhazian language belongs to the Abkhaz-Adyghe, north-western group of the Ibero-Caucasian language family. This group, along with Abkhazian, includes the Abazin, Adyghe, Kabardino-Circassian and Ubykh languages spoken by the kindred peoples of the Northern Caucasus: the Abazins, Adyghe, Kabardians, Circassians, and Shapsugh - united under the common name of Adyghe.

The language and ethnocultural closeness with the Adyghe does not mean any isolation of the Abkhazians from other peoples of the Northern Caucasus and Transcaucasia. From ancient times particularly close cultural and genetic ties linked the Abkhazians with Georgian tribes, their immediate neighbours in the eastern Black Sea littoral. This is confirmed by the archaeological remains of material culture (in particular, by the diffusion of the Colchian culture of the Bronze and Early Iron Ages throughout the territory of Western Georgia, including a large part of the present-day Abkhazian Autonomy), Georgian-Abkhazian ethnographic parallels, mutual borrowing of lexical and morphological elements in the languages, numerous coincidences in place names, etc. Even the earliest mention of the ancestors of the Abkhazians in Assyrian sources under the names of the tribe Abeshla (in the inscription of the Assyrian king Tiglath-pileser, 11th century B.C.) is found in immediate proximity with the listing of Georgian tribes Qulha (Colchians), Zevah (Jovah), Taochoi, etc. forming the mixed population of this region.

References to ancient Abkhazians (under the ethnonyms Abasgoi and Absili or Apsili) in classical authors, in particular Pliny the Younger, Arrian and other Roman sources of the first and second centuries, are also in permanent correlation with the listing of various tribes of Kartvelian origin (Mingrel-Chan and Svan). So, ancient Georgians lived with ancient Abkhazians on common land, engaging in complex ethnocultural interaction. The antiquity of origin and length of residence of the Abkhazians in this land is acknowledged by historical science: the idea that they are newcomers is out of the question. In the Abkhazian national mentality home is rightly felt to be this strip of rich land (8,600 square.kilometres.) between the Greater Caucasus Range and the Black Sea shore. It is bounded by the river Psou in the north-west and by the Inguri in the south-east, covering the woody slopes of the Caucasus mountains and the sub-tropical zone of the Kolkheti lowland, which, according to the administrative division of the USSR, was over the decades officially designated the Abkhazian ASSR (Autonomous Soviet Socialist Republic) within the Georgian SSR (Soviet Socialist Republic).

The right of the Abkhazians to consider this land to be their historical homeland - the ancient arena of their ethnogenesis - is beyond all question. However, any ideas that their ancestors were the only inhabitants of this land, and that there are no ancient roots of Georgian culture here, are absolutely erroneous and illusory.

The point is not only that the boundaries of the settlement of the Abkhazians in ancient times and throughout the Middle Ages were vague and transparent, but that they suffered considerable change and were eventually defined quite arbitrarily as the borders of the Abkhazian Soviet Socialist Republic. This claimed to be a state created on the basis of the right to national self-determination of the Abkhazian ethnos, though the Abkhazians constitute an ethnic minority on this territory.

In the Georgian national mentality this land is also rightly considered as their own territory, an organic part of the Georgian people who have lived here from time immemorial, formed their culture, gave their names to the mountains and rivers, towns and villages, fought side by side with the Abkhazian people against common enemies and were subject to common kings and princes. In the dramatic peripeteia of ancient and mediaeval history this, of course, did not rule out a shifting alignment of forces when related tribes and close neighbours fought against each other and argued over land, faith, crown and booty. Be that as it may, in 1917 on the territory of the future Abkhazian ASSR the Georgians totalled 42.1% of the local population, and the Abkhazians 21.4%. So, not only by virtue of historico-cultural association, but also ethnodemographically this land should be considered part of Georgia.

From the 6th century B.C. the territory of Abkhazia belonged to the most ancient Colchian kingdom of Western Transcaucasia, the heyday of which was in the 4th century B.C. This was the first attempt to unite all local tribes into a single ancient Georgian state. After the disintegration of the Colchian kingdom (2nd century BC), its territory became dismembered and its western lands of the Black Sea littoral, including Abkhazia, were captured by Mithradates VI, King of Pontus. Within the Pontic kingdom Abkhazia, like the rest of Western Georgia, in the 1st century B.C. became assimilated to Hellenistic culture which left here its vivid imprint and brought this region into contact with the northern Black Sea littoral and the Crimea.

(The Kingdom of Bosporus also became part of the Kingdom of Pontus at the end of the 2nd century B.C.) Eventually the Greeks were replaced by Roman legionaries, and already in 64 B.C. the lands of Abkhazia and Colchis together with the Pontic kingdom found themselves within the Roman Empire.

The local tribes waged a persistent struggle against Roman domination. Among the first to secede from the eastern provinces of the Roman Empire was Western Georgia where, at the end of the 4th century A.D., the Kingdom of Lazica (or Egrisi) came into being, comprising the territory of present-day Abkhazia and Ajaria (Atchara). Ancient Georgian tribes, known under the name of Laz, were by no means the only inhabitants of this multitribal and multilingual state. Unfolding in an endless struggle and with frequent wars both with late Rome and with the new powerful empires of Byzantium and Sasanid Iran, which sought to extend their domination to the eastern Black Sea area, the dramatic history of Lazica was a common landmark in the process of the becoming of both Georgian and Abkhazian statehood and early Christian culture. However, the processes of the diffusion of Christianity among the peoples of the Transcaucasus were not absolutely synchronous. Georgia is considered as having become christianized from 337, and Abkhazia much later - from 523.[6]

In the sixth and seventh centuries Western Georgia together with Abkhazia was within Byzantium and was actually the arena of incessant wars: between Byzantium and Iran for dominance on these lands, between the confederated local tribes and their Constantinople rulers, and between the warriors of the Caliphate invading the Caucasus and the forces opposing them such as the Khazars. At times the Arabs concluded temporary alliances but these soon broke up.

Towards the 730s an early feudal Abkhazian principality was formed as a stable union of Abkhazian and Georgian tribes. This principality consolidated its power in the battle of Anakopia (736), which put an end to Arab aggression. At the end of the eighth century the Abkhazian state freed itself from Byzantine vassalage, and the Abkhazian prince Leon II received the title of Abkhazian king (with the active help of the Khazar Khanate with which Leon was related through family kinship: his mother was the daughter of the Khazar Khan). The Abkhazian kingdom comprised the entire territory of Western Georgia, including Lazica. Its population was made up of

Abkhazian (the minority) and Kartvelian Georgian tribes (the majority: the Laz, Mingrels and Svans). At this period these tribes respectively contributed to the formation of the Abkhazian and Georgian nationalities. The capital of the kingdom was Kutaisi, and the whole territory extending from Nikopsia in the north to the Tchorokhi (in modern Ajaria) in the south, and from the Black Sea in the west to the Likhi (Surami) Range in the east. It was divided into eight principalities - Saeristavos: Abkhazian, Tskhumi (the old Georgian name of Sukhumi), Bedian, Svan, Racha-Takverian, Gurian, Kutaisian and Shorapanian.

The Abkhazian kingdom reached its acme in the ninth and tenth centuries (under Giorgi II and Leon III), becoming a powerful united state, polyethnic in population, with a prevalence of Georgians and Abkhazians - and a developed feudal society with a high culture. As correctly stressed by Stanislav Lakoba, referring to the studies of Academician G.A. Melikishvili: 'the kings of Abkhazia carried on active constructional work, erecting numerous churches, including those in western Georgia (Martvili) and even in southern Georgia (Kumordo) ... ; the capital of the Abkhazian kingdom, Kutaisi, became the capital of united Georgia, retaining this status for more than a century ...'[7]

In 978, after the death of the childless Teodosi, the dynasty of the Abkhazian kings and the kingdom of Abkhazia came to an end. However, the development of Abkhazian culture and statehood naturally continued within the broader, united Georgian state. The first to come to the throne was Bagrat III Bagrationi (978-1014) whose father was Georgian and mother Abkhazian, sister of Teodosi. Subsequently, throughout the Middle Ages, the process of the integration of Abkhazia and Georgia intensified in the political, economic, military and cultural aspects. It became traditional to conduct joint military campaigns of the Abkhazians and Georgians against aggressions threatening the Georgian kingdom, coming from the Seljuk Sultanate (the battle of Basiani 1205), the Abbasid Caliphate, and - with the expansion westward of the Empire of Genghis Khan and the Genghisids - from the Tatar-Mongol hordes whose invasion created a threat to the Christian civilization of Transcaucasia.

In the fifteenth century, Georgia, weakened by cruel feudal wars, disintegrated into several kingdoms and principalities (Kartli,

Kakheti, Imereti, Samtskhe-Saatabago, Mingrelia, Guria and
Abkhazia) which became the object of rivalry and wars between the
Shah's Iran and the Sultan's Turkey (16th-18th centuries). After a short
period of prosperity for the independent principality of Sabediano
(1470-1475) uniting Mingrelia (Odishi principality), Guria and a con-
siderable part of Abkhazia, Abkhazia came under the dependence of
Turkey and for almost 300 years (15th-18th centuries) was under the
Sultan's rule within the Ottoman Empire.

Three centuries of Turkish rule failed to break the primordial historical ties of Georgia and Abkhazia. Even the spread of Islam in
Abkhazia did not become a barrier to Georgian-Abkhazian cultural
and historical unity. Georgia, where Islam penetrated, affecting part
of the Georgian ethnos proper (Georgian Ajaria as well as the south
of the country: Meskhet-Javakheti), and some of the peoples and national groups settled there (Azerbaijanis, Turks, Tatars) did not show
religious intolerance towards the heterodox-Muslims or any other
religious minorities. As to the Abkhazians, the new religion did not
have a profound effect on their culture and national self-conscious-
ness. Characteristically, the article *Abkhazians* in the encyclopaedia
Narody Mira gives the following note: 'Believers: Muslim-Sunnites
and Orthodox Christians'.[8]

Actually, orthodox Christians are relatively few, and the mass
spread of Islam began as far back as the Tatar-Mongol period with
the penetration of the Golden Horde influence and the Empire of the
Timurids (14th-15th centuries). It gained force in the fifteenth to eighteenth centuries when Abkhazia was under the rule of the Ottoman
Empire and was completed during the Caucasian war and the Mahajir
movement (mass emigration of Muslim Abkhaz during the nineteenth
century under Tsarist rule. This altered considerably the demographic
balance in the area.) However, there has always been an indifference
towards religion in general - a rather rare phenomenon in the East.
Characteristically enough, there are actually no significant monuments of Islamic architecture on Abkhazian territory, though they
abound in the neighbouring Northern Caucasus, the Crimea and even
the Middle Volga Area (Bulgary, Kazan), to say nothing of such regions as Azerbaijan and Central Asia. The percentage of active believers among the Abkhazian population is very low. Suffice it to
say, for example, that in Sukhumi, the capital of Abkhazia, for more

than half a century there has never been a single functioning mosque, and nobody worried about it. Generally speaking, the Abkhazians could be considered heathen-pantheists rather than monotheist-Muslims or Christians.[10]

It is safe to say that the Abkhazians do not feel any particular 'co-religionist' closeness either to their Christian neighbours (Georgians, Greeks, Armenians, Russians and particularly Cossacks who appeared in the Caucasus in the 19th century), nor to their Muslim neighbours (Turks, Crimean Tatars, Azerbaijanis, and peoples of the Northern Caucasus). All demonstrations of solidarity or division occurred here, at least over recent centuries, on any other basis save religion. The religious division of most Abkhazians (Muslims) and most Georgians (Christians) did not lead to a rupture of their long-standing and stable ethnocultural ties or to any other political complications.

The fate of Abkhazia and Georgia in face of the spread of the power of the Russian Empire in the Caucasus proved to be common. They entered this Empire stage by stage with the conclusion by the Russian autocracy of separate treaties with local kings and princes. These were often then broken by the Russians as, for example, the shameless breach of the terms and principles of the 1783 Treaty of Georgievsk. The annexation of Georgia was carried out in parts, these colonial seizures being screened by a seemingly voluntary incorporation of separate territories into Russia. Elements of voluntariness did occur at all levels - from the ruling elite to the popular masses - for hopes were still alive that it would be easier with the Russians, and that the white Tsar would liberate them from the Turkish yoke and the imminent threat of Persian conquests. Nevertheless, this was a common and equally sad fate for both Abkhazians and Georgians. They could not withstand the onslaught of the Russian Empire and the conquest of the Caucasus.

The ideologues of anti-Georgian political movements in Abkhazia, and primarily the leaders of the Slav Home, are particularly fond of stressing that Abkhazia joined Russia in the nineteenth century independently of Georgia and voluntarily. In his *Essays on the Political History of Abkhazia* Stanislav Lakoba writes in this connection: 'As regards the Abkhazian principality (excepting the free Abkhazian communities of Aibga, Pskhu, Dal, Tsabal, etc.), it entered the patronage of the Russian Empire on February 17, 1810, as an independent state political unit. The Emperor Alexander I royally endorsed on that day "the points of appeal of the Abkhazian sovereign prince" the first of which reads: "I, the legitimate heir and sovereign of Abkhazia... am becoming the subject and entering the service as a hereditary subject of the All-gracious Autocrat of all Russia ..." Thus, from 1810 to 1864 the Abkhazian principality was part of the Russian Empire with the status of autonomy.[11]

Voronov builds an entire historico-mythological structure on the theme of a Russian-Abkhazian idyll. 'Slavic-Russian presence in Abkhazia', he writes, 'is attested from the 6th century A.D. Appropriate contacts developed after 965, with the establishment of the Tmutarakan principality in the north-western Caucasus. The Abkhazians supported Yuri Bogolyubski at the end of the 12th century; mediaeval Novgorod women of fashion combed their hair with combs of Abkhazian boxwood' (some historical argument!). In the sixteenth to seventeenth centuries the Abkhazians rendered assistance to the Zaporozhye and Don Cossacks in their inroads into Turkey. The commencement of the process of talks on Abkhazia's entry under Russian protection and the participation of the Abkhazians in the actions of Russian troops date back to the beginning of the 1770s. In 1806 the sovereign prince of Abkhazia, Keleshbei Shervashidze, resumed talks on Abkhazia's entry under Russian protection which soon cost him his life. In 1810 the Emperor Alexander I granted an investiture charter to Keleshbei's son Giorgi, according to which Abkhazia came under 'the supreme protection, power and defence of the Russian Empire'. The Abkhazian autonomous principality, transformed into the Sukhumi department in the 1860s, then into a district, was under Russian administration till 1917.[12] Thus in a nonsense version of history Abkhazia was under the power and protection (of Russia), and there were no national tragedies, no Mahajir movement, no national-liberation struggle of the Abkhazians with Tsarism, only the tenderest Slavic-Russian presence, a peaceful process of talks, and the unity of the Russians and Abkhazians in military actions. Zurab Achba borders on political delirium when he declares: 'Abkhazia is Russia. We can produce documents. Being a free and independent state we entered Russia in 1810. And we have never changed our choice...I was baptized by an old Russian woman named Manya... According to the constitution of 1925 the state language of Abkhazia became Russian...'[13]

This version of history which presents the incorporation of Abkhazia into Russia as an act of historical progress that put an end to the Turkish yoke and liberated the Abkhazians from a constant fear of invaders is developed by the authors of *Ethnopolis*[14], published by the Supreme Soviet of the Russian Federation.

It is necessary to shatter this myth and lay stress on the fact that there was no voluntary, progressive, independent-from-Georgia joining of Abkhazia to Russia; furthermore there was no autonomous Abkhazian principality within the Russian Empire. The conquest of the Caucasus was part of the colonial policy of the Russian Empire and various means were used in this policy, ranging from the exercise of military power to diplomatic deception and comical acts of bequeathing or presenting lands and bribing princes and nobles, the vast population having nothing at all to do with any of this. Dismembering the states to be annexed, playing on the clan, religious, dynastic and other contradictions, and seeking to set Christian and Muslim peoples against each other, Russian autocracy advanced in the Transcaucasus slowly, step by step annexing lands and countries, conquering its peoples, constantly alternating bloody violence with promises and acts of royal charity and tenderness to the new loyal subjects. Russia did not manage to annexe Georgia straightaway, the same being true of Azerbaijan and the Northern Caucasus. She had to crack and grab Georgia in parts: the kingdoms of Kartli and Kakheti in 1804 - the Kingdom of Imereti and the Gurian principality in 1810 - the Abkhazian principality, and only in 1878 - Ajaria (Batumi district) was wrested from Turkey and made part of Russia. At the same time expulsion began of Muslims residing on lands from Kars to Batumi. Georgia did not cease to be Georgia because of this, and the tragedies of all the peoples incorporated and subjugated by the Russian autocracy differed very little from one another. For the Abkhazian people this incorporation did not mean a mythical liberation from a constant fear of invaders, for it had not lived in constant fear, and its history was quite different until the beginning of the nineteenth century. Nor did it bring illusory autonomy (autonomy was out of the question in autocratic Russia), but the most brutal economic oppression, and moral and political humiliation. Not wishing to endure this condition, the Abkhazian people responded to the attempt at bringing it into the citizenship of the all-gracious autocrat by taking part in the Caucasian war and, after its defeat, by the mass tragic exodus of the Mahajir movement when thousands of Abkhazians left for exile in Turkey.

'This famous Caucasian war', writes A. Avtorkhanov, 'began back in 1817 and ended ... in the capture of the outstanding commander the Imam Shamil. No other war of conquest of alien peoples cost Russia so many casualties as the Caucasian war, and its duration (55 years) is in general unprecedented in the history of colonial wars. It began under Alexander I, continued throughout the reign of Nicholas I, and ended only under Alexander II.'[15]

In his work *Russia as a Multinational Empire*, Andreas Kappeler brings to light the real purposes of Russian autocratic colonial policy in the Transcaucasus which was considered to be 'a colony inhabited by uncivilized asiatics' and which, according to the 1873 decision of the Imperial State Council, was to form a single body with Russia and to bring the local population to a point at which it spoke Russian, and thought and felt in Russian. He emphasizes the exceptional importance of the 'protracted war of the freedom-loving peoples of the Caucasus against the attempt to dominate them ('the fact that small Muslim peoples waged such a long war with the mighty Russian giant became a symbol of anti-colonial resistance for many years - up to the Afghan war of the recent past'). Kappeler notes that whereas in the war headed by Shamil, Chechnia, Daghestan and Ingushetia were his main support, the peoples of the Adyghe community (Circassians) did not share their Islamic fanaticism and were not in a hurry to rally to the banner of the Hazawat or holy war against the infidels. After the defeat and capture (1859) of Shamil, when the resistance of the Eastern Caucasus seemed to have been crushed, the Russian colonisers had to face an enhanced resistance of the Circassians or, to be more precise, all the peoples of the Adyghe-Kabardino-Abkhazian community in the Western Caucasus.' Acting to some degree independently from Shamil and sharing muridism and its postulates only to a small extent, Circassian tribes nevertheless offered successful armed resistance to the Russian troops for decades. They relied on support from Ottoman Turkey with which they had long-standing links. Having defeated Shamil, Russia brought her entire brutal power to bear on the Circassians, and from 1864 she controlled the whole Caucasus, including its western edge. Populating the

Black Sea Coast and the fertile foothills of the Caucasus with Christian colonists, Russia destroyed the Circassians and drove them from their native lands. Some of them were exiled, others fled from Russian domination and emigrated voluntarily. In the 1860s-1870s, almost all the surviving Circassians (at least 300,000) emigrated to the Ottoman Empire. In 1897, there were 44,746 Circassians left in Russia.(According to other sources, the number of the Circassians that emigrated in 1860 reached two million.) The majority of Abkhazians linguistically related to the Circassians also emigrated to the Ottoman Empire. This emigration occurred in several waves during the nineteenth century... It was a tragedy which in a certain respect anticipated the forced deportation of peoples in the twentieth century.'[16]

Both the Georgians and the Abkhazians reacted to this strengthening of autocratic, social and national oppression with revolts, peasant uprisings, and political disturbances (the revolt in Abkhazia or Lykhny in 1866, which was cruelly suppressed by the tsarist troops under the command of the Governor-General of Kutaisi - Svyatopolk Mirsky). Mass actions of the Abkhazians in support of Turkey during the Russo-Turkish war of 1877-1878 caused fresh brutal repressions: by Royal Decree of 31 May 1880 the entire Abkhazian people were officially declared guilty, and thousands of Abkhazians were exiled to eastern and northern provinces of Russia, the wave of Mahajirs reaching 50,000. Central Abkhazia from the Kodori river to the Psyrtskha was almost completely deserted, as well as the lands once populated by Abkhazians in the Adler, Gagra, Sukhumi, and Gulripsh districts.

Furthermore, as noted by contemporaries, 'there was an order that Abkhazians should not settle in places between the rivers Kodori and Psyrtskha'. *The Memorandum on the Colonization in the Sukhumi District*, drawn up by its commander Colonel Brakker in 1895, clearly shows for whom these lands were intended. The memorandum reads: 'It is desirable to save as much free land as possible for the settlement of exclusively native Russian people.'[17] A little earlier Alexander II endorsed the plan drawn up by his Vice Regent in the Caucasus, Prince Michael Romanov, which envisaged the settling of the territory from the mouth of the Kuban to the river Inguri by Cossacks.[18] So much for the close historic ties unifying Russia and Abkhazia.

Not a trace was left of the illusory independence of the Abkhazian principality, the last sovereign of which in 1823-1864 was Prince Mikheil Sharvashidze (Chachba), a representative of an ancient Abkhazian aristocratic family. He had been granted the rank of general for his outstanding service to the Emperor. Georgia was divided into Tiflis and Kutaisi gubernias (provinces). In 1864 the Abkhazian principality was renamed as the Sukhumi military department. Broadened in 1868 through the inclusion of Pitsunda and Ochamchire districts, it existed till 1893 when it was transformed into the Sukhumi military district and was included in the Kutaisi military governorship. From 1904 till 1917 Gagra and its environs were excluded from the Sukhumi military district and subjected to the Sochi military district of the Black Sea coast province on the initiative of Prince Oldenburg, a relative of the Emperor. The concept of Abkhazia was restored only after the overthrow of tsarism and the disintegration of the Russian Empire.

It should be stressed that from ancient times Abkhazia emerged as a constituent part of Georgia. The ethnic Abkhazians as well as the Kartvelian tribes proper (the Karts, Egrians, Svans, and others) made a contribution to the birth of Georgian culture and statehood - common and unitary for this region. The integration of Abkhazia with other territories was due to geopolitical conditions and to the interests of the peoples. Here reference is not to a union of two different states isolated and opposed to each other. If small Abkhazia, occupying a narrow strip of the Black Sea littoral, had become a barrier to the powerful state drive of Georgia to the Black Sea, she might have been crushed by that larger and stronger state. However, in union with Georgia, Abkhazia preserved her ethnohistorical space and identity. Since ancient times all this land has been the zone of contact of the Georgian and Abkhazian ethnoses (tribes, nationalities, nations in the making). Historically the culture of the region was formed as a Georgian national culture with many common principles and parameters, despite the linguistic and religious peculiarities of the peoples inhabiting it.[19]

The Abkhazian Kingdom of the ninth and tenth centuries and the united Georgian Kingdom, experiencing its heyday in the eleventh and twelfth centuries, were, irrespective of the change of dynasties, structures of Georgian statehood. The tragedy of Georgia's disintegration into separate feudal principalities was a common tragedy of both the Georgian and Abkhazian peoples, for the disintegration was followed by attacks of enemies, predatory wars, occupation, break up of the common cultural zone, gradual annexation and finally colonization with all its tragic consequences including mass repressions and deportations. Both big and small nations in the Caucasus, Muslims and Orthodox believers, mountaineers and plainsmen, became victims of Russian autocratic colonial policy and Russian imperialism, hypocritically covering its real aims under its civilising or Christian missionary activities.

In this common calamity neither the Abkhazians nor the Georgians had any advantage over each other, nor is there any moral foundation to calculations of who fell victim to deceit or aggression earlier or later, who suffered more and who less.

1917 to 1931

The fate of the Abkhazians, Georgians and other peoples of the Caucasus was roughly the same. Even after the Revolution of 1917 the first sigh of hope, a brief dawn of freedom, and attempts at self-determination were followed by bloody Bolshevik terror. The Bolsheviks were particularly merciless to their flesh and blood and their close neighbours. Lavrenti Beria, who hailed from Mingrelia, Western Georgia, destroyed on his own initiative more than ten thousand of his fellow-countrymen, Mingrelians, and annihilated the pick of the Abkhazian nation, including its Bolshevik leadership of the 1920s and early 1930s, headed by Nestor Lakoba. For several decades the Georgian and Abkhazian peoples equally came under the grip of the Soviet empire with its operetta autonomies and Soviet republics deprived of real rights of self-determination.

Abkhazia had her own hell in this common nightmare - perhaps not the most terrible if one recalls the harder fate of the deported, punished peoples. However, this was small consolation for the people whose bitter resentments and national suffering accumulated over the decades. And this is the system to which the Abkhazian separatists wish to belong!

The most absurd thing to do is to represent the Soviet period in the history of Abkhazia in terms of the vulgar scheme proposed by Voronov: at first 'on the ruins of the Russian state system and culture (though unbelievable, it reads so!) there arose the Georgian Democratic Republic. The latter immediately occupied Abkhazia, the occupation lasting from 1918 till 1921. Then the Russian Red Army liberated Abkhazia, and the republic of peasants and workers, liberated in this way, acquired the status first of an independent, then of a sovereign Soviet socialist republic linked with treaty-based relations to Georgia. But Joseph Stalin began to hatch malicious and cunning intrigues against the Abkhazians from Moscow and, under his pressure, Abkhazia was included in the Georgian SSR as an autonomous republic.'[20] This kind of history is just incredible.

In reality the overthrow of tsarism and the Russian February Revolution of 1917 gave a powerful impetus to the rise of the national-liberation movements of all the peoples of the former empire. In the Sukhumi district on 10 March 1917 a Committee of national security, headed by Prince Shervashidze, was set up. New bodies of the Provisional Government, soviets of deputies (representatives) as well as national movements, parties and unions came into existence everywhere, to be the Union of the United Mountaineers of the Caucasus, founded in May 1917 at the First Congress of Mountaineers in Vladikavkaz. These bodies were formed by the revolutionary energy of the masses and their striving to break away from the grip of the empire and to find new forms of their own statehood. The Sukhumi Committee of National Security conducted its activities in contact with the democratic organisations of Georgia and Russia. In particular they showed considerable interest in the Union of the United Mountaineers of the Caucasus. The Abkhazian delegation attended the congress at the aul of Khakurinokhabl near Maikop in August 1917, where 'the question of the attitude of the mountaineers of Kuban region to the Abkhazian people' was considered; and in October 1917 the delegation was in Vladikavkaz where the setting up of the South-Eastern Union of Cossack Troops and the Mountaineers of the Caucasus and Free Peoples of the Steppes was announced.

On 8 November 1917 the Abkhazian People's Soviet was formed at a congress of the representatives of the Abkhazian people in Sukhumi. In the Declaration adopted at the congress the task was given to this Soviet 'to carry on work towards the self-determination of the Abkhazian people.' The concrete forms of such self-determination were not yet specified. Meanwhile the October coup in Petrograd and the Red Terror launched by the Bolsheviks created a palpable threat to democratic reforms in all regions of the country.

The Transcaucasian Sejm (under the chairmanship of N.S. Chkheidze) convened in Tiflis (now Tbilisi) on 10 February 1918 and, expressing the interests of all the peoples of this region, Abkhazia included,[21] adhered to the policy of establishing the Transcaucasian Federal Republic, independent of Russia: the Republic was proclaimed on 22 April 1918.

However, Abkhazia was one of the first regions in Transcaucasia to arouse an insatiable appetite in the Kremlin leaders and strategists of the 'World Proletarian Revolution', and to come under the attack of the Bolsheviks. She had to live through her first 'cursed days' as early as 16-21 February 1918, when the Military Revolutionary Committee headed by Efrem Eshba seized power in Sukhumi. The brutality and excesses committed by the Revolutionary Black Sea sailors (from the battle-cruiser *Dakia* and the torpedo-boat *Derzkii*) made the inhabitants of the sea-shore shudder with horror. The first attempt to establish Soviet Rule was brought to nought by the Abkhazian People's Council which demanded the liquidation of the illegitimate Military Revolutionary Committee.

In the spring of 1918 the Bolsheviks made a more disastrous and protracted experiment in the Sovietization of Abkhazia which had been turned by the All-Russian Extraordinary Commission (*VChK*) into a shooting-ground of execution and torture. Beginning on 8 April to 17 May, the Bolsheviks controlled the whole of the former Sukhumi district (with the exception of the Ochamchire area). At this time, the forces of the Abkhazian People's Council were not sufficient to liberate Abkhazia. The Georgian National Guard under the command of V. Jugeli joined the battle against the Bolsheviks. They acted in accordance with the mandate given by the Transcaucasian Democratic Federal Republic - the common state - in which the Abkhazian People's Council legitimately represented the population of the region. By 17 May Abkhazia had been cleared of the Bolsheviks. How little the operation undertaken by the Georgian National Guard resembled 'a bloody occupation' about which myths are being circulated by the present ideologists of Abkhazian separatism, is testified by members of the Abkhazian People's Council (D. Alania, M. Tarnava, M. Tsaguria, and others). In their letter of 29 September 1919 addressing the Georgian Government they wrote the following: 'For the first time Georgian troops appeared in Abkhazia during the fight against the Bolsheviks. This was the National Guard under the command of V. Jugeli and A. Dgebuadze. It gives us pleasure to note the impartiality and correctness with which the National Guard treated Abkhazia's whole population.'[22] It should be borne in mind that by 1918 the population of Abkhazia included 21.4% Abkhazians, 42.1% Georgians, 11.7% Russians, 11.7% Greeks, 10.2% Armenians and 2.9% of other nationalities.

Meanwhile, in the late spring of 1918, the days of the Transcaucasian Democratic Federal Republic were numbered. Thrown into a state of unrest by the advancing civil war and international turmoil (the Transcaucasian Sejm refused to accept the conditions of the Treaty of Brest), it was a very fragile, insecure political instrument, too feeble to be able to express and reconcile the various interests and desires of Transcaucasia's population.

So on 25 May 1918 the Georgian Democratic Republic was proclaimed (followed by the formation of the independent republics of Azerbaijan and Armenia), initiating the process of the consolidation of Georgia's independence and restoration of her statehood within her historical borders. The inclusion of Abkhazia in the political structure of the Georgian Republic was determined by the long traditions of their common statehood and also by the agreements reached on the eve of the opening of the Transcaucasian Sejm (on 9 February 1918) which envisaged the autonomy of Abkhazia within the borders of Georgia. It was also precipitated by the situation that had been created by the end of May 1918, when Abkhazia, liberated from the Bolsheviks for the second time, was actually part of the Georgian state and could defend herself only through the military aid of the Georgian National Guard.

This state of affairs was legally fixed by an agreement signed by the Government of the Georgian Democratic Republic and the Abkhazian People's Council on 8 June 1918. The agreement gave Abkhazia internal autonomy (self-government) and military aid in case of external aggression.

Considering these facts, all talk about Abkhazia's annexation or occupation by the Georgian Mensheviks is absurd. However, it would be incorrect to draw too idyllic a picture of the existing situation. The restoration of the single Georgian-Abkhazian state in the extreme conditions of nationwide disaster and imminent civil war progressed with great difficulty. Many mistakes, provocations, delusions, and crimes committed by political leaders of various orientations hindered this process, leading it into a deadlock of aggravating contradictions.

Bringing army divisions into Abkhazia 17-22 June 1918, and occupying the whole sea-shore from Tuapse to Sochi, General Mazniev (Mazniashvili) formed, as one might think, an indispensable beach-head against the Red Army threat, but unexpectedly this aggravated the situation in Abkhazia. The military command of Mazniev (he was appointed governor-general and commander of Sukhumi garrison) ignored the Abkhazian People's Council, oppressed the local population and violated the autonomous rights of Abkhazia, guaranteed by the agreement reached on 8 June 1918.

These Abkhazian-Georgian difficulties were exploited by both the Red Bolsheviks[23] and organisers of the Whites whose ultimate goal was the restoration of 'one and indivisible Russia'. In Sochi General M.S. Alexeev, commander of the Voluntary Army (*Dobrovoltsy*), received and attentively listened to the Abkhazian delegation whose request was to liberate Abkhazia from the armed intervention of Georgia. These complaints served as a good pretext for the general to start a war and bring back the lost territory under Russian rule. Vorobiev, one of the participants of this September meeting, a representative of the Kuban Cossacks, was quite outspoken about it: 'The question arises as to what motives the representatives of the Georgian Republic had when they seized the purely Russian Gagra area and Sukhumi district and, despite the demands of the commanders of the Voluntary Army - the representatives of great, one and indivisible Russia - and of the Abkhazian people, refused to clear this territory of their military troops ...It is not without reason that the Black Sea coast is called the 'Russian Riviera', ... 'a Pearl in the Russian crown', how to resist the temptation not to tear off from sick Russia one of her best regions, not to take advantage of the fact that there is no power as yet to defend this 'region'...'[24]

This sounds so familiar when compared with the invocations of the present Russian national-patriots who again are in need of the 'Russian Riviera'. The tragedy of history is repeating itself.

The independent Georgian Democratic Republic existed for less than three years (from May 1918 to April 1921). Moreover, it may be stated that all her short history was full of a dynamic search for optimal relations with autonomous Abkhazia, based on the people's will and the norms of a democratic constitution. Force was used only in exceptional cases, particularly when an attempt was made to engineer a coup d'etat in Abkhazia during General Denikin's operation (January 1919). Denikin, responding to the appeal of the conspirators to liberate Abkhazia from the Georgian troops, launched an attack on Sukhumi. He presented his arguments to the Georgian government, claiming that Abkhazia belonged to Russia. But in the spring of 1919 the Georgian forces repelled this aggression.

Notwithstanding the wartime tension, immediately after the dissolution of the old composition of the Abkhazian People's Council (which had been in secret negotiations with Denikin), in the autumn of 1918, preparation for the elections to the new Abkhazian People's Council began. And these very elections, carried out on a democratic basis with the participation of the whole population of Abkhazia, resulted in the formation of a new Abkhazian People's Council, a legitimate government body, which at its first sitting on 18-20 March 1919 passed a resolution to the effect that Abkhazia entered into the Georgian Democratic Republic as its autonomous subject. On 20 March 1919 the government of Georgia approved the Act on the autonomy of Abkhazia that had been passed by the People's Council.[25]

It was a bitter irony of fate that the principal proposition on the autonomous government of Abkhazia was adopted by the Constituent Assembly of Georgia on one of the last days of her independent existence. The troops of the 11th Red Army, obeying the orders of Trotsky and Ordjonikidze, invaded Georgia and pushed towards Tbilisii. However, the Constituent Assembly - elected through a nationwide ballot - fully performed its civic and historical duty to the people of the Republic: on 21 February 1921 the principal proposition on Abkhazia's autonomy and the Constitution of the Georgian Democratic Republic were adopted. This is *the Constitution of 1921* which the Georgian people have succeeded in restoring only after seven decades. Ideologists of Abkhazian separatism are fond of asserting that this Constitution did not specify the existence of autonomous Abkhazia. This is a downright lie. The proposition on the autonomy of Abkhazia was adopted by the Constituent Assembly even earlier than the Constitution as a whole, and article 107 of the Constitution clearly announced the right of Abkhazia, as an integral part of Georgia, to have 'autonomous government in local affairs'.

At the close of the winter of 1921, the period of the first democratic revival of Georgian statehood, involving the Abkhazian autonomy, came to its end.On 25 February the Georgian SSR was proclaimed, and on 4 March Soviet power, the Bolshevik dictatorship, was established in Abkhazia. On 6 March notorious Abkhaz revolutionaries - enjoying the special personal favour and confidence of Stalin - arrived from Turkey. They were the so- called *Exes*, experts in plunder and expropriation, terrorist activity, and in training the Comintern secret service from the foreign diaspora in the Middle East. They formed a Revolutionary Committee (a three-member group consisting of Eshba, chairman, Lakoba and Akirtava). Having established a local Extraordinary Commission (*ChK*) and Organisation Bureau of the Russian Communist Party of the Bolsheviks (*RCP/B*) in Abkhazia, they started energetic activity to turn Abkhazia into a Soviet Socialist Republic. On 31 March 1921, the Abkhazian SSR was officially proclaimed. From now on the political history of Abkhazia, as of the whole of Transcaucasia, was directed from the Kremlin. It is noteworthy that the USSR was not yet in existence, neither the Union nor Union Republics, but Ordjonikidze ruled the Caucasian Bureau of the Central Committee of Russia's Communist Party of Bolsheviks (RCPB), and gave the orders in Georgia, Armenia and Azerbaijan. Moscow took the line of setting up a federation - a union of the Georgian, Armenian, Azerbaijani SSRs in a Transcaucasian Socialist Federative Soviet Republic (proclaimed on 12 March 1922). It entered the political structure of the USSR in December 1922, and existed in such status for fourteen years until the new Stalin Constitution, adopted on 5 December, 1936, determined the fate of Transcaucasia in a different way. Probably at this new stage it seemed to the leader more expedient to rule Georgia, Armenia and Azerbaijan separately. Thus they were given the status of independent union republics. Abkhazia had to enter the TSFSR and then together with it, through Georgia, the USSR. Delegating her authorities to Georgia, Abkhazia in fact entered the USSR as an autonomous republic, as part of the Georgian SSR. However, the term 'autonomy' in reference to Abkhazia was not used in official documents in the first Soviet decade (1921-1931).

On 16 December 1921 Georgia and Abkhazia signed an appropriate agreement and in February 1922 the first Congress of the Abkhazian Soviets ratified the state union of the Abkhazian and Georgian SSR. The Abkhazian and Georgian Soviet Constitutions, adopted in 1925, also registered this political union. 'The Soviet Socialist Republic of Abkhazia on the basis of a special treaty, enters the Georgian Soviet Socialist Republic and through her the Transcaucasian Soviet Federative Socialist Republic,' states the Constitution of the Abkhazian SSR. However, the status of Abkhazia was often defined in peculiar political jargon: a 'treaty' republic (it is clear though that the term 'treaty' might have been used in reference to Georgia as well). Finally things were made clear when on 11 February 1931 at the 6th Congress, convened simultaneously by the Georgian and Abkhazian SSR, a resolution was passed on changing the 'treaty' Abkhazian Republic into the Abkhazian autonomous Soviet Socialist Republic within the Georgian SSR. This proposal was confirmed by the Stalin Constitution in 1936.

1931 to the Present Day
In reality all of this was of no consequence. For, irrespective of how often definitions were changed or what words were used in constitutions and declarations unanimously adopted by congresses, convened one after another in the country of the Soviets (the word *autonomy* is, of course, far more attractive than the obscure *treaty*), all these treaties, autonomies, unions and all the widely announced civil rights they were supposed to enjoy, served merely as a screen concealing an absolute lack of civil rights, a cruel enslavement of personality, ethnos and civil community of the population of any republic, be it Union, federal, or treaty in the general system of the totalitarian regime.

Pilipe Makharadze, Chairman of the Council of People's Commissars of Georgia, was very accurate and outspoken in characterizing this state of affairs in his speech delivered at the 12th Congress of the Party in 1923: 'They talk', he remarked, 'about independent Soviet republics...we all understand what kind of independence is meant. You know, we have a single party, one central organ which makes all the decisions for every republic, even the smallest ones; it does absolutely everything, and gives general directives, right up to appointing executives.'[26]

After being changed from a treaty republic into an autonomy, Abkhazia actually neither gained nor lost anything, not a single kopek for her budget, not a single inch of her land (enthusiastically being turned into an All-Union health-resort, mercilessly devastated ecologically, but no longer hers), nor any bit of freedom, for there was no trace of freedom in that country.

After receiving within a few years the Order of Lenin and the Sun of the Stalin Constitution as a gift for the fifteenth anniversary of the Republic, Abkhazia was plunged into the most atrocious, bloody horror of repression. There was a rapid succession of events: the secret murder of Nestor Lakoba, Chairman of the Abkhazian Central Executive Committee, on 16 December 1936; the posthumous announcement of his being an enemy of the people; the merciless elimination of his whole family, including his children and comrades-in-arms, their terrible torture in torture-chambers of the People's Committee of Internal Affairs (*NKVD*); impetuous countrywide collectivization within a year, from the horror of which Lakoba tried, more or less successfully, to protect the agriculture of Abkhazia till 1936; the complete elimination of the Abkhazian intelligentsia, the most important link ensuring the mutual understanding and reciprocal influence of Georgian and Abkhazian cultures, and the fundamentally prepared decision on the mass deportation of the Abkhazian people from their native country (by sheer luck it was not fulfilled, though the people of the Northern Caucasus, the Crimea, Meskhetian Turks, Kurds, Khemshils, and Pontic Greeks had to suffer this misfortune).

Against the background of these huge crimes came the programmes to cripple the Abkhazian language, to restrict the sphere of its application, bringing to nought its role in the people's culture and memory.The replacement of Abkhazian writing first with Georgian and then Cyrillic scripts (1937),[27] and the abolition of the Abkhazian language at secondary schools and in the system of preliminary education, with a provocative substitution of Abkhazian lessons by obligatory lessons conducted in Georgian - all this formed part and parcel of the national policy of the Communist Party and the Soviet State.

All the peoples of the USSR found themselves in the orbit of this policy regardless of the status that was conferred on - or arbitrarily taken away from - a republic, region or any other territorial unit; regardless of the borders that were drawn and re-drawn, of the high-flown words about equality, freedom, autonomy, and friendship between the peoples that were solemnly pronounced on different occasions and forgotten at once, and of many other fine things that had nothing to do with reality.

At the same time, the card, deftly played in Abkhazian political history, aimed at a gradual transformation of a republic formed on a treaty basis into an autonomous one, was not a futile exercise, and though these words were devoid of juridical sense, political reality, value and truth, playing with them proved to be surprisingly easy in order to maintain in the public consciousness and psychology the sense of wounded dignity, jealous envy of their neighbours and a host of political myths that, for the communist dictators, facilitated the task of dividing and ruling in a multi-national country.

In the Abkhaz social consciousness, a myth was cultivated that Abkhazia - because of the malicious intent of its neighbours, the Georgians - was fraudulently deprived of the status of a sovereign republic and artificially turned into an autonomous republic in 1931.

However, under the totalitarian regime, neither the so-called union republics nor any other autonomous formations possessed any genuine autonomy and the human and ethnic rights of the peoples were equally flagrantly violated on the whole territory of the Soviet Union. Yet the difference between the two administrative formations was appreciable.In the union republics far more favourable conditions were created for the titular nations than in the autonomies which were under double subordination - first to the republic centre, in the present case in Tbilisi, and second, to the All-Union authorities in Moscow. The resentment was even more irritating because of the striking difference between the standard of living of the Georgians in Georgia (including the level of their cultural development) and that of the Abkhazians, who felt oppressed in every respect in their own homeland.

It was not difficult to make the people labouring under a totalitarian regime, whose best intellectual part was almost completely exterminated, who had been driven to despair and who were not well-versed in political science or realpolitik, believe that all their misfortunes resulted from a loss of sovereignty and its replacement with the humiliating status of autonomy.

It goes without saying that for several decades after such a replacement many concrete steps were taken that infringed upon the national rights and offended the national dignity of the Abkhazians, whom Communist power skilfully set against the neighbouring peoples, first and foremost against the Georgian people. Further carrying on the tsarist policy of ousting the Abkhazians from their historical homeland, the Soviet Government continued this policy by the hands of the Georgians. It gave the Georgian settlers in the western and eastern regions of the republic the most fertile lands, allotted to them plots for country-cottages, houses and flats (in conditions of an overall housing shortage in the resort zone); it opened the doors of prestigious higher education institutions to Georgians (in conditions when the demands of the youth of Abkhazia were not satisfied); it appointed Georgians to lucrative posts and jobs (in conditions of latent unemployment and overall poverty); finally, it granted to Georgians the leading posts in the Party and government structures. Having long since turned into a national minority within the boundaries of Abkhazia, and despite their natural population growth, every year the Abkhazian people found themselves increasingly surrounded by other nationals, primarily Georgians, and the number of Abkhazians began to decrease steadily.[28] Divide and rule, the tactics of the Communist leadership, are plain to see.

The leading posts in Sukhumi, especially from the mid-1930s to the mid-1950s were occupied not even by local Georgians but by people from other regions who were not familiar with the situation in Abkhazia and indifferent to all the problems of the Abkhazians.

Both the exploitation of the resort zone and the denigration of Abkhaz culture naturally stirred up a feeling of bitterness among the Abkhazian people, summed up recently by Aslanbey Gozhba: 'We live in Abkhazia, but we do not possess it.' [29]

All this happened here in the same way as in the national outlying districts of the Soviet empire, from Lithuania to the Far East. At this time causes for resentment were not all invented by some nationalist-extremists but had real substance; they accumulated through several decades, turning into an explosive mixture of suppressed resentment, popular anger and civil protest. With the collapse of the totalitarian regime, much depended on how and by whom that destructive force would be directed.

It should be said that attempts to direct rising popular resentment and impatience along a safe channel had been made a long time before. To what extent and by whom these attempts were organised, how much came from a spontaneous, sincere impulse or naive hope ('We shall leave Georgia and it will make our life easier'), and how much was based upon a subtly calculated provocation which gave those concerned a chance to search for and punish culprits after each political démarche, are questions that call for a thorough historical analysis in each case.

Without going too deeply into the matter, I simply remind the reader that as far back as 1931, a stormy meeting of many days (18-26 April) - the so-called national rally of the Abkhazians - in the village of Duripsh voiced the people's protest against the transformation of the Abkhazian Republic into an autonomous one. The fate of many orators who had dared to give vent to their sentiments and emotions at that meeting was really deplorable.

Later, after Stalin's death, the Abkhazian question cropped up with a surprising regularity every ten years, and perhaps this helps provoke the teasing thought that advanced planning and organisation were at work. It may have been thought a good idea to let off some steam after each decade, allowing the Abkhaz anti-autonomists to make one more declaration concerning the unjust inclusion of the Abkhazian SSR within the Georgian SSR. Perhaps from time to time an object lesson and a pretext were needed for a new campaign against nationalism (both Georgian and Abkhazian) and to 'strengthen the ideological work towards an international education of the working masses'. Nationalistic passions were so much aroused that heartfelt collective letters were written and sent to various official departments: to the regular Congress of the CPSU, the Supreme Soviet of the USSR, or personally to Comrade Khruschev, Comrade Brezhnev, and so on. Anyhow in 1957, 1967, 1978 and finally in 1988 (when the notorious Abkhaz letter that became the detonator of the first tragic events of 1989 was written) the Abkhazian question recurred.

Any changes in the highest echelons of power and any change in the home policy served as a stimulus for raising this question anew. As is seen in the chronological chain of events, the Abkhazian question was discussed shortly after the 20th Congress of the CPSU, then after the removal of Nikita Khruschev, later in connection with the adoption of the new Constitution of the USSR, and naturally at the time when perestroika was in full swing. Collective letters, individual public speeches, small-scale meetings (it had not come to larger-scale demonstrations yet) were promoted by narrow circles of functionaries directly interested in raising their republican status, who managed to inspire not only the youth but the romantically disposed Abkhaz intelligentsia with this idea. The main body of the population of the republic, the so-called 'working mass', did not take part in these political games. These speeches did not produce any radical changes, as the state system of the USSR remained indestructible for the time being; but these actions did leave some traces.[30]

Permanent tension in Abkhaz-Georgian relations was maintained: and it is not difficult to understand in whose long-term interests this was done. A not so subtle blackmail of the Georgian leadership was resorted to at a high level: 'If you don't behave yourself we shall punish you by cutting off Abkhazia from Georgia'. This was usually followed by the exposure of some suspicious trouble-making nationalists among the Abkhazians. (Those who signed petitions in the Soviet tradition were always among those who suffered.) Then came 'filtration' of the 'unreliable elements' throughout the whole republic. Every act of shake-up and reshuffle, every resolution of the regional committee or the Central Committee of the Georgian CP, following yet another attempt at revising the status of the autonomy, promised pragmatic advantages to all those who stood behind the scenes.

Meanwhile the situation in Abkhazia changed and in those changes there were certain things that inspired hope, and certain other things that caused anxiety. The Abkhazia of the 1950s, 1960s, 1970s and especially of the 1980s no longer looked like the Abkhazia of 1936-1938 or 1944-1949 - the humiliated, mute country, crushed by terror and deprived of its national intelligentsia and of its native language. Sukhumi State University became the engine of lively scientific ideas; the scientific-research institutes of the republic gave birth to some important schools engaged in technical and humanitarian studies and in the unions of writers, artists, journalists and architects, the Abkhaz creative intelligentsia was worthily represented.

I would not like to lapse into the tone of an official festive report or a prospectus on Soviet Abkhazia, but the above, after all, did correspond to reality: the Abkhazian Theatre with a rich repertory in Sukhumi, some talented amateur art groups, the Days of Abkhazian Culture in Georgia (10-13 April 1980), the national press, independent television and broadcasting not controlled by Moscow or Tbilisi, four magazines issued in the Autonomous Republic, the largest number of books per head in their mother tongue. It has been calculated that in terms of titles (4.3 book editions per 10,000 people) Abkhazia ranked first in the USSR (Estonian and Latvian book-publishing offices excelled this figure by the circulation index, and not by titles). In the 1980s both the Abkhazian language and the history of Abkhazia were taught at the schools of Abkhazia.

At the same time the situation in Abkhazia changed for the worse. If in Stalin's time advantages and privileges were artificially conferred on the Georgians, after 1956 the situation went to another extreme and now the ethnic Abkhazians began to supplant the Georgians, the Russians and representatives of other nationalities and to form a ruling and representative elite on the basis of family, clan and blood ties. In search of ways to satisfy the career ambitions of some Abkhazians, the nationalist argument was very frequently put forward.

At one of the last plenary sessions of the CPSU Central Committee (in September 1989), the first secretary of the CP of Georgia, G. Gumbaridze, emphatically announced: 'The fact that at present in multi-national Abkhazia, where the Abkhazians constitute only 17% of her total population, the national Abkhaz cadres hold 40% of places in the local elective bodies and more than half of the leading political and executive posts, speaks for itsel'.[31]

At the Abkhazian D. Gulia Institute of Language, Literature and History, which (especially after Ardzinba's appointment as its director in 1988) became the hotbed of theories of 'Abkhazia for the Abkhazians', 'Abkhazia is not Georgia', and the ideological headquarters of Abkhaz separatism, 75% of its scientific personnel are Abkhaz nationals.

The dismissal of Georgian specialists from many offices and especially from leading posts had become almost a norm in the political life of Abkhazia by the end of the 1980s. For example, the activists of the Abkhaz national movement unleashed a baiting campaign, demanding the resignation of the secretaries of the regional Committee of the Communist Party of Georgia in Gagra (including T. Nadareishvili) only because of their nationality.[32]

Without closing our eyes to these very real contradictions, we can draw the following conclusion from the review and analysis of the ethnopolitical situation in Abkhazia towards the end of the 1980s. There was not a single problem that could not have been solved without resorting to military force. There were no objective reasons for the collision of the two peoples in an armed conflict and a civil war. There was no great warp in the state system of Georgia or in the autonomy of Abkhazia that must necessarily be corrected by a radical severing of the historically established geopolitical and ethnopolitical ties in this region.

At the same time the situation was complex. There was real social tension: links between the Autonomous Republic, the Union Republic, and the Centre, were far from ideal. There was no real political culture in the country; the ethnopolitical factors and the scars which still lived in the people's memory, all created favourable ground for the seeds of conflict. The only thing needed was the emergence of forces interested in such a conflict to turn potential problems into out-and-out war.

Chapter 3

The War of Words

I would ask the reader to pause here for breath. In this chapter I shall discuss the background to the Abkhazian war in terms of the propaganda war conducted in the media. The enormous importance that propaganda plays in the political life of the territories of the former Soviet Union, cannot be over-emphasized.

The range of sources used in the present work does not correspond to the conventional academic idea of a solid source base for an historical investigation. State archives with their well-ordered files do not contain materials on the current political process. I had to obtain documents from the offices of state institutions, from public organisations and from private individuals. I had to obtain copies of decrees sent circularly to different offices and to take extracts from the shorthand reports of proceedings, some of which were only to be found in the desks of the secretaries of the chairmen who had signed them. Also I had to use references, communiques and statements distributed at various press conferences.

To be sure, while referring to sources of this kind, complications arise, one problem being that of authenticity. In a scholarly work one can expect all sources to be referenced. Unfortunately here I sometimes have to refer to a 'xerox copy at the author's disposal', where for ethical or political reasons I cannot say who gave me access to the source material. Sources of this kind, of course, were never intended for publication.

I had the opportunity to study many of the documents referred to while working at the Supreme Soviet in Abkhazia; others come from files of various public organisations such as the Abkhazian People's Forum *Aidgylara*, the Slav Home society, the International Permanent Mission of Civic Diplomacy on the Conflict in Abkhazia, the International Fund of Humanitarian Initiatives, and the Association *Grazhdansky Mir* - the Fund for the Revival of Georgia.

Many pages of this book have been written on the basis of direct personal impressions, records of my conversations with state and public figures and all that I was able to observe with my own eyes in the Caucasus from August to October 1992.

The most important source for this book was the stream of Abkhazian political material in the mass media: from the general mobilisation declared by Ardzinba and Shamba in the afternoon of 14 August 1992 and the first appearances of Russian politicians debating the 'Abkhazian question' on Russian television (*Itogi* 23 August) right up until the last televised meeting of Ardzinba and Andrei Karaulov on the programme *Moment Istiny* (Moment of Truth) on 28 June 1993.

There were also, of course, the many publications in the Russian, Georgian and Abkhazian press.[33] What characterized them more than anything else was the way in which they not only quite monstrously contradicted one another, but also themselves. Newspapers no doubt often print unchecked facts, even fabrications; some aspects of an event are hushed up, others overstated. Nevertheless newspapers served as an important source for this book: by using them I was able to reconstruct the sequence of events and to take the temperature, to understand the aims, intentions and feelings of whichever side they happened to represent.

Some newspapers were of special value as the only source for rare documents of major importance. For example, the newspaper *Pod Nebom Gruzii* (Under the Georgian Sky) published the complete shorthand record of the meeting in Moscow of the heads of the republics of the Caucasus region on 3 September 1992.[34] The newspaper *Yuige Igilik* was the only one in Russia that printed the draft of the 'Conception of National Policy of the Russian Federation of the Northern Caucasus' which had been prepared by the Security Council (directed by Yu.N. Skokov) and which disclosed plans for the re-colonization of the Caucasus.[35]

The most important steps taken by the Georgian leadership were consistently reflected in the pages of the newspaper *Demokraticheskaya Abkhazia* (Democratic Abkhazia) published since August 1992 in Sukhumi. Directives from the government, orders of the commandant of the city, reports from the front and much other such data were printed here.

In studying the background to the military conflict, the newspaper *Aidgylara* (Unity) from the People's Forum of Abkhazia, which began to appear in Sukhumi in 1989, serves as an indispensable source. It gives a consistent and frank acccount of the separatists trying to 'tear Abkhazia away from Georgia'. In addition, some of the official and independent pre-war papers like *Sovetskaya Abkhazia* (Soviet Abkhazia) and *Respublika Abkhazia* (Republic of Abkhazia) are also very interesting in this respect.

Behind all this there is also a vast historical and ethnographic literature on Abkhazia, created long before the dramatic events of 1992. A list of the principal works of this literature is given in the Bibliography. While not wishing to get bogged down in this, any study of present events is not possible without some knowledge of the former history of the Abkhazian people, their ties to Georgia, their relationship with Russia.

It must be said that most of the Soviet works of recent decades have been dreadfully distorted by ideological dogma and the stereotypes of Soviet historical science. This is especially true of any description of the revolutionary period in Abkhazia when ludicrous references were made to the 'indestructible family of the fraternal peoples of the Soviet Union', the 'prosperity' of the Abkhazian SSR and so on.

It has been possible, however, to balance such distortions by the use of foreign studies of Abkhazian history, primarily the work entitled *The Tragedy of the Abkhazian People* by S.Danilov who managed to survive through 1937 in Abkhazia. This study appeared in the *Munich Proceedings of the Institute for the Study of History and Culture in the USSR*. There was also the work of the British Sovietologist Darrell Slider *Crisis and Response in Soviet National Policy: The Case of Abkhazia* published in 1985.[36]

Even recent works published in the ex-Soviet Union, in the post-perestroika press, are considerably politicised and hopelessly partial. Books and articles by Abkhaz and Georgian historians, by journalists and scholars of all kinds, prefigured the imminent conflict. In the pages of seemingly neutral studies of remote historical events, one could frequently see the raging of present passions. Art, archaeology, ethnography - all could be appropriated.

Historical literature has long been the battlefield of those with a vested interest in the Abkhazian conflict. Some authors urge the reader to conclude that there are no grounds whatsoever for the geopolitical union of Abkhazia and Georgia, for these are different peoples, different cultures and different state systems. Georgians on Abkhaz soil are characterized as 'colonizers' and 'invaders'. Others try to deprive the Abkhaz nationalists of any history or ethnocultural originality separate from Georgia.

This historical controversy is old and extremely politicised. As far back as the beginning of the century, on the wave of political reaction following the defeat of the 1905 revolution, there appeared such writings as *Abkhazia is not Georgia* by L.Voronov (St. Petersburg 1907) and N.Vorobyev's manifesto *On the Untenability of Georgian claims to the Sukhumi district - Abkhazia* published in Rostov-on-Don 1919, just at the time when General Denikin, the commander of the Voluntary Army, was discussing with General Briggs, head of the British Military Mission in the South of Russia, the prospects and grounds for the 'liberation' of the Sukhumi district from Georgian troops and its incorporation into 'indivisible Russia'.

Four decades later, at the time when the mass deportation of the Abkhaz people, following that of the Pontic Greeks, seemed about to become reality, the Georgian press published chapters of P. Ingoroqva's book *Giorgi Merchule - Georgian Writer of the 10th Century 1949-1951*. In these extracts the author asserted that the ancient Abkhaz/Abasgoi, known from ancient and medieval sources, were in fact Georgian tribes and had nothing to do with the present day Abkhazian population which had penetrated into Georgia from the north relatively recently, in the eighteenth or nineteenth century. These are ideas which still have currency.

Over the decades chicken and egg questions about the 'ownership' of Abkhazia, about the 'original' inhabitants, about who had come from where and when, were tossed like a ping pong ball between the authors of ethnographic and historical works. In the years of perestroika such matters found their way from bulky scholarly journals and specialist historical tomes into the pages of newspapers and the arena of popular publishing including the unofficial, independent press. And as political passions increased, they grew more simplified and unbalanced.[37]

Typical in this respect is Alexei Gogua's article *Our Concern*, printed in the magazine *Druzhba Narodov* (Friendship of the Peoples) 1989 (see note 38). In this he represents the existence of Abkhazia within Georgia as a national tragedy for the Abkhazians: 'Having preliminarily exterminated or bled white the intelligentsia, closed down Abkhazian schools, resettled more than 200,000 inhabitants from other parts of Georgia onto the best Abkhazian lands, which resulted in the assimilation of part of the native population, they plunged one of the most ancient people of the Caucasus and its culture into a state of shock, turning its autonomy into a mere facade.'[38]

Among the passionate and indignant responses to Gogua's article, which really did cause a state of shock among the intelligentsia of Georgia, I shall single out M. Lordkipanidze's thorough paper in which she emphasised that 'since ancient times Abkhazia has formed part of the Georgian State and the Georgian cultural and historic world' and 'we - Georgians and Abkhazians - cannot live without each other. We have to live together on the same land.This has been predestined by History.'[39]

Naturally these questions acquired a particular edge at this time of approaching calamity. The article entitled *Georgia and Abkhazia have a common destiny* by the historian Viktor Sichinava, published in the newspaper *Demokraticheskaya Abkhazia* after the outbreak of the war can be seen as a desperate attempt to counteract extremism. 'The multifaceted links of the Georgian and Abkhazian peoples', writes Sichinava, 'their unity, has served over the centuries as a powerful means of ensuring their national independence and freedom in their fight against all sorts of encroachments.'[40]

'In a large-scale anti-Georgian campaign', wrote the historian Zurab Papaskiri, analysing the wave of pre-war publications, 'particularly great importance was attached to the falsification of the history of the Georgian and Abkhazian peoples. The Georgian State and the Georgians were declared...guilty of all the misfortunes that had befallen the Abkhazian people throughout their history...; the Georgians were regarded as the newly-arrived, non-native population of Abkhazia.'[41]

One of the recent studies claiming to introduce clarity into these historical controversies is Stanislav Lakoba's book *Essays on the Political History of Abkhazia*, published in Sukhumi in 1990. Interesting in many respects, particularly for a novel description of Abkhazian themes in Stalin's time - in which he looks at the attitudes to Abkhazia of Stalin, Beria, Trotsky and Lakoba - the book is based on a wealth of archival material and extensive historical literature. However, in one respect this book displays extreme prejudice: it is militantly anti-Georgian. Its whole thesis is reducible to the idea that Abkhazia is, was and will be a state independent of Georgia and any Georgian aggression, occupation or 'autonomization' of Abkhazia is historically unjustified and doomed.

Characteristically the author, who treats Nestor Lakoba's memory with such respect, carefully forgets to mention the stand taken by Lakoba while he was Chairman of the Central Executive Committee of the Abkhazian Republic, on its entrance into Georgia as an autonomy. Nestor Lakoba wrote: 'Historical and economic conditions demand that Abkhazia and Georgia form a single whole... For the working masses of Abkhazia the question is answered once and for all: Abkhazia and Georgia have a single destiny.'[42] There is not even the slightest hint of this position in Stanislav Lakoba's Essays.

The popularity of these Essays among separatist political circles and their endorsement by the ideological leadership in Abkhazia was, not surprisingly, opposed by Georgia's scholarly community. During the first months of the war a document based on these Essays was circulated and the newspaper *Svobodnaya Gruzia* (Free Georgia) published a sharp review by the Tbilisi historian Avtandil Mentshashvili which exposes the consistent falsification of history in the Essays.[43]

One of the most interesting publications on the Abkhazian question is a booklet published in Moscow in early 1993 by Olga Vasilyeva: *Georgia as a Model of Post-Communist Transformation*. Abkhazia gets a few pages in here in the chapter on national problems. Nevertheless the author's assessment of the situation and her political position are extremely interesting. The character of this book, orderly and precise, reveals its provenance: it is one of those analytical, 'operative' documents, as they were called, which were traditionally prepared by qualified experts and specialists of the old power structures like the KGB or the CPSU Central Committee or the State Emergency Committee. It is a real replica of those operative documents, written in a military, clear and formal language, which were sent 'upward' in large numbers by the relevant departments in the crisis situations of

April 1989 (the document on Tbilisi), December 1989 (the document on Lithuania), August 1991 (the document on Moscow), and so on.[44]

The main purpose of Vasilyeva's book is to identify the weaknesses of the democratic bloc that came to power in Georgia after the Tbilisi Revolution of 22 December 1991 - 6 January 1992 (see Chronicle of Events), to trace any incipient internal discord between the parties and the various military groups and their leaders (Shevardnadze, Sigua, Kitovani, Ioseliani) and to assess all the political, economic and military problems that faced Shevardnadze's new order. She describes the inter-ethnic tensions within Georgia and any relevant external matters of foreign policy and also identifies the foci of opposition to Shevardnadze. Naturally, South Ossetia and Abkhazia are closely scrutinized in this connection: bases for opposition where civil war had already been unleashed. Vasilyeva is openly cynical about measures to end the war in Abkhazia, like the Moscow meeting and the 3 September 1992 agreements, and frankly expresses her hopes for the continuation of hostilities in Georgia. The ultimate aim is to create a model for 'post-communist transformation' and 'federalization' which will ultimately destroy both democratic Georgia and democratic Russia.[45]

There were a plethora of articles, reports, eye-witness accounts, analyses, speculations and appeals in the press about the situation in Abkhazia. The demarcation of forces was fairly obvious. The Georgian central press (*Svobodnaya Gruzia, Novaya Gazeta, Droni, Mimomkhilveli, Resonance* and others) and *Demokraticheskaya Abkhazia*, which started in August 1992, unequivocally supported the activities of the State Council of Georgia. These papers condemned the political steps of the Abkhaz separatists, the military crimes of the bandit units of the Confederation of Mountain Peoples of the Caucasus and the double-faced policy of Russia in breaking her proclaimed neutrality.

The mass media controlled by the Supreme Soviet of Abkhazia,on the other hand, poured scorn and curses on the 'fascist regime' of Shevardnadze and his 'thugs', and pushed out a furious tide of anti-Georgian propaganda and misanthropic rage. The tone of much of this can be inferred from a brief quotation that appeared in many Russian newspapers: 'The Georgians can live here no longer; in Abkhazia they can only die.'[46]

Siding with the Abkhazian media were various unofficial public associations of a nationalistic character and orientation, vigorously opposed to the leadership of Georgia and Russia. For example, since the beginning of September 1992 articles had been published in *Nart* (a newspaper founded by the International Circassian Association), justifying the actions of the Confederation of Mountain Peoples in their support 'for the liberation of Abkhazia'.[47]

The 'fascist junta of Shevardnadze' came under attack from the Georgian newspaper *Pod Nebom Gruzii* (Under the Sky of Georgia) which supported the ex-president Zviad Gamsakhurdia (*he died in strange circumstances in January 1994*). However, this paper was not published under the sky of Georgia but in Grozny, the capital of the Chechen Republic, and was edited by Mzia Shervashidze who proclaims herself a 'representative of an ancient Abkhazian princely family.'[48] Under the heading *You, Abkhazia, My Suffering!* this paper published the most extreme speeches and threats ('the whole Caucasus will be consumed by fire.'etc.) and lengthy fabrications on the allegedly planned annihilation of the Abkhazian people by the State Council of Georgia.

As for the central Russian press, the most authoritative and popular of the mass media concentrated in Moscow, it has always shown a tendency to sympathise with the Abkhazian separatist side and to condemn the 'Georgian aggressors'. Occasional attempts by Russian journalists, scholars or political figures to achieve some sort of balance, mostly in papers of a democratic orientation, never really got to the essence of the problem. There seemed to be a general unwillingness, for instance, to recognise the truth of Russian complicity in this war.

Perhaps the most striking example of an objective analysis was a paper by the political-scientist Emil Pain: *The Russian Echo of the Caucasian War*. He writes: 'One need not think long on the causes of the revenge of Russian national-patriots.They explain these causes themselves, saying: Shevardnadze destroyed the Soviet Union, let his Georgia be destroyed now.'[49]

Though Pain disagreed with the decision taken by the State Council of Georgia to send troops into Abkhazia to secure the release of a number of hostages (we shall come to this later) and called it a 'strategic mistake', he understands the essence of the Abkhazian tragedy:

'Is it permissible to have an alternative policy - that of ultimata, the encouragement of terrorism, the use of political instability in Georgia - to strengthen one's personal power in Abkhazia? All this transpired in Ardzinba's actions and these actions placed the Abkhazians - to no lesser extent than the actions of the Georgian troops - on the verge of ethnocide.'[50]

Viktor Kuvaldin in *Moskovskiye Novosti* (Moscow News) drew attention to the dangers of dragging Russia into the Transcaucasian conflict and to the temptation of accepting Abkhazia into her fold: 'The annexation, in some form, of South Ossetia and Abkhazia and the possible break-up of Georgia will soon boomerang on Moscow... Scared by its great-power expansionism, all former Soviet Republics will forsake Russia... We shall return to the times of the cold war, doomed to an ignominious defeat.'[51] The sad example of the Abkhazian adventure of July 1992 allowed him to conclude: 'The Caucasian collisions show the absurdity of the extremist interpretation of the right of nations to self-determination that does not wish to take account of reality nor of the legitimate rights of other peoples.'[52]

However, the Russian press was on the whole one-sided and limited. Horror stories of marauding, of dreadful violence and of casualties among the civilian population were a reality for both sides in this conflict, but they were consistently reduced to a catalogue of complaint against the 'Georgian occupationists'. No attempt was ever made to go into the causes of all this and there were many terrible distortions of the truth.[53] It is extraordinary that so many publications from all shades of the political spectrum, including the democratic free press, seemed to have swallowed whole the extreme right-wing formulations of the ultra-patriotic pro-communist press, like Prokhanov's paper *Den* (Day).[54] One can understand on whose behalf Alexandr Nevzorov was speaking when he cursed Shevardnadze and blessed 'heroic Abkhazia' in his TV programme *600 Seconds*. But it is hard to understand why fascist ravings were echoed by the most progressive of journalists like Alexander Podrabinek in his *Express-Khronika* (Express Chronicle). He published Saida Bigvava's reports from Gudauta as some sort of gospel account of developments in Abkhazia. They were in fact just reworkings of the propagandist directives of the separatist leadership.[55]

There was a peculiar blindness and deafness where Abkhazia was concerned.[56,57] Perhaps this had something to do with a feeling in Russia that now one is obliged to side with the underdog in any dispute, that it is difficult to escape from the idea that a small nation must be the victim, a larger - the oppressor.[58] Even the bogeyman of an Islamic Fundamentalist Front in Abkhazia[59] soon gave way to anti-Georgian sentiment.

However, the real reason for this attitude is, I think, clear. The Abkhazian leaders have continuously, almost desperately, declared their loyalty to Russia, their desire to be placed under Russian protection. The Georgians, on the other hand, have always made plain their desire for independence. How can the Russians resist such blandishments, when Russia itself is being cast by the separatists in the role of good guy: 'We are with Russia', 'We are under Russia's wing', 'It is time to understand that Abkhazia is Russia.'

Zurab Achba, a deputy of the Supreme Soviet of Abkhazia and close friend of Ardzinba, gave a revealing interview in this vein to the newspaper *Den*. His monologue was a strange mixture of wild invention, crude lies and sheer demagogy, but within it lies a clear formulation of separatist aims: the destruction of the integrity of the Georgian state, the joining of Abkhazia to Russia, the return of Russia to her former imperial geopolitics, and the settling in Abkhazia of Russians, primarily military personnel of a patriotic orientation. He said: 'Moscow is all the time pushing us towards a federal treaty with Georgia, but we have simply returned to the Constitution of 1925 according to which Abkhazia was proclaimed a Soviet Socialist Republic. I don't think this federal treaty with Georgia is an optimal solution. Perhaps the presence of a fairly large number of Russians will open up some other political bearings for Abkhazia...We have conducted negotiations with the business circles of Russia and they are ready to help us create work opportunities for Russian settlers...It is beneficial for Russia too and it is high time for her to stop disintegrating and return to traditional geopolitics...The people who come to us will become citizens of Abkhazia...Many Cossacks have arrived and they have actively joined artillery and infantry units...There are many officers of the Soviet, now Russian, army who arrive here for their vacation: for a month or two they devote themselves to war...People must understand that Abkhazia is Russia.'[60]

Much of this is just open political bargaining with the reactionary forces in Russia. This prominent Abkhazian statesman concludes that 'Abkhazia is a promising republic in this region and if we gain military victory, I am sure...it will be of great significance to Russia and for all those who come to live here. After all, Abkhazia has sea ports and magnificent resorts!'

Democratic Georgia is clearly losing the information war. In Russia we see, day by day, a weakening of the new democracy under the onslaughts of extreme nationalism, right-wing patriotism and the attacks of the *Black-Hundreds* press (right-wing, anti-semitic, fascist imperialist press). It becomes all the more urgent, therefore, to know what is really going on in Abkhazia, to understand clearly which forces are at work.

Chapter 4

The Web of Conspiracy

By the end of the 1980s national movements, triggered off by perestroika, had surfaced everywhere in the USSR. Long-standing contradictions that had been driven deep into the state structure of the country were suddenly exposed and most regions were agitated by the tensions that this provoked. In one way or another these processes had affected the whole territory of the USSR - the aggregate of Soviet nations and nationalities, which had been declared 'a new historic community of people - the Soviet people' by the communist ideologists of the Brezhnev era. These processes also had a bearing on the whole ugly system of Union and autonomous republics, regions and areas, as well as of the territories where whole ethnic and national groups were doubly deprived of civil rights and did not enjoy even an illusory autonomy. Neither Georgia as a whole, nor Abkhazia within Georgia were exceptions in this respect.

All these national movements in the USSR that had declared themselves by 1988 differed from each other. They might seem to an outside observer homogeneous and similar in their motive force and essence, but this is only superficially true. In every concrete national or multi-national region the civic and ethnic communities were faced with specific political, economic, ecological, cultural problems and tasks; the circumstances in different regions were not the same; the local and historical traditions differed; the ethnic communities had different opportunities for the consolidation of their forces; the authority of their leaders differed from one ethnic community to another; the intellectual potential of the ideologists of these movements were not the same. Finally, every people had its own grievance, its own pain and its own hopes, its own needs and claims against the authorities, its neighbours, and so on. Furthermore, the tactics, the forms, and the political culture of the national movements in different republics were totally dissimilar. That is why, though in its essence it was a common, single process of the inevitable and dramatic disintegration of the Soviet empire as a multi-national power, it is useless and wrong to apply the same standard to all alike: to the Baltic Republics or the Ukraine, to Nagorny Karabakh or Tatarstan, to the Central Asian or Transcaucasian republics.

But, more than this, there were essential differences in the political direction of these various movements. The expiring Soviet Union found itself riven by national movements which were by no means directed at the same ultimate goal: the disintegration of the USSR. Some of them converged, while others opposed each other. Acting within the same area, they were bound to collide and were irreconcilably hostile (in spite of their common nationalist colouring) by the very essence of their ideological attitudes and programme of aims. This fundamental demarcation equally refers to ethnic and multi-national, civil movements. The latter unite several peoples, the Caucasian mountaineers, for example, according to the principle of geographic, linguistic and religious closeness or according to shared ideological conviction as with the various communist *interfronts* (shortened version of Russian: *internationalny front* = Eng: international front=fifth column), as they were called, which opposed the Popular Fronts in Latvia, Estonia and Lithuania.

Any separation of modern national movements by merely opposing them - some belong to the right, others to the left; some are progressive, others are reactionary - is too simple. The true historical picture is incomparably richer and more complex than a scheme of this kind can be, because even the most progressive movement sometimes reveals inconsistency, inner contradictions, discrepancy between what is said and what is done, or an inability to reach the ideal declared by the movement itself. Besides, a national, civil movement often undergoes such tremendous transformations during its existence that finally it turns into something completely different. The political history of Georgia from the late 1980s to the early 1990s presents many such distressing examples and the same is also true of other republics.

The confusing plethora of names gives no clue, either, to political direction. All the fronts, forums, centres, revivals, unities, round tables and so on are no more indicative of purpose than the various religious or linguistic tags which differentiated these movements: Christian, Muslim, Slavic, Turkic and so on. They were characterized, however, by their objectives. Either they aimed at the destruction of the totalitarian empire or at its maintenance, at the overthrow of communism in all its forms or at the continuation of the communist experiment and the strengthening of the Soviet socialist form of government.

In Georgia, Abkhazia, and in other regions of the former Soviet Union, the national movement faced the only alternative: it had to become the basis for a powerful democratic movement, able to sweep away the resisting remains of the socialist regime and return its own people to the road of civilization, free from communist experiments (as the Lithuanian *Sajudis* did successfully in 1989 and in the 1990s, or *Democratic Russia* in the formidable August days of 1991). The other way implied the transformation of the national movement into a base for national-patriots or national-fascists, irrespective of whether they came from large or small nations, who would inevitably join the defenders of the socialist choice and the communist regime, and would attempt to restore the Soviet empire and its colonial policy under the pretext of patriotism.

And if it is true that all happy families are alike, but each unhappy family is unhappy in its own way, national movements too proceeded to their bitter, unhappy end, towards fratricidal wars and bloody conflicts in their own way. They sharply differed from one another in their arguments, in the demagogy of their many dishonest politicians and the sincere delusions of the people who had, simply, lost their bearings. It will finally become clear that the Russian organisation *Pamyat*, calling for the saving of Russia from 'Jews and masons', the Tatar party *Ittifak*, ready to declare *hazawat*, or holy war, against all the Russians in and around Tatarstan, and the *boeviks* (militants) from the Popular Front in Tajikistan, aiming fire on all the 'enemies of the nation', both from Islam and from the democratic opposition, have the same roots, the same masters, the same ultimate goals. It will turn out later that the greatest nationalist-patriot, Zviad Gamsakhurdia (the first post-communist President of Independent Georgia, later deposed), who discriminated fiercely against the ethnic minorities of Georgia and who has caused much bloodshed in his own country, and the greatest nationalist-separatist, Vladislav

Ardzinba (the eventual leader of the Abkhaz separatist movement), who in the name of his ambitious plans has sacrificed his native land to civil war, are, in fact, the closest soul mates and found themselves discussing joint plans for a war against their own peoples in the hospitable quiet and coolness of a private mansion in Grozny.

So far, however, in the crucial 1988-89 period, when various civil movements were being formed and diverse political groups emerged, their natures had not yet shown themselves distinctly. Nor did many people realise that the People's Forum of Abkhazia - Aidgylara (Unity), appearing on the political scene so inconspicuously, not only differed politically from the 'extremist' groups striving for the separation of Georgia from the USSR, but was directly opposed to them.

The emergence of Aidgylara was by no means spontaneous. It did not suddenly arise from below, on a wave of resentment against the regime. However, account was taken of the fact that the people were discontented, and that the power structures of the local regional committees of the Communist Party of Georgia and local Soviets were incapable of ruling the country in the old way. In 1988-89 the Communist Party of the Soviet Union felt a real threat to its absolute power. Ignoring the liberal and reforming aspirations of many Politburo members, as well as the will of the communist rank and file, and relying on reactionary groups within the Party, in the military and the KGB, it started organising interfronts - fifth columns - in the republics where mass national movements had already raised the question of the secession of those republics from the USSR. For the communist regime Estonia, Latvia, Lithuania, Moldavia, and Georgia naturally became areas of heightened threat. Already in January 1989 the Constituent Congress of the International Front of the workers of the Latvian SSR was held in Riga. The Congress adopted its Charter and Declaration proclaiming the 'inexhaustible possibilities' of the socialist system and obligatory membership of the USSR for the Latvian SSR.[61] The public organisation Unity, formed in Lithuania as a counterbalance to Sajudis, first tested its strength on 15 February 1989. A fifteen thousand-strong rally was held in Vilnius in protest against Lithuanian being granted the status of official language and against the celebration of the Independence Day of Lithuania on 16 February.

The fact that these interfront and unity groups and their activities followed one and the same common pattern, and were well organised and premeditated, is attested by the last head of the KGB, V. Bakatin, a most reliable source: 'The Security Committee was at the source of the formation of those international fronts in the Republics that displayed obstinacy in their relations with the Centre.The vicious logic of divide and rule stimulated the splitting of these republics into two irreconcilable camps, leading to an intensification of social tension... The following scheme worked: If you don't want to obey, then you will get an interfront instead, which will call for strikes, raise the question of the frontiers of the republic and the legitimacy of the government bodies elected there. Then the activity of these interfronts was presented by the Security Committee as the manifestation of the whole nation's will', writes Bakatin.[62]

It should be noted that the organisers of interfronts had special problems with their national composition. It was rather difficult to create a semblance of an international association out of local marginals. Thus, although it was solemnly announced at the Latvian interfront's founding congress that the 713 delegates were representatives of 19 nationalities, it turned out that there were 535 Russians and only 26 Latvians among them. It was awkward and politically disadvantageous to set up Russian interfronts against the native peoples of the republics. Therefore, wherever possible, they tried to form all sorts of unities, forums and fronts from representatives of the native nationalities and ethnic minorities of the given region. In Lithuania, the 'Polish question' was being thoroughly worked out: the possibility of involving the Polish population of the Vilnius area - whose problems for almost half a century had been completely neglected by communist Moscow - in combating 'Lithuanian nationalism'. In Moldavia, besides the Russian *Dniester* area, the *Gagauz* districts were identified as a possible base in the struggle against the champions of Moldavia's independence, its secession from the USSR and reunification with Romania. For those in Georgia who were preparing to deliver a blow at the 'extremists', all the autonomies and districts forming parts of Georgia with a non-Georgian population - primarily South Ossetia and Abkhazia - turned out to be real finds.

It was less difficult to organise counter-movements in those places since people of different nationalities actually felt that they were treated unfairly. They did, indeed, suffer from a lack of national rights and from social injustice, but naively thought that the real cause of all this was not the system itself but the evil will of their immediate neighbours. They announced themselves ready to defend their historical rights. All this and the general lack of a real political culture, the vacuum of moral values formed over decades of 'international and patriotic education of the working people', the spread of false conceptions about the past, created additional conditions favouring the implementation of those projects worked out in the studies of the *Staraya Ploshchad* (Central Committee of Communist Party HQ) and in the *Lubyanka* (KGB HQ) in Moscow.

The climate was favourable. In Georgia, many people of different nationalities - Abkhazians, Ossetians, Armenians, Turks endeavouring to return to Meskheti, and Azerbaijanis were scared by the threat of Georgian nationalism. They were sincerely indignant and saw their oppressors in their Georgian neighbours whom they called enemies or invaders or imperialists. They believed that they were fighting for the lofty ideals of national freedom, the right to self-determination, autonomy and reunion with their brothers across the Georgian border or the Caucasus Range. There was no lack of fine formulations of these ideals. Furthermore, the organisers of anti-Georgian actions consistently and skilfully used the errors of the Georgian national movement itself which had openly put forward some dreadful formulations about guests and hosts on Georgian land. Communist reaction acted in the same way in all the republics of the Soviet Union without exception, wherever a national-liberation movement strengthened and tendencies developed towards secession from the USSR. Communist organisers and propagandists, trying to form diverse 'intermovements' and to oppose them to the national fronts in Latvia, Moldavia, Estonia and to Lithuanian Sajudis, skilfully manipulated the declarations of the leaders or the press of the various national independence movements. Many of these manifested not only glaring narrow-mindedness and scornful attitudes to the vital interests of national minorities, but also much open belligerence.

The leaders of Georgian unofficial groups, intensely active in 1988-1989 (primarily such figures as Zviad Gamsakhurdia, Merab Kostava, and the leaders of the bloc of parties of the Round Table) turned out to be involuntary assistants of imperial forces that sought to form an anti-Georgian coalition on ethnic and religious grounds by uniting all non-Georgians residing in Georgia, and partly Muslim Georgians (Ajarians, Meskhetians) too, by the common fear of Georgian nationalism and fanaticism. Statements were, indeed, made proposing to abolish all the autonomies, putting forward categorical demands for immediate and overall change to the Georgian language, telling the 'newly-come' peoples to leave the ancient Georgian land, and proclaiming the special mission of Christian Georgia as an advanced post of European civilization in the Muslim East. Such disregard for the humanitarian principles of tolerance and fraternity really scared people and roused the indignation of the non-Georgian and non-Christian population of the republic.

All this made it easy for communist provocateurs to create an anti-Georgian 'international' coalition in which the Abkhazians were, from the very beginning, assigned the striking role. They had the required 'Caucasian temperament', an historical right to their native land, affiliation to Islam, ethnocultural differences from Georgians and there were long-standing frictions and contradictions on social, demographic, administrative and political grounds. The Georgian press, Georgian mass media, and Georgian journalism must undoubtedly bear a measure of responsibility for the intensification of interethnic tension, for disseminating the fear of pan-Georgian chauvinism in the minds of the national minorities: the Ossetians, Abkhazians, Russians, Armenians, Azerbaijanis and others residing in Georgia. It would be quite incorrect to pretend that there were no grounds for this. A fascist-minded author writing in the Georgian newspaper *Komunisti* on 21 November 1988 recommended that: 'For a balanced propagation of separate nations living in Georgia: to keep to the limited level of their simple reproduction (two children). To those who wish extended reproduction: to grant the right to leave for a place of residence outside the republic.'[63]

Unfortunately, there is no deficiency in the Georgian press and literature of examples of a scornful attitude to Abkhazians, Ossetians or Meskhetian Turks. One could often read ignorant and scientifically unfounded articles, according to which, for example, the Abkhazians, or some of them anyway, came to Georgia from somewhere else, from Central Asia or from the Northern Caucasus.[64] Absolutely arbitrary hypotheses were being advanced on how and why the Abkhazian, Ajarian and South Ossetian autonomies were created in Georgia. It is asserted that the Bolsheviks, or sometimes Stalin himself, gave these autonomies to Abkhazian and Ossetian revolutionaries as a reward for their help in the annexation of Georgia. Therefore, all the autonomies must be abolished and such a demographic policy carried out in the future that will ensure a stable majority of the Georgian population in all regions.[65]

So it was not difficult to find crazy statements in the Georgian press. Perhaps this is not so surprising at a time of such great tension and difficulty. The organisers of the Abkhazian war and the supporters of Ardzinba liked to brandish such statements to scare their compatriots. They used them to justify their own actions. However, such a use is absolutely wrong. This is like, say, justifying - let us assume for a moment such a terrifying scenario - some pre-emptive strike upon Russia by the USA on the grounds that the Russian press of a definite type (such as the newspaper *Den* and the like) is full of anti-American, anti-Semitic and other nasty statements. The policy of Georgia regarding the peoples of Georgia and the autonomies within Georgia, cannot be assessed on the basis of selected quotations from certain lunatic nationalist papers, even though a definite layer of the Georgian national mentality is, indeed, represented here.

Those who planned the Abkhazian war and who waged it, skilfully played on the national feelings of the Abkhazians who were striving to assert their own identity and their unique right to possess this land. Hence the abundance of fantastic versions in Abkhazian historiography and in the media developing ideas about the autochthonous Abkhazian people and their unique millennial, or even multi-millennial rule of this land. There is also much about the superiority of Abkhazian culture over Georgian and so on. They turned to advantage the errors and delusions of some of the Georgian authors who showed a staggering deafness to the pains, hopes, and interests of the ethnic minorities of Georgia. Any call for 'de-Armenianization', 'de-Turkification' of Georgian land, the 'abolition of all autonomies', 'state control of the birthrate of non-Georgian populations', the banishment of all Ossetians to Ossetia, Russians to Russia, and so on (such calls were made at rallies and in the Georgian press) was manna from heaven for the reactionary forces interested in doing away with the democratic movement in Georgia.

The first foundations for open conflict were laid in the summer of

1988. On 17 July, representatives of Abkhazian intellectuals, Alexei Gogua was the most active among them, sent a statement to the Presidium of the forthcoming 19th All-Union Party Conference - later known as *the Abkhazian Letter* - requesting a decision on subordinating Abkhazia directly to the Central bodies of power in Moscow.[66] By that time (literally the day before: on 15 June 1988) the Supreme Soviet of the Armenian SSR had adopted the decision to satisfy the request of the Regional Soviet of the Autonomous Region of Nagorny Karabakh (*ARNK*) to reunite Nagorny Karabakh with Armenia. Nobody could predict what a tragic turn events would take in Karabakh and such a solution to the problem seemed quite possible at the time: to secede from one republic and join another, to form a new Union Republic, especially if Moscow consented to it.[67]

This time Moscow kept silent. The Abkhazian Letter had no apparent consequences. Hardly anybody in Abkhazia was aware of the letter except a rather narrow circle of persons initiated into Party and state secrets. Naturally no polls were conducted to ascertain public opinion before or even after the Letter. It could have remained a private affair for the group of writers and journalists who signed it, and could have been consigned to oblivion, as was the case with many previous appeals to the top by the leaders of the Abkhazian ASSR who were displeased with the system of dual subordination and preferred to have direct dealings with Moscow.

The Abkhazian Letter was remembered in *Staraya Ploshchad* in the autumn of 1988, when a wave of unsanctioned rallies swept Georgia with tremendous force. It was precisely then that the Abkhazian People's Forum Aidgylara began to be formed, concurrently with the interfronts (those organisations formed with the express intent of countering any move towards independence and democracy) of the Baltic Republics, the All-Russian National-Patriotic Front (*ARNPF*), and similar associations.

The first draft of its programme, drawn up in Moscow and replete with arguments in favour of a socialist order and the indivisible and unbreakable Soviet Union, stated that Socialist Abkhazia must become a constituent part of the Soviet Union on the basis of Lenin's principle of the right of nations to self-determination. The draft was formulated by Doctor of Law Taras Mironovich Shamba, an Abkhazian by nationality and lecturer at the Academy of Social Sciences attached to the Central Committee of the CPSU. His works: *Party guidance of the organs for guarding Socialist law and order*, *The law and order of developed Socialism*, and even *The CPSU and organs guarding law and order*[68] had already enormously enriched Soviet humanities!

Understandably, a specialist serving in such a rarefied sphere would not waste his precious time on drawing up programmes for any dubious organisation of *neformalny* (informal groups which sprang up during the epoch of perestroika who aspired to change and freedom from the old system) even for his former compatriots (Shamba had long lived and worked in Moscow) unless he was ordered by his direct chiefs or their proxies. In the best tradition of nepotism, mastered by the Party and Soviet nomenclature, the younger brother of Taras, Sergei Mironovich Shamba, Cand. Sci. (History), was elected chairman of the People's Forum of Abkhazia Aidgylara (*PFA*) at the Founding Congress in Sukhumi.

As if by magic, money was found to issue, from 1990, the newspaper *Aidgylara* both in Russian and Abkhazian. The headquarters of the PFA received spacious rooms in 44 Frunze street. A little later rooms were given to the leaders of the PFA in the building of the Supreme Soviet of Abkhazia. The complicity between the Abkhazian separatists and the old communist elite could not have been made clearer.

It is noteworthy that the programme of the People's Forum Aidgylara differed little from the official standpoint of the Party and Soviet leaders of Abkhazia. The popular fronts, movements and associations of many Union and autonomous republics were formed in 1988-1989 as forces opposed to the governing structures, primarily the CPSU. Often they were directly connected with former dissident circles which advanced more radical political demands than the aims of local central committees and regional committees of Communist Parties. However, the Forum Aidgylara merely echoed what was expressed by the Party organisation in Abkhazia, hardly affected by perestroika, and all that was advocated in the pages of the official newspaper *Sovetskaya Abkhazia*.

Their position was most concisely expressed in 1989 by T.N. Tsushba, a party functionary from Sukhumi, in his article *The tasks of the Party in perfecting interethnic relations in the conditions of Perestroika (As exemplified by the Abkhazian SSR)*.[69] He emphasised their loyalty and readiness 'to be steadfastly guided by the resolutions of the 27th

Congress of the CPSU, January 1987, the Plenary Session of the Central Committee and the 19th All-Union Party Conference.' He wanted to strengthen 'the sacred principles of Lenin's national policy and the might of the USSR', for 'the USSR is our common and native home. It is indestructible.There is no alternative here.'[70] Protestations of loyalty to and love of the Big Russian Brother are combined in this article with sharp attacks upon some of the leaders of the Ilia. Chavchavadze Society[71] for their request to use the Georgian language along with Abkhazian as the language of state business and 'deprive Russian of that function'. The idea of transforming Abkhazia from an autonomous to a union republic with direct entry into the USSR is persistently adhered to in the article. 'After the adoption of the Party documents it will take at least ten to fifteen years to improve interethnic relations. If there is no progress in this direction then there is only one way out ... to return to discussions launched in 1923[72], i.e. to grant all Soviet national-state formations the right to join directly the USSR, for the uppermost idea or paramount mission of a socialist federation is that all enjoy equal rights, entering the federation on an equal footing.'[73]

The true political objectives of Aidgylara can best be seen in the huge number of anonymous bulletins, the 'information', carried in its publications. For those who understand the genre, these bulletins are strongly reminiscent of the political denunciations which were regularly sent at apposite moments to government departments by organisations with an axe to grind or a signal to send. Here is one such from Aidgylara in July 1990: 'The extremist elements, using the great gains of perestroika, glasnost and democracy, in their antipopular and selfish interests are seeking to direct this process into the channel of anti-sovietism, separation, aggressive nationalism and chauvinism. This is attested by the events in the Baltic republics, in the republics of Central Asia, Moldavia, and Transcaucasia, particularly the Georgian SSR. All this is against the political frame of mind of the Abkhazian population which is loyal to the ideas of October, Leninism and internationalism.'[74]

But the political masters directing this performance demanded from the PFA Aidgylara more resolute and more impressive actions than mere protestations of the loyalty of the Abkhazian population to the 'ideas of October'. The first such action followed in March 1989.

It was a 30,000-strong rally, held on 18 March in the village of Lykhny, Gudauta district, on the initiative of the PFA Aidgylara. Of course, it was sanctioned and not simply sanctioned but held with the 'participation of the leaders of the Party and Soviet authorities' of the autonomous republic. As though enacting a scenario written by the KGB, (there is disobedience in the republics, so organise an interfront that will call for strikes, raise questions about the borders and so on...) the Lykhny gathering adopted an appeal to the Central Committee of the CPSU, to the Presidium of the Supreme Soviet of the USSR and the Council of Ministers of the USSR, requesting the restoration of the status of the Abkhazian SSR of 1921-1931 thereby, naturally, altering the present borders of the Georgian SSR.

As early as 24 March a somewhat edited Appeal of the Lykhny gathering appeared, as if by magic, all at once, in all local Abkhazian and Russian newspapers - the organs of the regional committees, district committees, the Supreme Soviet, and the executive committees of district soviets of the Abkhazian ASSR. Let me remark in passing that a rally could be held by the will of the people, but to publish the appeal, adopted there, simultaneously in all the newspapers of the republic was feasible in 1989 only by the will of 'the leading and directing power' namely the CPSU.

A carefully composed reference was subjoined to the appeal, which first appeared in February 1989 in *Bzyb*, the district newspaper and organ of the party district committee and the executive committee of Gudauta district. It was an excursus into the history of Abkhaz-Georgian relations, arguing that Abkhazia was not part of Georgia. The Lykhny appeal, as openly admitted by its initiators, was 'to deliver a blow' to the 'leaders of unofficial associations from Tbilisi, Sukhumi and other towns, to all who try to tear Georgia away from the USSR.'[75]

This well calculated provocation proved the detonator to an explosion that involved the whole of Georgia. The first protest rally by the Georgian population, 12,000-strong, was held in the regional centre of Gali on 25 March, and it was followed by rallies in Sukhumi, Leselidze (1 April) and other towns of Georgia. The activists of the PFA Aidgylara assiduously tried to expose the instigators of these rallies, wrote down the names and speeches of the orators, compiled 'information' they signalled 'upward' in time and then published in the Aidgylara. One such 'information' on the Ilia Chavchavadze society, set up in Sukhumi and headed by the artist, Nugzar Mgaloblishvili, was reported to various institutions: 'On behalf of the National-Democratic Party of Georgia (*NDPG*) this society distributed leaflets of anti-Soviet content, calling for the proclamation of 25 February 1921 (the day of establishment of Soviet power in Georgia) as a day of national mourning, to boycott the elections, to protect their children from the Soviet school, to forbid the children to join the October Pioneer and Komsomol organisations'[76] Analogous information was fabricated about the Leselidze rally (1 April).

Then, on April 1st, a group of specially trained activists of the PFA attacked a bus on the Bzyb-Sukhumi road, brutally beating up the Georgian passengers. And that is how Georgia stepped into her tragic April, into a continuous unsanctioned but entirely peaceful (till the end) rally lasting for many days in the square in front of the Government House in Tbilisi. And this was how the steamroller of Soviet history moved inexorably towards the Bloody Sunday of 9 April 1989. Slogans such as 'USSR - a jail of peoples' and 'Away with the Communist regime!' were raised above the huge gathering. The mass character of this rally, the passion, determination and national solidarity it showed, made it impossible to put the blame for it on a band of extremist agents-provocateurs and scared the central authorities so much that they decided to resort to military force for the very first time in Tbilisi. At the command from Moscow, special troops (*Dzerzhinski* division) and a regiment of airborne landing forces were brought into action against the peaceful population. The military operation, with the motive of 'clearing the square in front of the Government House', was carried out by the Commander-in-Chief of the Transcaucasian military district General Rodionov and was marked by extreme cruelty, using shovels and poison-gas, including CS, against the peaceful population, which resulted in many casualties and more than 20 dead. General Rodionov had fulfilled the secret orders of Yegor Ligachev, Viktor Chebrikov, and Marshal Dmitri Yazov, the Defence Minister. It is now clear that the decision to use force was taken in Moscow on 7 April 1989, at a meeting chaired by Ligachev. Later, Ligachev himself called it 'a sitting of the commission of the members of the Politburo, comprising three fourths of the whole body ...'[77] The essence of the decision was defined by another member of the commission - Viktor Chebrikov, the former chief of the KGB and member of the Politburo of the Central Committee of the CPSU: 'We provided some military force in order to help them to decide on the spot what to do.'[78] This decision and the subsequent use of force eventually brought about a result quite opposite to that expected by the reactionary ruling clique and the military command. Gorbachev dissociated himself from the actions and decisions of his companions-in-arms, and if their plans actually envisaged 'the aggravation of the situation so as to lead to the reversal of perestroika and ..., moreover, to the replacement of the leader',[79] the plans ended in a complete failure. After the Tbilisi events those who were the most desperate opponents of perestroika were obliged to leave the political arena: the first was Chebrikov in 1989 (then Chief of the Committee on Legal Policy of the Central Committee of the CPSU); a year later Ligachev's turn came, when the 28th Congress of the CPSU, at which he had to answer for his role in 'the Tbilisi syndrome', did not support his candidacy for the General Secretary of the Party and retired him on a pension. A year later it was followed by a complete collapse of Marshal Yazov's political career after the failure of the August Putsch. (All three were engineers of the August coup against Gorbachev.) The leaders of the Central Committee of the Communist Party of Georgia were also dismissed (the first secretary Jumber Patiashvili, the second secretary Boris Nikol'ski). They were especially compromised after Lukyanov read aloud the cipher telegrams sent from Tbilisi to Moscow with the request to assign troops to establish order.

The retirement from the political arena of those bearing the blame for the tragedy in Tbilisi, naturally, was not an adequate punishment for the monstrous crime and in some cases was nothing but a cover for corruption. Thus, the very same General Rodionov, found guilty of the bloodshed in Tbilisi by the decision of the 2nd Congress of People's Deputies, was soon transferred from the Transcaucasian military district to Moscow and was appointed Chief of the Academy of the General Staff of the Armed Forces of the USSR. The system protected those who proved loyal to it. Yet this still powerful communist system suffered a crushing defeat after 9 April 1989.

The atmosphere of the First Congress of People's Deputies of the USSR, opened on 25 May 1989, was charged with the spirit of this defeat. Contrary to the plans and intentions of the leadership, it was opened by Vilen Tolpezhnikov, a deputy from the Latvian SSR, who, taking advantage of a pause while the chairman of the Central Electoral Committee was sorting out papers, mounted the rostrum and suggested honouring the memory of the casualties of 9 April 1989 in Tbilisi with a minute of silence. Perhaps that very minute when the whole audience, ignoring the confusion of the top leaders, rose to their feet, marked the beginning of a disobedience which in a strikingly short period of time led to the complete collapse of totalitarianism and the communist regime in this country.

Everything that followed it, namely the attempts to investigate and reveal the truth about the massacre at Tbilisi, continued to turn the screws on this regime. The latter still resisted. The reactionary part of the corps of deputies wildly applauded General Rodionov who plainly declared his hostility to 'the Georgian variant of perestroika and pluralism of opinions'. Military deputies distributed anonymous leaflets, containing the outright lie that such 'horrors with blood-stained shovels is pure invention'. Party and Soviet functionaries and the military leaders who sent forces to Tbilisi contradicted themselves and one another in an attempt to extricate themselves from the affair. But their moral defeat was already a foregone conclusion. The 2nd Congress of People's Deputies of the USSR laid stress on the findings of the special commission of deputies set up for the investigation of the events in Tbilisi, headed by Anatoly Sobchak. The whole world became aware of the crime committed against the Georgian people and the name of the principal culprit was clearly pronounced - the totalitarian, communist system.[80]

One thing became obvious: Georgia would not remain in this system. The proud, freedom-loving Georgian people would never forgive the Soviet executioners the bloodshed on the night of 9 April 1989 in Tbilisi. Georgia would leave the empire and maybe even sooner than the rebellious Baltic republics. And, in fact, in the days of mourning, while the victims of Bloody Sunday were being buried, the Georgian people came to this decision.

As it turned out, it took little more than a year: the November elections of 1990 determined the political future of Georgia as an independent state, declaring its intention to secede from the USSR. But in that year the system, still alive and kicking, all its power still intact (the army, intelligence service, KGB etc.), with all the financial and economic levers in its control, using the well tested methods of ideological blackmail, deception and provocation, did everything possible to plant the seeds of future conflict and political complication. This minefield primarily involved the regions of Georgia with her multi-national population where the ethnic factor could be brought into action, playing, as we have seen, upon national feelings, old grievances, territorial disputes, religious, language and cultural differences.

Abkhazia was not the only place where communist reaction started to flex its muscles. Other possibilities were also carefully examined, such as Ossetia (which had worked earlier) and Ajaria (which did not work). Account was taken of the possibility of setting different groups of Georgians against each other: Mingrelians, Svans, Kakhetians, Gurians, Ajarians. Special attention was given to Mingrelia, the home of the President, Zviad Gamsakhurdia. The ground was prepared in outlying districts of the country as well as in the towns with a considerable Armenian, Russian, and Greek population. Hopes were pinned on difficulties arising from the return of Meskhetians to Georgia, exiled under Stalin to Central Asia (the bloodshed in Fergana, causing a stream of refugees of Turkish origin from the places of their old Central Asian exile, was arranged immediately after the Tbilisi syndrome in June, 1989). Yet the Abkhazian bridgehead appeared to the strategists especially convenient and full of potential from the very beginning.

Prospects for the restoration of the Soviet-communist regime appeared most favourable here. Russia was close at hand, literally just next door. There were powerful military bases of the Armed Forces of the USSR in Abkhazia and if they were not used openly in military actions, there was a chance of using them to apply pressure against the Georgian side. There was a particularly favourable social environment, a rich soil for the realization of the policy of restoring the regime: around the elite departmental and governmental sanatoria, country-cottages, zones of recreation and tourism, service clans had taken shape over decades, involving a greater part of the local population. Especially formidable in these clans was the stratum of military guards traditionally linked to the services of the Union ministries. Thousands of people whose income and well-being were directly connected with the prosperity of the 'communist paradise' proved to be a reliable potential reserve. But the crucial point is that in Abkhazia, more than anywhere else and more acutely, real inter-ethnic contradictions made themselves felt, which could be used in the desired direction: towards the restoration of the empire.

The aims of political revenge here could acquire a flawless ideo-logical mask: the Abkhazian question did not spring up yesterday or today, but had long since worried this region, where the people were unsatisfied with their political standing. In almost every decade of the last fifty years the problem became aggravated; the form of So-viet Socialist autonomy hardly answered the interests and hopes ei-ther of the Abkhazian ethnos or of the multi-national population of Abkhazia, the demographic and migrational processes took a com-plicated course. All these could easily serve as proof that anti-Geor-gian activities and conflicts had natural and reasonable grounds.

After the Tbilisi events, tension quickly escalated.On 14 May 1989, the Council of Ministers of the Georgian SSR issued an order requir-ing the formation of a branch of Tbilisi State University in Sukhumi. This instruction met the requirements of Georgian students and pro-fessors who had protested in April against systematic insults to their personal and national dignity, had left the Abkhazian university and were now actually on strike. Their action was widely supported by demonstrations and marches organised by the workers of the plant *Sukhumpribor*, by the locomotive depot and other enterprises, by peas-ants' gatherings in the Georgian villages of Kochara and Tsagera and so on.

The old Abkhazian University was not closed down by anybody and the opportunity to receive instruction in the Georgian language, at the new branch of Tbilisi University, as well as in Russian and Abkhazian in such a multi-national town as Sukhumi should have only enriched its cultural and scientific life and put an end to some of the tension arising on ethno-psychological grounds. However, the opening of the new higher school was used as an excuse to organise mass anti-Georgian actions by the leaders of the Abkhazian move-ment (now it was headed by the First secretary of the regional com-mittee of the Party V.D. Khishba).

On 15 May, the leaders of the republic and the activists of the PFA Aidgylara organised a huge rally. The obscurantist speeches against the opening of the University for Georgian students in Abkhazia (in a re-public with an overwhelming majority of Georgians in the population) must have been agreed upon with the Soviet structures in the Centre, since the Procurator General of the USSR, Alexandr Sukharev, by that time already notorious for many anti-democratic acts, including the persecution of the investigators (into corruption at a high level in Uzbekistan) - Gdlyan and Ivanov - abolished the order of the Council of Ministers of Georgia regarding the establishment of the branch of Tbilisi University in Sukhumi.

The voices of the leaders of Aidgylara joined those of the supporters of tough military measures who came out against the celebration of 26 May, Georgia's independence day, by the population of Sukhumi ('under Menshevist anti-soviet slogans' - as the Aidgylara newspaper reported to the authorities).[81] They also objected to the placing of a memorial plaque in the town of Ochamchire in commemoration of those killed in Tbilisi on 9 April. On 8 July 1989, the PFA Aidgylara made public an appeal to the Chairman of the Supreme Soviet of the USSR, Mikhail Gorbachev, which read: 'under the circumstances the only way out is to arrange a special form of administration in Abkhazia with direct subordination to the Centre.'[82]

But Gorbachev was not in a hurry about 'direct subordination to the Centre', realising perfectly well the magnitude of upheaval it might cause among the Georgians. As for the politicians from Aidgylara, they needed just such an outburst; so they provoked the first bloody incident. On the early morning of 15 July a group of unidentified persons destroyed the temporary stand with the photos of those killed on 9 April in Tbilisi which had been recently placed in Karl Marx Street in Sukhumi. 'The People's Forum of Abkhazia appealed to Gorbachev personally, to the Supreme Soviet of the USSR and the Ministry of Internal Affairs of the USSR and requested that troops be brought into Abkhazia.'[83]

That very night a group of Abkhazian elders was sent to the First Secretary of the regional committee of Abkhazia, informing him that 'special brigades of Abkhazian youth have been organised' and 'if measures are not taken, the Abkhazian part of the population will block the regional committee of the Party and the building housing the new branch of Tbilisi University.'[84]

However, they decided not 'to block' the regional committee of the Party (for they found understanding and support there) so they turned instead to the Georgian secondary school N 1, which in those summer days housed the examination commission of Tbilisi State University. The following day they made a vandalous pogrom of the school, wildly beating up the professors who were members of the examination commission. Sergei Labanov, correspondent of *Rossiya* (Russia) newspaper, a journalist who can hardly be accused of any special sympathies for Georgians, describes the Sukhumi events in the following way: 'On 15 July the town was in a fever. Small skirmishes started here and there. A well-organised string of buses kept arriving from different parts of Abkhazia; strongly-built young people with red flags and portraits of Gorbachev got off the buses... The trouble started about 6 p.m. near Rustaveli Park. Use was made of pieces of steel, stones and wooden clubs. At about 10 o'clock the first shots rang out in the square and the town was soon in turmoil. That night fourteen people were killed - nine Georgians and five Abkhazians. One of the first casualties was V. Vekua, leader of the Sukhumi branch of the Ilia Chavchavadze Society.

And so it began. Following these events, a well rehearsed campaign aimed at a prolonged confrontation was started. Impassive border-guards recorded the following: '...during the day of 16th and the night of 17th July 1989, people armed with side-arms, automatic rifles, also with bottles of incendiary mixtures... batons, metal rods, etc., boarded boats unhindered. Six boats transported nine hundred persons from Gudauta to Ochamchire.'

'The Abkhazian leaders', writes S. Labanov,' needed armed resistance and bloodshed in order to force the Centre to impose a state of emergency on the territory of the autonomous republic. In this case Georgia would automatically lose control of the region, and new national structures of power could be formed under the fraternal wing of the Soviet army. Who knows how much blood would be needed for the realization of this undertaking...'[85]

In the summer of 1989 the time had not yet come for such bloodshed. However, two tactics for future operations to be conducted on a much wider scale were being tested and mastered. First of all, armed detachments of militants (*boeviks*) of the Abkhazian People's Forum Aidgylara were involved in these actions for the first time. Secondly, techniques for neutralizing the police and the military border detachments were rehearsed, as well as possible co-operation with them in any joint offensive against Georgian units. The Police time and again simply did not interfere in the skirmishes and pogroms. Officers of the State Traffic Inspectorate and the Water Transport Police pretended that they did not notice buses and boats full of Abkhazian militants. But the Soviet army remained. Colonel-General Shatalin, for example, succeeded in separating the sides involved in an incident near the village of Ilori, without a single casualty. He clearly did not wish to follow the example of General Rodionov and carry out punitive 'military operations' against the Georgian population.

The organisers of the July bloodshed could draw the following conclusions: for operations on a wider scale they needed full authority and power to issue orders rather than having to negotiate with the hesitant Regional Committee through Abkhazian elders. They also needed 'their own' Supreme Soviet, 'their own' police, 'their own' army, fully controlled by them. Thirdly, it became clear how serious the resistance of the 'anti-Soviets' and the Georgian population would be.

This was probably the most important lesson of July. Having realised that the resistance would be desperate, the civil war fierce, and the balance of forces not in favour of the Abkhazian side - remember the population figures - a new concept of the 'solidarity of mountain peoples', and 'the help of the fraternal peoples of the Northern Caucasus' began to take shape. The leaders of the People's Forum of Abkhazia (PFA) Aidgylara - zealous defenders of socialist law and order - had not dreamt of it before.

Informants from the PFA, supplying the Central Committee of the CPSU, the Procurator's Office of the USSR, Ministry of Internal Affairs of the USSR, and other offices with reports on the July events in Abkhazia, with unconcealed fear specified details of the resistance to the terror unleashed by Abkhazian militants. On 16th July Georgian 'unofficials' took under their control the streets of Sukhumi, seized bridges and organised their headquarters at the cinema *Apsny*. The population from Western Georgia rushed to their aid. At dawn 180 prisoners were released (according to other sources they broke away) from Zugdidi jail.[86] In summing up the information used by the analysts of the USSR KGB, the following inconceivable statement was made: '... at the battle near the river Ghalidzga (town of Ochamchire) ... a 300-strong detachment of Abkhazians stopped a 20,000-strong force (including 180 criminals who had broken away from the Zugdidi jail) from Western Georgia.'[87]

If this was an obvious tragicomic exaggeration, the clear realisation of the deficiency of their own forces ('the whole of Western Georgia will come to help them') was another important conclusion drawn by the leaders of the PFA in the July of 1989. They immediately informed Moscow about this. From that time, a new political orientation began to take shape. New organisational structures began to be formed and considerable regrouping of forces took place.

This orientation of the most reactionary circles, still in power or close to the central authority which hoped to keep Georgia within the USSR and block its centrifugal forces, was now directed not so much towards the People's Forum Aidgylara (for some time it kept in the background) but towards the legitimate organs of power in Abkhazia. In 1989 Vladislav Ardzinba, R. Arshba, R. Salukvadze and K. Cholokyan were all elected to the Soviet of Nationalities of the Supreme Soviet of the USSR. They and their colleagues amongst reactionary groups like *Soyuz* began to look at ways to unite the ethnic groups in Georgia with their fellows throughout the Caucasus.

The democratic forces in Georgia understood the situation clearly. The Appeal of 21 July 1989 by the Popular Front of Georgia to her countrymen said: '... the real instigators of these events are reactionary external forces which for decades artificially created the Abkhazian question and set the Abkhazian people against the Georgian. Georgians and Abkhazians can preserve their ethnic and cultural originality only together. Only together can they achieve full national independence.'[88]

There are many explanations of this cessation of the Abkhazian-Georgian conflict which seemed so threatening in the middle of July 1989. The military pointed to the efficiency of their actions as peacemakers in the separation of the conflicting sides. Local authorities ascribed this to themselves, noting the timely introduction of a 'special regime of the conduct of citizens' on 18 July. The Party leadership of Georgia, probably for the last time, displayed optimism, reporting at the Plenary Session of the Central Committee of the CPSU in September 1989 that the investigation of the Abkhazian events was going on successfully 'under the strict supervision of the Procurator's Office of the USSR', and also that there was 'the beginning of an inter-ethnic dialogue in Abkhazia, and great determination by the communists of the regional organisation, the whole population of the autonomous republic - Abkhazians, Georgians, Russians, Armenians, Greeks - to overcome the difficulties. (This) fills us with confidence and optimism ...'[89] Some journalists conducted their own criminal investigations, which convinced them that a 'third force' had interfered. A peculiar internationalism was shown in this situation by the criminal world for which the resorts of Abkhazia had always been a goldmine: they did not want to have their business undermined in the middle of the holiday season. The mafia had forced a truce! 'And the conflict was localized without much noise, but not in the rooms of party authorities, nor at the meetings of the leaders of unofficial unions of the opposing sides, but in a coffee shop near Sukhumi harbour - at a gathering of thieves on the 19th of July. Having discussed the situation, the criminal bosses went to the districts in trouble and a day later passions calmed down.'[90]

In any case, a big war against Georgia did not take place in the summer of 1989, the forces being inadequate. Meanwhile, work started on other kinds of pressure on the republic and on the leaders of its democratic movement. In August unexpected tension developed in districts with a predominantly Armenian population in the south of Georgia. Rallies were held in Akhalkalaki and Bogdanovka, demanding the creation of an Armenian autonomy on the territory of Georgia and a ban on the immigration of Georgians to Javakheti from districts affected by avalanches. However, this potential conflict was settled peacefully with the participation of the leaders of Armenia. Georgia offered aid in foodstuffs to the neighbouring republic which was suffering a blockade at that time, and the demands of the participants of the rallies were dropped.

The centre for the preparation of new anti-Georgian actions was drifting to South Ossetia.[91] The leaders of the Ossetian movement and *Adamon Nykhas* (People's Conversation) stepped up their efforts to make closer contacts with the PFA Aidgylara and to create a united anti-Georgian front along the Sukhumi-Tskhinvali axis, with hopes of involving other peoples of Georgia in the near future.

Analysis of documents coming from Tskhinvali as early as 1989 convinces one that the ideologues of separatism were fully aware of the importance of uniting anti-Georgian movements in the Armenian and Azerbaijanian districts, in South Ossetia and Abkhazia into a single chain, thus creating a coalition hostile to Georgia.

Cries of 'to us all' and 'we all' - from Aidgylara to Adamon Nykhas - are highly characteristic both of messages coming from Tskhinvali, published in the first issue of the newspaper Aidgylara, and for other anti-Georgian movements, all of which began in 1989. There is no doubt that the Centre, Moscow, was steering these movements, punishing rebellious Georgia which had created so many problems for the defenders of the 'single and indestructible Soviet Union' in the spring of that year.

Asserting this, however, we should bear in mind that the thousands of people participating in the July clashes in Abkhazia, in the *Borchalo* movement for Azerbaijanian autonomy (June-July 1989), in the August rallies in Akhalkalaki and Bogdanovka (Armenians), and in the defence of Tskhinvali on 23 November, were by no means all 'agents' of the Communist Centre fulfilling tasks set by the Central Committee of the CPSU, KGB or military structures.

While organizing these mass movements one after another, the reactionary forces of the old regime played on the sincere feelings of the different nationalities. The actions carried out in Sumgait and Fergana in the summer of 1989 vividly showed that the level of accumulated resentments against unbearable living conditions and political repression was very high in all parts of the USSR. At the same time, there was such obfuscation and such a lack of real information that the flood of popular resentment could be manipulated very easily. Thus the pogroms of Armenians, Turks, Crimean Tatars, Jews, Russians, Uzbeks, Kirghiz and so on. The range of possibilities was exceptionally wide.

In Georgia this flood had to be directed against the Georgian version of perestroika, against the Georgian people. In April 1989 Georgian 'extremism' failed to be crushed by military force. Hence it was desirable to continue the anti-Georgian war, constantly blackmailing the leadership of Georgia and desperately trying to keep the republic in the Soviet empire by any means possible.

Thinking, and with good reason, that the Abkhazian-Ossetian alliance would not be very reliable, the leaders in Moscow, on the eve of the collapse of the Soviet Union, began to explore the ground for more productive lines of conduct. Indeed, in all this time it had proved unfeasible to organise a single joint or at least simultaneous Abkhazian-Ossetian action against Georgian 'unofficials' or, later, against independent Georgia.Geographical remoteness and divisions within the local Party nomenclature hindered unification. There were also psychological differences. The Abkhazians had long been instilled with the idea of their superiority over the 'newcomers', and the Ossetians with the idea of their exclusiveness as the representatives of Christian civilization on both sides of the Caucasus Range.

However, two simultaneous scenarios were being planned. The first one envisaged the unification of the Abkhazian, Russian (Slavic), Armenian and other national movements into a common interfront within the Abkhazian Autonomous Republic against Georgian anti-Sovietism, rigidly controlled and supervised by the Communist party and forces of socialist law and order. The other scenario planned the consolidation of mountain peoples of the Caucasus against the 'mini-empires of Transcaucasia', primarily against Georgia.

The first scenario worked slowly, but on the whole successfully. The society of Russian culture, the Slav Home, was formally registered only in April 1991, but already from autumn 1989 its future leaders, Yuri Voronov, Viktor Loginov and others, acted resolutely to suppress any Georgian aspiration for independence. At the same time, from the very beginning, Big Brother assumed the role of ideological leadership of the Abkhazian and other national movements. Voronov notes with satisfaction that 'after the July events (1989) a rapprochement of a part of the Russian diaspora with other national groups of Abkhazia became evident. At the referendum of the 17th of March 1991 Russians together with Abkhazians, Armenians, Greeks, Jews, many Georgians, and representatives of other communities voted for the preservation by Abkhazia of common political, economic and cultural space with Russia.'[92]

However, in the second scenario - consolidation of the mountain peoples - sudden unexpected developments occurred. These developments, obviously not foreseen by the authors, were reminiscent of the well-known story of the djinn freed from the bottle.

The Confederation (or initially Assembly) of the Mountain Peoples of the Caucasus proved to be an uncontrollable force. The fierce anarchic love of freedom of the mountain peoples, and their reluctance to live either in the Russian, or Soviet empire, made it very difficult to direct this force only against democratic Georgia. For this, acrobatic feats of reasoning and considerable demagogy were needed.

1. *Eduard Shevardnadze and Tamaz Nadareishvili (Georgian ex-Prime Minister of Abkhazia) whose family and village were wiped out.*

2. *Shevardnadze in Sukhumi.*

3. *Vladislav Grigorievich Ardzinba.*

4. *A recent photograph of Ardzinba.*

5. *Evacuation of civilians from Sukhumi.*

6. *Evacuation from Sukhumi of civilians on to Ukranian ships.*

7. *Ship from Ukranian navy in Abkhazia.*

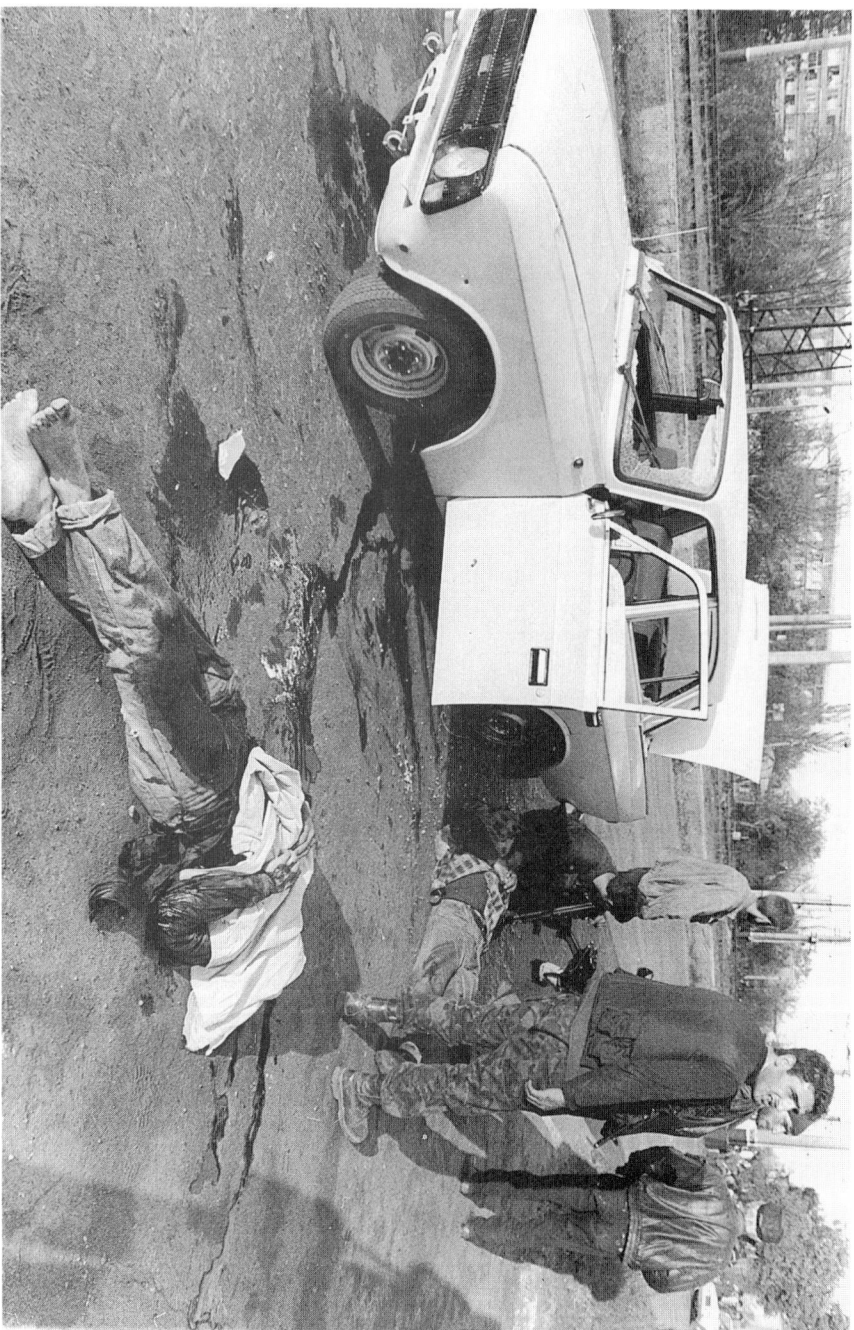

8. *Georgian casualties from car bomb attack.*

9. *Georgian homes on fire in Sukhumi.*

10. *Georgian family in the rubble of their home.*

11. Local Georgian residents in Sukhumi defend their city.

12. *Georgian soldiers in Sukhumi.*

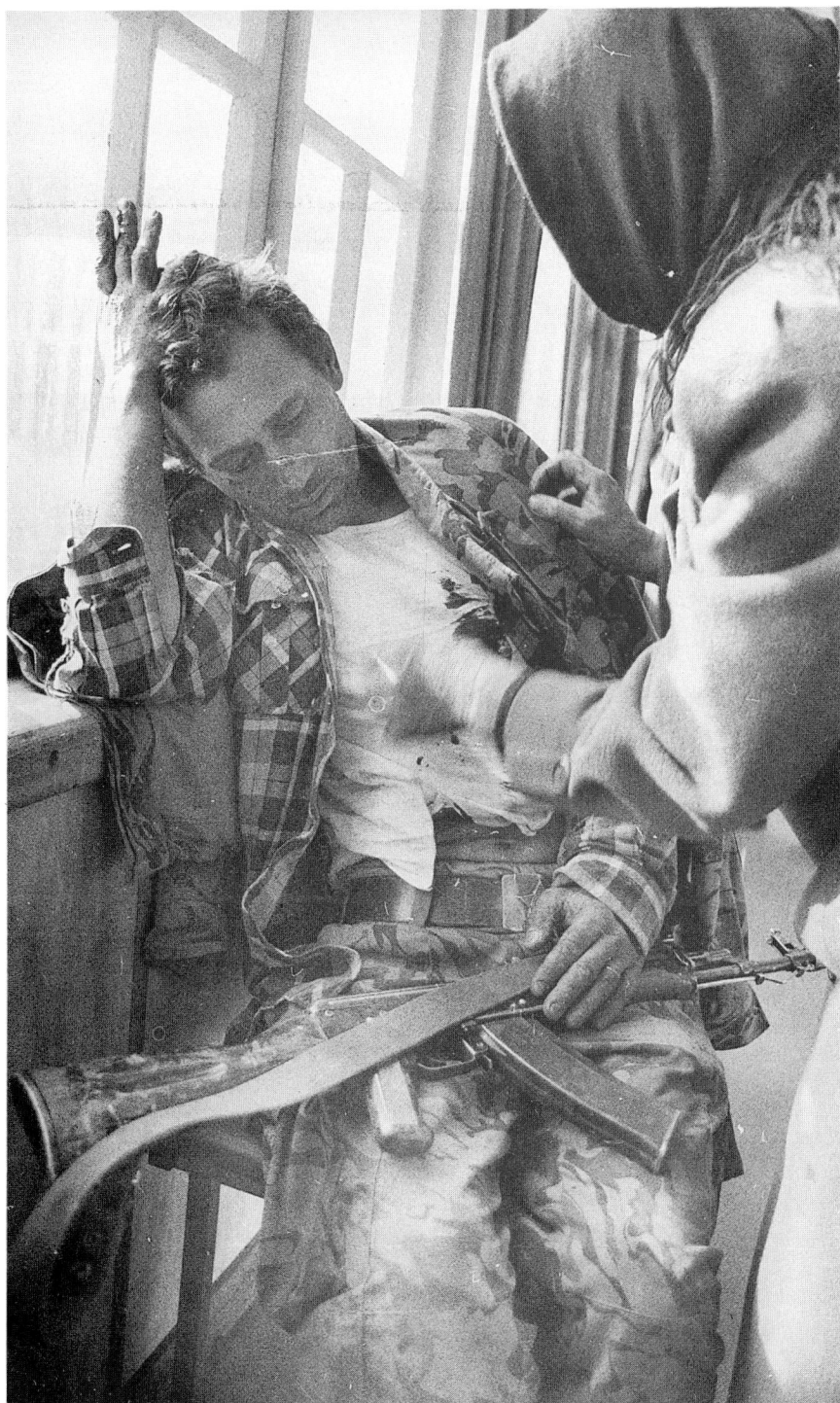

13. *Wounded Georgian soldier in Kutaisi Hospital being tended by his mother.*

14. *Georgian civilian defending Sukhumi near the airport.*

15. *The bodies of Abkhazians, Chechen and Russian mercenaries awaiting burial.*

16. *Old Russian woman in Sukhumi.*

17. *Sukhumi cinema on fire.*

18. *Georgian soldier.*

19. *Georgian dead.*

20. *Georgian civilians at Sukhumi airport.*

21. *Georgian soldiers in Abkhazia.*

22. Georgian soldiers.

23. *Dead Georgian soldier.*

24. *Georgian child in Sukhumi.*

The mountain people were reminded of the hostility of Christian Georgia to the Muslims, of its aspirations as a 'mini-empire', and similar nonsense. Sergei Shamba suddenly discovered that: 'Abkhazia stands for a sovereign federation of the mountain peoples within the USSR.'[93]

The fundamental values towards which the Confederation of the Mountain Peoples was orientated did not include either the USSR, memorable to many peoples of the Caucasus for the terrors of the Stalin deportations, or Communist ideology or 'socialism with a human face'. Anti-democratic and anti-Georgian passions could often be heard in the speeches of the leaders of the Confederation along with manifestations of Islamic fundamentalism, fierce anti-Russian (anti-Slavic) and anti-Semitic feelings. Anti-Georgian passions were especially important for those who stood at the cradle of the Confederation, for those who held its first Congress in Sukhumi in August 1989. The Confederation was carefully fostered - of course it was dangerous, for it could blow up in their faces - but useful, if thrown in the right direction, primarily against rebellious Georgia.

Later, when independent democratic Georgia became Shevardnadze's Georgia and independent democratic Russia Yeltsin's Russia, the Confederation of the Mountain Peoples of the Caucasus, with great energy and an impetuous readiness for any actions of political banditry, terrorism and cruelty, acquired more definite aims: the confederates would be ready to fight according to the laws of Holy War and Blood Feud, with all their concommitant medieval savagery.

But all this was still to come. On 25 August the First Congress of the Representatives of the Nationalities of the Caucasus was convoked with the sanction and hospitality of the local Party and Soviet authorities, the activists of the People's Forum of Abkhazia Aidgylara showing special animation.

The first to arrive were the delegations of two Caucasian ethnic communities - the Adyghe and the Vainakhians, i.e. Abazins, Adyghe, Kabardians, Circassians, and the Chechens and Ingush. Neither the Ossetians nor the Turkic peoples of the Caucasian region participated in the first congress. However, the congress was named an assembly of 'national-democratic movements and parties of the Northern Caucasus, Abkhazia and Daghestan'. It adopted a decision on the establishment of an

Assembly of the Mountain Peoples of the Caucasus (*AMPC*).

The Assembly elected the Coordination Council chaired by the Kabardian Musa (Yuri) Shanibov, 52 year-old assistant professor of the Kabardino-Balkarian University, Cand.Sci.(philosophy) from Nalchik. The Assembly's proclaimed aim was the restoration of the Mountain Republic with Sukhumi as its capital and the regeneration of the Community of the Mountain Peoples of the Caucasus which Shanibov even called 'the Caucasian ethnos'. He wrote in the first issue of the AMPC newspaper: 'The question is the restoration and development of the Caucasian ethnos. The mountain peoples, coming out of the same cradle of the proto-Caucasus, must primarily revive their spiritual and cultural unity... as a uniting force, religion is the last but not the least.'[94]

'Yes, we declare our determination to restore our Mountain Federation', Yusup Soslambekov, another leader of the AMPC, explained. 'This federation had been proclaimed and received international recognition earlier than the Georgian Republic. We declare that it was annexed as a result of a collusion between Russian and Georgian Generals. As a consequence our southern region, Abkhazia, with the traditional capital of the Caucasus, fell to Georgia, while the rest of our territories went to Russia. Yes, we shall restore our state and it will never join any other one ...'[95]

The tone of the first documents adopted by the first founding Congress of the Assembly of the Mountain Peoples of the Caucasus in Sukhumi was rather restrained. In particular, the tone of the appeal to the 'Abkhazian and Georgian Peoples', which expressed its regret on the occasion of the July events, called to 'the fraternal peoples to shake hands.'[96] But their North Caucasian neighbours, on behalf of individual organisations and parties belonging to the AMPC as well as the AMPC itself, interfered much more unceremoniously in Abkhazian-Georgian relations. Accusing and threatening Georgian unofficial military units, they appealed to Moscow to give a political assessment of the situation in Georgia and, apparently, asked them to organise one more punitive expedition to Tbilisi.

The Statement of the Popular Front of the Checheno-Ingush ASSR on assisting the reconstruction read thus: 'The policy of abetting the so-called informals by the Soviet and party bodies of Georgia... with the connivance of the Centre brings us closer to another tragedy - to the mass indignation of all the peoples of the Northern Caucasus... Because of the country's top leadership, too slow in the political assessment of the situation in Georgia, the Abkhazian people are still in danger of new aggression. This disturbs our peoples who cannot view with indifference the unjust situation in which the Abkhazian people has found itself. In this connection we record a resolute protest to the Chairman of the Georgian National Democratic Party, Gamsakhurdia,[97] who in his appeal to the Georgian people went as far as to say that Abkhazia is on Georgian land, as if Abkhazia did not exist twelve hundred years ago...[98] Gamsakhurdia with his provocative statements ranked Abkhazia with the recently created autonomous region in Khabarovsk Krai.[99] All over Abkhazia Gamsakhurdia's hard core supporters are launching an unbridled campaign of persecution of the Abkhazian people, hoisting Georgian Menshevist flags throughout Abkhazian land...'[100]

The telegram on behalf of the general meeting of the Kabardian National Democratic Movement, *Adyga Khase*, is of a more categoric tone (21 September 1989). Assembled in distant Nalchik, the activists of Adyga Khase having discussed the situation in Abkhazia, urgently and without delay demand:

1. To grant Abkhazia the status of special rule like Nagorny Karabakh.
2. To form a commission of the Central Committee of the CPSU and the Supreme Soviet of the USSR for any objective analysis
3. To remove urgently the flagrant injustice... lying in the fact that Georgia, one of the sides of the conflict, is granted the opportunity to establish the truth regarding the facts of infringement of the law... to transfer the conduct of the affairs to a neutral team of people from other regions of the USSR.[101]

A delegation of the Georgian Popular Front headed by Professor Nodar Natadze was invited to the Third session of the Assembly of the Mountain Peoples of the Caucasus which was held on 4 November 1989 in Nalchik. The crude pressure to which the Georgian delegation was subjected forced it to make a statement on the impossibility of conducting a dialogue on the Abkhazian issue. Under the pretext of defending the interests of the Abkhazian people the leaders of the AMPC openly strove to provoke and induce the Centre to take measures against Georgia. They threatened that otherwise blood-shed would be organised by the mountaineers of the Caucasus. The appeal adopted by the AMPC to the Supreme Soviet of the USSR and the Georgian SSR reads: '...the example of Abkhazia shows that the Centre does not take effective measures... The Centre does not wish or cannot fulfil the obligations it has assumed... If the deepening process of depriving the Abkhazian people of their rights guaranteed by law is not stopped, it may lead to a new wave of bloodshed.'[102]

Summing up the events of 1989, it may be said that Georgia, transformed by a strong wave of democratic movements, realized the impossibility of remaining within the grip of the Soviet Union. But, having risen against the totalitarian system, Georgia received a whole set of counter-strokes and 'measures of pressure'. These measures, as attested by V.V. Bakatin, were carefully thought out in advance and planned at the Central Committee of the CPSU and the Committee of State Security. They included: direct violence (9 April) and peculiar interfronts in the shape of various movements: Abkhazian, Ossetian, mountaineers of the Caucasus. These raised the question of the re-carving of the borders of the Georgian State. They threatened blood-shed and organised the first clashes on ethnic grounds. They called the first strikes which destabilized the economic situation. Twice in the spring and summer, passenger and transport trains had to stop for several days in Sukhumi. Normal railway communication with Russia was disrupted;[103] in September, in response to the calls of the PFA Aidgylara, several plants in Abkhazia announced a strike. On the 14th of September twenty persons, including five women, went on hunger strike 'in protest against the infringement upon the rights of the Abkhazian people.'[104]

Thus, in 1989, the rehearsal for a counter-revolutionary Vendée was held in Abkhazia. However, the denouement was somewhat delayed because from the end of November 1989 South Ossetia, supported by the Communist leadership of the North Ossetian ASSR, became the main arena of organised anti-Georgian actions.

Chapter 5

Deliberate Provocations 1990-1992

For almost two and a half years, from the beginning of 1990 till the summer of 1992, the fifth column against democratic Georgia was being formed. It was being provided with personnel, finances and organisational and ideological backing. Outwardly this period was not full of striking events that would have drawn the attention of the international press and public to the Abkhazian region. During this time South Ossetia was the main trouble spot in Georgia. Here the tension spiralled: cities were ruined, villages were burnt - ninety three totally - and thousands of refugees left the area. Georgians fled to neighbouring areas of Georgia, South Ossetians to North Ossetia. The Russian army and the Georgian Guard were getting increasingly involved in the armed conflict.

Our focus, however, is Abkhazia, which seemed to be relatively peaceful, though some clashes between the Abkhazian and Georgian population did occur and internal tension was constantly maintained. These clashes were deliberate provocations by the boeviks - PFA activists who, for example, organised the attacks in Gagra on 26 May, Georgia's Independence Day. These were against demonstrators and representatives of the local administration for 'disrespect to the Abkhazian flag'. The assailants were not punished. Such incidents, however, remained of local significance.

Meanwhile, consolidation and help for organisations supporting Abkhazia's separation from Georgia continued from above. Mass rallies, scholarly conferences, plenums of artistic and literary associations were devoted to strengthening and substantiating the great idea of separation, and to stirring up anti-Georgian sentiments. Thus, addressing the plenum of the Union of Writers of Abkhazia, Alexei Gogua declared: 'The patience of Abkhazian writers is running out and there is no sense in continuing any contacts with the Georgian

Writers' Union'. Earlier Gogua had become well-known as the author of devoted works of Soviet Realism: *The River is hastening to the Sea, Taste of Water, Wild Azalea*, in which he advocated a Soviet Abkhazia, happy in the bosom of the fraternal family of the peoples of the USSR.

At that time propaganda justifying the complete independence of Abkhazia was produced constantly. Abkhazian patience was running out, it was declared. More than 'a hundred thousand people (Georgians) had been resettled on the best lands of land-starved Abkhazia', wrote *Aidgylara*.[105] In 1990 the publishing house *Alashara* issued Stanislav Lakoba's *Essays on the the Political History of Abkhazia*. Here both the history of the so-called 'independent' joining of Abkhazia to Russia and the instigative role of Turkey in the complication of Russo-Abkhazian relations, were systematically falsified. The establishment of Soviet power in Abkhazia on 4 March 1921 was interpreted as a deliverance from occupation by the Georgian Democratic Republic and the repressive regime of the ruling Menshevik party.[106] This is an appalling travesty of the truth.

From the 26th May and the Declaration of Independent Democratic Georgia, the Abkhazian press escalated their attacks. From the very beginnings of Bolshevik dictatorship till the present day, great efforts have been made to expunge the memory of Georgia's previous independence from the minds of its people. The Georgian Mensheviks[107] were villified and presented as 'hirelings of imperialism', 'bloody invaders', 'interventionists', and so on.[108] Obliging journalists and scholars with diplomas prepared the way for further enmity between the Georgian and Abkhazian people: 'The consanguinity of the Abkhazian and Georgian peoples is an empty word for science... There is no blood relationship between these peoples', wrote Alexi Papaskiri, assistant professor at the Abkhazian State University.[109]

Day after day from 1990 to 1992 in the Abkhazian nationalist press, radio and television, in the lecture rooms of the University, in institutes and schools, wherever Abkhazian History was taught, the activists of the PFA stirred up national hostility and prepared the way for the secession of Abkhazia from Georgia.

So the image of Georgia as the enemy was created in the public consciousness. This enemy was any Georgian, including the next-door neighbour. He was blamed for all the troubles of the Abkhazian people, for the lowering of the standard of living, for the breakdown of the regular rhythms of the holiday season, for the shortages of essential goods. He, allegedly, grabbed everything, robbed everyone. He drank the blood of Abkhazia and pumped all its wealth into Tbilisi. The average Georgian was portrayed as a bandit, a murderer, a cruel sadist. Georgians of the past as well as the living came in for their share of calumny. The democrat was held up as the perpetrator of all evils, for it was the democrat who had destroyed the great Soviet Union, who had brought 'blood, starvation and cold', and who had destroyed this contented Abkhazian Riviera.[110]

When it proved possible to unite these two monsters, the democrat and the Georgian, in one person, the image was doubly frightening. When Gamsakhurdia fled and Shevardnadze became head of the State Council of Georgia, all the fury of the reactionary and nationalist forces became focused on one man.[111]

Meanwhile the People's Forum of Abkhazia was persistently trying to write its charter. This involved considerable amending to take account of changing circumstances, especially during the disintegration of the Soviet Union and the extraordinary turnaround when the Communist Party became the opposition, almost an underground party. The former zealous expressions of loyalty to the principles of Marxist-Leninism and to the indisolubility of the USSR had to be quickly extirpated, though the essence of its ideology remained the same. This had, after all, been born within the walls of the Central Committee of the CPSU. Nothing really changed for Aidgylara; it is interesting to see that in the final draught of the charter, attitudes to property, for example, remained as they had always been: 'The PFA Aidgylara considers that it is too early to introduce private ownership of land.'[112]

Section one of the charter was devoted to the idea of Abkhazian statehood: 'Abkhazian statehood is rooted in hoary antiquity. The state has proved to be the highest form of self-determination of the Abkhazian people. Each time the Abkhazian state fell under the pressure of external forces, the Abkhazian people were subjected to genocide. For many centuries historical tradition shaped the Abkhazian mentality in such a way that the highest... value of our people is the national state, without which the existence of the Abkhazian ethnos loses all meaning. At the present historical stage, following the

disintegration of the USSR, the Abkhazian state is facing two tasks: se-
curing constitutionally the Declaration of State Sovereignty of Abkhazia
and the building of a state governed by law. Unfortunately, the fulfil-
ment of these and many other tasks facing Abkhazia is impeded by the
national-chauvinistic forces in the Republic of Georgia. However, the
counteraction to the sovereignty and democratisation of Abkhazia on
the part of Tbilisi can only be of a temporary character.'[113]

The final draught of the Charter[114] turned this 'public and political' movement into an organisation based on strict centralist principles, just like the communist party with the same controlled membership enrollment, expulsion, fees - and with local, district and ur-
ban 'cells' whose network was to embrace the whole of Abkhazia.

Alongside Aidgylara other organisations sprang up in Abkhazia,
sometimes acting independently, sometimes uniting with it. By the
summer of 1992 the main structure which united all the anti-Georgian and anti-democratic forces assembled in Abkhazia, was the Slav
Home. It was officially registered on 23 April 1991 as *the Society of
Russian Culture in Abkhazia*, and later renamed *the Community of the
Russian People in Abkhazia*.

This highly political organisation with its close connections with
commercial and often partly illegal structures, was really a front and
had little to do with cultural matters, Russian or otherwise. A document sent by the Chairman of its board, Viktor Loginov, to Abdulatipov, Chairman of the Council of Nationalities of the Supreme
Soviet of the Russian Federation in April 1992, graphically proves
this point:

'The renunciation of the objectives of the former USSR, as well as
the existing destructive tendencies inside the Russian Federation,
inevitably lead to the necessity of creating a state institution to defend the interests of the Slavic-Russian population and their communities not only in Russia, but outside as well.

In this connection primary importance is attached to the creation
of conditions for a commercial and industrial social stratum consisting of the local Russian population, as well as the recreation
of...national structures...that it is deprived of at present. The task will
be greatly aided by the legislation of the system of privileges...for the
organisations participating in the restoration of the Russian
community...In its turn, it is necessary to create a regime of the least

favourable conditions for the persons, organisations and states infringing the rights of Russians on the territories of near, far and internal abroad.In the light of the foregoing...it seems necessary to:
1. Open a Russian consulate in Abkhazia...
2. Open a Russian cultural centre on the territory of Abkhazia...
3. Open branches of the Abkhazian Slav Home, vital for the Russian-Caucasian economic and cultural integration as well as for uniting the Caucasian Russians, in the following cities: Sochi, Krasnodar, Stavropol, Rostov-on-Don, Moscow and St.Petersburg.
4. Open in Abkhazia representations of Russian federal lands, branches of banks etc.
5. Include the municipal, public and other structures of Abkhazia in non-governmental, inter-regional formations (Associations of South Russian Cities etc.)
6. Create Russian-Abkhazian committees to organise celebrations of the three hundredth anniversary of the Russian Navy, the Day of Slavic Culture and Writing etc.
7. Establish a system of subsidies, privileges and the assignment of credits on liberal terms to public organisations representing the interests of Russians on the given territory - the Community of the Russian people in Abkhazia, the Slav Home and its subsidiary structures: the Russian Cultural Centre of Abkhazia, the Association of Cossacks of Abkhazia, and the Charity Fund of Smetsky.'[115]

Nothing could be clearer. The ideology of the Slav Home was defined from the start, and its main political objective plain: to wrest Abkhazia away from Georgia. While it still seemed possible to rely upon the party structures of the USSR, such an objective could be realized within the Union. Either Abkhazia could leave Georgia and enter the Russian Federation as an autonomy, or she could sign the Union Treaty with Russia and Georgia on an equal footing. The collapse of the Soviet Union did not change the plans of the leaders of the Slav Home. The goal remained the same, only the reference points became different: Russian trading, commercial and industrial structures, with their liberal subsidies from the Russian budget, would become the main levers in the scheme. Hopes lay also with the paramilitary

Cossack groups from South Russia and with the political forces in the Supreme Soviet of the Russian Federation that were interested in 'Russian-Caucasian integration'.[116]

Various Russian 'cultural societies' were founded quite properly to satisfy the cultural needs of Russian communities living outside the boundaries of the Russian state. The Slav Home, however, had from the start performed a different function: that of Big Brother and leader to the People's Forum of Abkhazia. Viktor Loginov, one of the central figures in the Slav Home, an historian by training, had directed the preparatory ideological work for all the destabilisation, the eventual declaration of Abkhazian independence, and the subsequent war. It was here, in the Slav Home - which had, by the spring of 1992, quite literally occupied all the commanding heights in the building of the Supreme Soviet of Abkhazia - that Abkhazian policy was determined, even down to questions of what should or should not appear in Abkhazian newspapers.[117] Naturally it was bad to stay with Georgia, good to secede and join Russia, though not the new Russia of Yeltsin and the democrats, (the leaders of the Slav Home had declared quite openly their determination to 'hang Yeltsin and Shevardnadze side by side from the same tree') but a restored Russia 'mighty and great', Soviet and Socialist.[118]

The Slav Home did not limit its activities to merely slavic problems. It was turning into an ideological and political organisation with claims to lead all the national movements in its desired direction - the restoration of the old regime. Military matters, namely forming and equipping the Cossack armed forces, were given closest attention. Regulations for various associations of a paramilitary nature were worked out and conferences, gatherings and quasi-military reviews were held.

Thus, under the aegis of the Slav Home, on 14 June 1992, two months prior to the outbreak of war, a gathering (*skhod* or *krug*) of the Abkhazian Cossacks was held. A new Cossack association was formed and its ataman, V.I. Shmalii, was elected. It is noteworthy that, according to the charter worked out by the Slav Home, the age of membership for young men was eighteen (the age of military conscription) and orthodox christening for all recruits was compulsory (to prevent undesirable aliens from joining). On the eve of the events of August, the Cossacks could muster three hundred sabres.[119]

Not content with their own Cossack army, the leaders of the Slav Home sought contact with the powerful armed groups of the Don and Kuban Cossacks which were being formed towards the end of 1992. The association (*rada*) of Kuban Cossacks particularly, was originally fostered as a potential fighting partner of the Abkhazian Slav Home and was initiated by the former chairman of the Krasnodar regional party committee, N. Kondratenko. The polling carried out by the Supreme Soviet of Russia in August 1992 showed the potential here: approximately one million Kubanians considered themselves Cossacks; less than 40% of the Kuban Cossacks supported the idea of land ownership (in comparison, 82% voted for it in the whole of Russia); every tenth Cossack was sympathetic to communist ideology. Alexandr Rutskoy, (*since imprisoned and then released for his part in the plot to overthrow Yeltsin in 1994*) proved to be their most popular Russian politician. Traditional adherence to order and authority was demonstrated by their readiness to actively support the fight in the Dneister area and in their categorical 'no' to the request to shelter refugees in their area, among them Armenians, Azerbaijanis, Meskhetian Turks and Crimean Tatars.[120]

Along with the Slav Home, smaller organisations came into being in Abkhazia. They were formed according to ethnic background (the Armenian *Krunk*, the Ossetian *Alan*) or were similar to those parties and organisations whose political objective was to oppose the democratic forces in Georgia. They were characterised by their attitude towards communist ideology, Soviet power and the future Union or Federation of Republics.

Initially the PFA was seen as the hub of all activity in the area, but as the multi-party system grew, a pluralism of public organisations became a feature of everyday life. However, it was not the intention of those who had reared and cherished it that it should be lost and scattered among the various parties and national committees. By the spring of 1992 *Soyuz* was formed here incorporating the PFA Aidgylara, the People's Party of Abkhazia, the Slav Home, Krunk and several minor organisations united by the common ideology of separatism. The very name Soyuz reveals a sort of nostalgic longing for the defunct Soviet Union and shared interests with the old Soyuz bloc in the former Supreme Soviet and sessions of the USSR People's Deputies. It is worth remembering that at those sessions Ardzinba and his colleagues in the Abkhazian corps of deputies actively tried to attach themselves to the most reactionary representatives of the military-industrial complex, Army Generals, the Party Apparat and agents of the State Security Committee - the KGB.

This consolidation was meant to demonstrate universal support for Ardzinba's policies in Abkhazia. But this did not in the least coincide with the stand of the majority of the population with its diverse ethnic strata. Small groups were seeking the protection of the new leadership and loudly claiming to represent the interests of the Russians or Armenians or Greeks, but in fact the public opinion of the peoples of Abkhazia had never been studied. There had never been a referendum and no polling was ever carried out. An Armenian from the Gulprish district, Gregory Mosikyan, wrote to the newspaper *Demokraticheskaya Abkhazia* after the war began:

'These leaders have announced the independence of Abkhazia and its secession from Georgia without consulting all the peoples inhabiting the republic...I, an Armenian, support the integrity of Georgia, have always condemned those political parties and public organisations that approved and abetted Ardzinba in his separatism, leading to the aggravation of the situation.These are the Slav Home, the Ossetian Alan, the Sukhumi Society of Internationalists, the Human Rights Society as well as the Armenian Krunk, the leaders of which claim to be talking on behalf of the Armenian population, though we, Armenians, have never given them this right.The leadership of the Krunk have been defending their own interests, not those of the Armenians.'[121]

Between 1990 and 1992 ties between the anti-democratic forces in Abkhazia and the Assembly of Mountain Peoples were strengthened. Their second and third Congresses (October 1990 in Nalchik and November 1991 in Sukhumi) were characterised by feverish planning aimed at tearing away a large chunk of Russia, and of course Abkhazia, and the creation of a Mountain Republic with an autocratic regime. The 'Chechen Revolution', which took place between the second and third congresses in 1991, was the first attempt to realise their programme - though so far only on Chechen territory. Within three years the Assembly had considerably expanded its composition: from six to sixteen of the different peoples of the Caucasus.

At the third Conference the Assembly was transformed into the Confederation of the Mountain Peoples of the Caucasus (*CMPC*) and its tough administrative body was formed, including the offices of President (the Kabardian Musa Shanibov retained the post) and sixteen Vice-Presidents, as well as the Committee of Caucasian Associations. This latter was, in fact, a government, for these associations had charge of the economy, defence, culture, external relations and so on. The Chechen Yusup Soslambekov was elected head of the Caucasian Parliament and the Abkhaz Zurab Achba was given charge of the Arbitration Court of the Confederation. The goal of the CMPC was the setting up of a Mountain Republic that would establish its relations with Russia, Georgia, Armenia and Azerbaijan as an equal. According to the plans of the leaders of the Confederation, the road to the achievement of their goal lay through the independent national states of the CMPC which would first secede from Russia and Georgia and then unite with each other.[122]

The Confederation ever more resolutely showed itself to be an aggressive and extremist organisation, ready to unleash a war against anybody who stood in their way.[123] 'Multifaceted is the evil standing in the way of the rapprochement of our peoples,' declared Musa Shanibov, 'Struggle with this evil is one of the most important tasks...'[124]

From the Centre in Moscow the Confederation was becoming uncontrollable. The waves of fury and obscurantism that rose from it threatened to swallow much of the work of those who prepared the anti-democratic putsch in Abkhazia. Communism itself, with all its objectives, Russia's state interests in the Caucasus, the rights of Russians and Cossacks in the region, were all under threat in the Confederation. It was only with great difficulty that the leaders of the CMPC preferred not to accentuate any orientation towards Islamic Fundamentalism and even stressed their goal was not 'an Islamic Union but a secular state with religious toleration', and that 'the Imamate has no ground to the West of Chechenia.'[126]

In spite of all the contradictions, the alliance between the leadership of the Confederation and the Abkhaz separatists was cemented by their hatred of Georgians, democratic Russia and the 'Jews and Masons' for whom the CMPC searched everywhere. Even so the Confederation itself was hardly as united as it would appear; it never came to any understanding with the Ossetians and remained highly suspicious of the Turkic peoples - Balkars and Karachais - about whom Shanibov remarked with irritation that they played the role of a Trojan Horse.[127]

The more the CMPC ceased to be a purely public organisation, as the Assembly had been, the more menacing the Abkhaz-CMPC alliance became. The CMPC claimed to have its own government and parliament, its own territory, its own armed forces and, what is most important, its outlet to the Black Sea through Abkhazia. They had declared their capital in Abkhazia, Sukhumi - part of Georgia, remember - and sewn their own flag: a green flag with seven stars symbolizing Abkhazia, Ingushetia, Daghestan, Adyghe, Kabardia, Circassia, and Chechenia.

'As for Abkhazia, we regard it as a territory occupied by Georgian forces', declared the future Chairman of the Caucasian Parliament, Yusup Soslambekov in 1990, 'and we shall do everything in our power to bring Abkhazia back into the Caucasian Federation and to return its capital, Sukhumi, to the Caucasian Federation'.[128] This was the cold war that was underway along the entire political front prior to the outbreak of conflict on 14 August 1992, and Abkhazia was the prize.[129]

And so events developed in the Caucasus along similar lines as in Russia: the communist reactionaries preparing the Moscow putsch in 1991 and nursing new revanchist plans under the banner of the National Salvation Front, closed ranks with the black-hundreds, the monarchists, the national-chauvinists, even though these were often hostile to communist ideology and incompatible with it. Similarly the PFA Aidgylara, initially conceived of as a pro-communist international front, found common ground with their 'blood relatives', Russia's enemies from the CMPC, while under the aegis of the Slav Home. The irony is profound. The Slav Home were, of course, agents of the KGB, sent to Sukhumi with instructions to defend the constitutional system of the USSR. In so doing they fraternized with 'patriots' from the criminal world and Cossack atamans only sceptically disposed to the Constitution of the USSR and intending to impose their own order on the Caucasus with the help of a whip and a sabre.

These were strange bedfellows indeed. However, if we look at the situation in Latvia, Estonia, Moldavia or Pridnestrovye (the Dneister area), in Azerbaijan or in the Republics of Central Asia, we see the same thing: personnel from the official state structures, members of the Supreme Soviet, the KGB, the Omons (Special Police Units) joining hands with the most shady fascists, nationalists and mafioso groups of all kinds. This was characteristic of the years between 1980 and 1990.[130]

The peculiarity in Abkhazia was that such a fusion of forces was done on the legitimate level of local authority. This was not a unique situation; roughly the same happened later in South Ossetia and Pridnestrovye. It became clear that it was relatively easy to strangle democratic movements at birth through these local authorities. Abkhazia happened to be one of the first territories of the former Soviet Union where it proved feasible to constitute a new Supreme Soviet with a clear reactionary, separatist policy.

However, in the summer of 1990 the old Soviet power, which never took any steps without instructions from the Communist Party, was counting its last hours in Abkhazia as in the whole of Georgia. The session of the Supreme Soviet was suspended till winter and the deputies dismissed. There had not been unanimity on the Declaration on the State Sovereignty of the Abkhazian ASSR of 25 August, a number of deputies voting against it and, officially, no-one in Sukhumi raised his voice against the resolution of the Presidium of the Supreme Council of the Georgian SSR of 26 August which annulled the decisions of the Abkhazian Supreme Soviet as they violated Georgia's territorial integrity and ran counter to her constitution.

This lull, however, did not mean that nothing was being done. On 22 September 1990 the first Congress of the representatives of all former SSR's, autonomous regions and areas, was convoked in Moscow. This was done at the height of the election campaign in Georgia, the results of which would define Georgia's relations with the Union.

The main objective of the Congress was to work out how to deal with the autonomies and the 'peoples having no statehood of their own' in case the new democratic authorities were unwilling to sign the Union Treaty and attempted to secede from the Soviet Union. At the Congress particular activity was displayed by Vladislav Ardzinba.[131] Abkhazian forces were brought into play to back the idea of the Union. B. Ketsba, the holder of a chair at Sukhumi University, was the main speaker and I. Akhba was confirmed as the manager of an association of all the participating delegates. The Chairman of this association was Musa Shanibov who was also the head of the Assembly of Mountain Peoples; together they were to bring strong pressure to bear on Georgia on the question of her joining the USSR. The closer Georgia approached her goal of secession, the greater the Centre pinned its hopes on the Abkhazian authorities being able to counteract this goal.

On 28 October 1990 a bloc of left-wing parties, *the Round Table*, headed by Zviad Gamsakhurdia, won the general election to the Supreme Council of the Georgian SSR. So ended sixty eight years of Georgia's membership of the USSR. Long before the collapse of the USSR at the end of 1991, it had become evident that Gamsakhurdia's signing of the Union Treaty was out of the question. And so the Abkhazian card was brought into play.

On 4 December 1990, after a three month-break, the tenth session of the Supreme Soviet of the Abkhazian ASSR resumed its work. The first action taken on that very day in response to the changed situation in Georgia, was the election of Ardzinba to the post of Chairman of the Supreme Soviet. From the spring of 1989 to August 1991 the so-called emissaries, mostly new people, gradually started to group together as a political shock troop. They were set tasks by the still all-powerful KGB, and received the blessing of the Central Committee of the CPSU and Anatoly Lukyanov's Supreme Soviet of the USSR. These tasks were differentiated according to 'lines' (as the main directions and areas of work are customarily called in the KGB): some people were responsible only for the ideological provision of the future putsch and an appropriate engagement of the mass media; others were involved with the organisational work for the election campaign; others held the strings of the economy, supplies and transport; some were to establish contacts with the army, to buy arms and replenish secret arsenals, to train and instruct the boeviks, to guard ammunition depots.

A special function was to be performed by 'messengers' whose task was to make contact with unofficial organisations, on whose assistance they could rely in a Georgian war. These messengers ran constantly between Sukhumi and Moscow where they had contacts with Pamyat, the powerful organisation of Russian patriots of an extreme fascist tendency. They acted, in particular, under cover of the Fund for Slavonic Writing and Culture and with the editorial board of the newspaper *Den*. They were also closely in touch with the Formation of Cossacks in the Northern Caucasus, in Nalchik and in Grozny and with the staffs of military groups like *Fighting South Ossetia, Fighting Dneister* and so on.

A particular 'line' of work was the preparation of international public opinion, the activation of foreign contacts through the myriad different Friendship Societies which had proliferated so bemusingly in the USSR. Contact was made with people of the right political disposition at academic centres throughout the Soviet Union and abroad. When the bloodshed started, 'defenders' on the level of international observers, TV commentators, specialists of institutes, should be prepared to stand up for the Abkhaz side. This did in fact happen when immediately after 14 August, all blame was heaped upon Tbilisi.

The main load in the preparation of Abkhazian events was given to staff of the former KGB. Almost all of them got appointments in Abkhazia under cover of neutral establishments which had nothing to do with their real activities. To distract attention, various ruses were resorted to, such as the private exchange of apartments, or the necessity of moving one's place of work to Abkhazia due to a sudden deterioration in health. In those years a peculiar number of able-bodied men of military bearing appeared in Abkhazia who, for medical reasons, could no longer live outside its subtropical climes. People who had absolutely nothing to do with culture found themselves employed under the roof of some cultural organisation, or in sanatoria, theatres, health establishments - even in literary and artistic associations.

There was an extraordinary level of infiltration throughout Abkhazia. This 'invasion' made it possible to send dozens of specialists from Russia: some acted openly, occupying leading ministerial posts and prominent positions on committees and in the apparatus of the Supreme Soviet. Some, on the contrary, went deep underground. Nobody could guess that a modest guard or worker in a sanatorium or on an empty state dacha was, in reality, a major or lieutenant-colonel in the KGB, responsible for a strategic military facility.[132]

Thus the process of gathering the necessary people in Abkhazia had long been under way. Yet a key figure was still missing: a leader of the nation.Vladislav Ardzinba was a priceless find. Combined in him were the correct origin, imposing appearance, youth, education, a career unblemished by direct relations with the former party nomenclature[133] and, what was most important, practically unbounded though hitherto unrealised ambition. He was also an eloquent speaker and proved a great manipulator of the nationalist vote.[134]

The starting conditions for Ardzinba's activities in Sukhumi were extremely favourable. From early December 1990 the conflict in South Ossetia was gaining strength. Both sides - the Ossetian separatists, guided by a devoted communist-Leninist who refused to renounce his principles, and the Supreme Council of Georgia, led by Zviad Gamsakhurdia, did everything to pour petrol on the fire. The elections of the Supreme Council of the South Ossetian Autonomous Republic on 9th December, then the law on the abolition of the South Ossetian Autonomous Region passed by Tbilisi on 11th December, the introduction of a state of emergency in the Tskhinvali and Java districts the next day, were swiftly followed by blockade, mayhem and blood.

When the military opposition in South Ossetia slackened slightly towards spring, the danger of a second front in Ajaria immediately arose. In April the Vice-Chairman of the Supreme Soviet of Ajaria, Nodar Imadze (a personal friend of Gamsakhurdia) was dismissed; he was shot in May by bodyguards in an attempt on the life of Aslan Abashidze - the President of Ajaria. There was no trust between Tbilisi and Batumi; neither did Gamsakhurdia expect anything good from Ajaria where, at the elections of October 1990, the Round Table received less than 20% of the votes, while the Communist Party of Georgia got 55%. Certainly the people of Ajaria enjoyed little peace under Gamsakhurdia's rule and from the beginning of that summer, opposition to his regime intensified in Tbilisi.

In these circumstances Ardzinba was practically given a free hand. Even had Gamsakhurdia understood the forces that were grouping in Sukhumi, he was losing support so rapidly that he could hardly have countered them effectively. However, he lacked such insight and throughout 1991 the Abkhaz separatists strengthened their position. In fact he helped them do so, for his regime provoked an eruption of wounded national self-esteem. Even before coming to power, Gamsakhurdia had become notorious for his attitude to national minorities though he did make some attempts to correct this afterwards.

However, he connived at the most flagrant violation of democratic norms and civil rights in Abkhazia, at the most appalling actions of Ardzinba and his entourage who had quite openly passed what can only be called apartheid laws. They made their separatist declarations, mercilessly sacked Georgian personnel and paved the way for an ethnocratic dictatorship.

Ardzinba's efforts were directed in the first place towards the modification of the law on the elections to the Supreme Soviet of Abkhazia. He hoped to purge the old Soviet of opposition and pinned his hopes on the new elections to create a majority obedient to his will. It was impossible to achieve this in a normal and honest way: the people of Abkhazia did not want a war with Georgia, nor secession. Without deception and violence at the elections, he could not form a sufficiently large group of deputies that would follow the separatist programme. Ardzinba was afraid of any kind of referendum or plebiscite because he knew perfectly well what the outcome would be. He wished to impose his own will on the people, but with the semblance of legality. This could only be done by limiting the electoral rights of the majority of the population. By blackmail and demagogy, juridical trickery and with the connivance of Gamsakhurdia, Ardzinba and his colleagues managed to push the electoral law of 9 July 1991 through the Georgian Parliament. This permitted the creation of prerogatives and restrictions on a solely ethnic basis in the formation of the new electoral districts. Shevardnadze wrote later that:

'The electoral law of 9 July 1991 totally ignores the norms and practice of modern parliamentarianism. What is this if not apartheid de jure, the striving of the minority to dictate its will to the majority, deliberately provoking the threat of inter-ethnic clashes? The restriction of electoral rights on the basis of nationality put the Georgians living in Abkhazia, and making up almost half the population, as well as Russians, Armenians, Greeks and other national minorities, in an obviously unequal position. This was pure racial discrimination and the establishment of an ethno-dictatorship.'[135]

The elections were organised in two rounds (October and December) with the second round taking place in eleven electoral districts and determining the final composition of the corps of deputies. It was held on 1st December and the Abkhazians won 28 seats, the Georgians 26 and representatives of other nationalities 11. In fact the true ratio of voters in the republic was: Abkhazians 18%, Georgians 46% and others 36%. Abkhazian districts with a small number of voters were equated with other districts, predominantly non-Abkhazian and with a far greater population. Both districts could elect only one deputy to the Supreme Soviet. And so the Supreme Soviet was formed according to ethnic quotas with guaranteed prerogatives for Abkhazians. All types of democratic opposition were cruelly suppressed, more often than not on Ardzinba's direct orders.

The situation became especially strained at the turn of 1991-1992. In spite of the complex alignment of political forces and the variable mood among the Georgian population of Abkhazia (there were supporters of Gamsakhurdia, now in his last days as President), the main thrust of Georgian political activity in Abkhazia was pro-democratic and anti the regime in Tbilisi, with which the Supreme Soviet of Abkhazia got on perfectly well.

On 17 December 1991, five political groups,[136] which on the whole united the Georgian population of Sukhumi, created a common co-ordination centre and adopted a Declaration sharply condemning the regime of Zviad Gamsakhurdia. It said that the President had established a 'neo-totalitarian, anti-democratic rule' and that 'in Georgia dissidents are persecuted, there are political prisoners and prisoners of conscience, the mass media are monopolised and an unbridled and slanderous campaign of terror is being waged against the opposition. The violation of human rights has been raised to the level of state policy.'[137] All this, of course, resulted in the Tbilisi Revolution (see Chronicle page 155). The attitude of the Georgian democratic opposition was also unambiguously expressed in the Declaration. It stated that the Supreme Soviet of Abkhazia had been formed as a result of a deal between Tbilisi and Ardzinba and that it had degenerated into a 'local institution of modernized neo-totalitarian government.' The Coordinating Council called for 'peaceful political opposition to the Supreme Soviet and civil disobedience to the government of Abkhazia[138] in order to establish democratic principles and defend human rights.'

Ardzinba was infuriated by the Declaration and decided to institute criminal proceedings against its authors.[139] Matters grew worse when the Progressive-Democratic Union of Georgian Parties of Abkhazia published an Information Bulletin in Sukhumi in the spring of '92. The first issue carried an appeal to the peoples of Abkhazia to 'declare a vote of no-confidence in the usurpers of power in the Parliament of Abkhazia.'

On Ardzinba's orders the Vice-Chairman of the Supreme Soviet, A.G. Topolyan, sent in April a demand to the Prosecutor of Abkhazia, Anri Jergenia, 'to punish according to the law' the publishers of the bulletin for their attempt to 'discredit the Supreme Soviet, especially those of Abkhazian nationality'. Commenting later on this, the lawyer M. Patsia wrote: 'Our native power could not put up with criticism. It never understood (nor wanted to understand) that their attempt to monopolize power, to become the only and infallible voice for the aspirations of thousands of people would create opposition. Any attempt on the part of the population to persuade the authorities by peaceful means to observe the law, caused an angry backlash and demands for legal action against persons and organizations which they disliked.'[140]

After the collapse of Gamsakhurdia's bankrupt regime, the new leadership in Georgia was able to analyse correctly the true nature of the Abkhazian situation. Shevardnadze, particularly, saw that what was happening in Abkhazia was no less than the institution of a system of apartheid.[141] When Alexandr Kavsadze, the Vice-President of the government of Georgia, addressed a session of the UN Security Council on January 23,1993, in New York, he spoke out about Abkhazia:

'The local administration is headed by Vladislav Ardzinba, former deputy of the Supreme Soviet... Mr Ardzinba and his like-minded colleagues, refusing to recognise the supremacy of the laws of the Republic of Georgia, pursued a policy that ran counter to these laws, a policy of apartheid. They predominantly appointed Abkhazians to the leading posts..a National Guard was formed, being manned according to the ethnic principle. Subsequently this became the nucleus of the insurgent detachments. Laws were passed that restricted the freedom of movement for persons of non-Abkhazian nationality...'[142]

I have documents at my disposal that confirm the truth of this and convince me that, during 1991 and the first half of 1992, Ardzinba really was systematically and intentionally preparing for war.

Among such documents is the Decree of the Presidium of the Supreme Soviet of Abkhazia, adopted on 29 December 1991, and signed by Ardzinba, on the deployment of military units, the offices of border and internal troops and naval forces, and the introduction of changes into the order of their functioning on the territory of Abkhazia[143] (Also see Appendix 1 for text.) References to the 'will of the people' and the 'constitution of Abkhazia' contained here are sheer demagogy. No constitution of Abkhazia - and the only one in force at that time was the 1978 constitution of the Abkhazian ASSR - envisaged usurpation by the Supreme Soviet of Abkhazia of the control of military units of the former USSR, in other words, the armed forces that were stationed in Abkhazia and which only belonged to the competence of the successor state to the Soviet Union. Only Georgia - and by no stretch of the imagination an autonomy or region within Georgia - could be such a state along with the other fifteen republics that had formed the Soviet Union till 1991.

By a stroke of the pen, Ardzinba declared the property of the Soviet Army the property of Abkhazia. He simply decided that military units of the former USSR now came under the control of the Supreme Soviet of Abkhazia. He hurried to lay hands on units, equipment and arms, taking advantage of the chaos in Tbilisi where street-fighting had broken out (22 December) and the President was in hiding.

However, neither the temporary paralysis in Georgia during those days of the Tbilisi Revolution, nor Ardzinba's unscrupulousness could possibly have allowed him to take such daring decisions unless those decisions had been guaranteed by the relevant commanding officers. They themselves must have had appropriate instructions from the very top. With extraordinary ease they subjected themselves to the competence of the Supreme Soviet of Abkhazia. With the confidence of a Commander-in-Chief, Ardzinba made colonels and lieutenant-colonels of the Soviet Army, members of the Provisional Council headed by himself. These officers should simply not have been subordinated to the Chairman of the Supreme Soviet of Abkhazia. All this was one single concerted action, planned in the upper echelons of the military-industrial complex. Ardzinba's correspondence with top officials from the former Ministry of Defence of the USSR (who all received new posts from the end of '91) is a striking illustration that he was quite at home here.

In a letter of 21 May 1992 addressed to Colonel-General A.N. Kalinichenko, head of the Humanitarian Academy of the Armed Forces of the CIS, Ardzinba, with amazing self-assurance, wrote:

'The Supreme Soviet of the Republic of Abkhazia asks you to ap-point the graduate of the Air-Defence faculty, Major V.G. Agumava, to the post of Assistant Commander of the Special Regiment of the internal troops of the Supreme Soviet of the Republic of Abkhazia, for service with the staff of Military Unit 5482, stationed in Sukhumi. We ask you to decide the above mentioned request through the Central Personnel Board of the Combined Armed Forces of the CIS, and the Personnel Board of the Air Defence. Major Agumava is recommended to the post by the decision of the Provisional Council for the co-ordination of activities of mili-tary units, under the Chairman of the Supreme Soviet of the Re-public of Abkhazia.'[144]

So military unit 5482, stationed in Sukhumi, had already been trans-formed into a Special Regiment of internal troops. This was an un-lawful military formation, not provided for by any of the constitu-tions, military regulations or agreements within or outside the CIS. Not embarrassed by this illegality, and confident in the protection of the top Army Generals, Ardzinba openly engaged in manning the commander's staff of this unit and passed through the Central Per-sonnel Board's recommendations of the Provisional Council, set up unlawfully under his personal direction. He appointed Major Klimov, commander of unit 5482, as a member of this Council and shortly afterwards, ordered that this unit be provided with foodstuffs at the expense of the Autonomous Republic.[145]

In the winter of 1991-92, when the provision of food for the civil-ian population became catastrophically inadequate and the tragic countdown of deaths and suicides due to starvation began, the boards of trade and the co-operatives of Abkhazia were ordered to provide 'five hundred people' free of charge for '366 days' with thousands of kilogrammes of flour, cereals, macaroni, meat, fish, butter, sugar and so forth. In other words, the people of Abkhazia had to pay for what became Ardzinba's personal guard, called, in the tradition of revolutionary language, the Special Regiment.

Ardzinba was not content with this. He signed another decree: (N46-X11, 31 March 1992) 'On the calling up for military service and measures on the enforcement of the law on general military duties on the territory of the Republic of Abkhazia'.[146] He threatened the heads of a number of enterprises, organisations, collective farms and educational establishments, with severe penalties for not organising the training of young people of conscription age (and under) for active military service. A spring call-up for the army was announced. That Ardzinba was organising a call-up at this time is all the proof one needs that he was preparing for war.

It is hard to imagine a more outrageous situation. Into which army was he conscripting his young men? Abkhazia, legally, had no army of her own and Georgia had abolished compulsory military service. Of course, this was going to be a separatist army, the recruits intended in fact, for that same Special Regiment which he had already appropriated by sleight-of-hand. This desire for troops was obviously motivated by intent to use them, but the call-up did not proceed smoothly. As one might expect, many of the young men wilfully tried to avoid military service under the pretext of starting to work or study: 'Despite the measures taken by the Presidium of the Supreme Soviet of Abkhazia...law enforcement bodies are adopting a passive position in the preparation of the mobilization of reserves, registration of citizens at the calling stations, calling up youths to active military service, thereby breaching the law on 'general military duties.'

So the Presidium of the Supreme Soviet of Abkhazia passed another decree to ensure that the call-up for military service proceeded and that the law on general military duties was strictly observed. (See Appendix 2) Lists were made of the ethnically suitable and call-up committees were rigorously controlled.

Along with its military efforts, the leadership of Abkhazia strove to concentrate in its own hands the entire legislative and executive power. It was necessary to lay hands on all levers of management, all financial and economic structures, anything that could provide a source of income, including the entire resources of the resort zone. Everything was gathered into a single iron fist. A law on the 'subordination of certain bodies to the State Administration of the Republic of Abkhazia' was adopted without discussion or voting, and was signed personally by Ardzinba. (See Appendix 3)

All the appointments to the leading posts of the republic made by Ardzinba, who had mastered Stalin's credo that 'personnel determine everything', were directed towards the creation of a team of tested people, personally devoted to himself. Their professional qualifications were of secondary importance to their shared ideology, national origin, kinship, family ties, and official recommendations from the Slav Home or the Presidium of the PFA. The latter, particularly, provided testimonials without which, as in the Soviet past, promotion was practically impossible. A recommendation from Aidgylara was a guarantee of political reliability. For example:

PFA Aidgylara N.55   13 May 1992

TO THE SUPREME SOVIET OF THE REPUBLIC OF ABKHAZIA

The People's Forum of Abkhazia Aidgylara, having discussed at its meeting (prot.N11, 13 May 1992) the candidates to the post of Minister of Education and Culture of the Republic of Abkhazia, decided to support Nodar Chanba.

N.V. Chanba is an active member of the PFA Aidgylara. During the formative stages of the Forum he showed his formidable organising abilities: he can unite people, is full of initiative, has a wide outlook and modern thinking.

Vice Chairman of the PFA Aidgylara
R. Ebjznou
Presidium of the Supreme Soviet of the Abkhazian ASSR
incoming number N41-210/6   10.06.1992[147]

There was one more 'line' in the preparatory activity of the Abkhazian leadership that is worthy of note: their recruitment of support, both in diplomatic and human resource terms, from abroad. I quoted above the speech of the Vice-Premier of Georgia, Alexandr Kavsadze, in which he said that there were cases of the breaching of the existing passport laws and that Georgian passports had been issued to foreign nationals. I have at my disposal xerox copies of instructions sent from the Presidium of the Supreme Soviet of Abkhazia to town and district executive committees, primarily to the Sukhumi Executive Committee and to the Ministry of Internal Affairs of Abkhazia, on the registration of citizens wishing to arrive and take up permanent residence in Abkhazia, and multi-page lists of such citizens with data on their old and new addresses.[148]

These are mainly citizens of the wide Circassian diaspora, arriving from Turkey, Iraq and other Arab countries, from the autonomies of the Northern Caucasus, as well as Russians - mostly servicemen and their families. Migration per se is a natural process and even the fact that during the registration of settlers, some laws of the Republic of Georgia were violated, (they were granted dual citizenship) and the necessary formalities were not observed, might be regarded as forgivable negligence in the young administration. However, this migration was rigidly controlled and pursued with definite political objectives. Thus, according to the data of Nugzar Mgaloblishvili, deputy of the Supreme Soviet of Abkhazia, who conducted his own investigations of what was happening, 70% of the Russian citizens registered in 1991-92 in Abkhazia were members of Vladimir Zhirinovsky's so-called *Liberal-Democratic Party*. The Chairman of the Human Rights Committee of the Supreme Soviet of Abkhazia, Yuri Voronov, guaranteed a large group of activists residence in Abkhazia, lodgings in Sukhumi, plots for summer cottages, registration with rights to retain their Russian citizenship, according to lists especially agreed with Zhirinovsky. In addressing the meeting of the UN Security Council, Alexandr Kavsadze expressed somewhat mildly his concern over these links: 'Ardzinba controlled the processes with Zhirinovsky... As is known, the most active opponents of democratic movements and reforms in Russia were concentrated in the Soyuz bloc and in Zhirinovsky's Party.'

It would be absurd to reproach the Abkhazian leadership for trying to establish links with the Abkhazian diaspora abroad, or for seeking the return of their people to their historical homeland, or for counting on their support. Indeed, one has special sympathy for them when one remembers the mass emigration of Abkhazians caused by the tsarist government after the insurgent Mahajir movement in the 1860s.[149] This is not the question. The question is: to which compatriots, circles and political forces did Ardzinba and his colleagues address themselves?[150]

The search for the Abkhazian diaspora led the Abkhazian leadership along a slippery path. A considerable stratum of ethnic Abkhazians in Turkey and other countries of the Middle East appear to have been ignored, particularly the settled middle class, loyal to their own countries. Instead, terrorist elements reared and bred by certain pro-communist regimes in the Arab world, often directly connected with the old Soviet Secret Service, were particularly targeted. Such links were best established with Abkhazians in the capital of Syria, Damascus.

From 1989 the *Aidgylara* newspaper carried, from issue to issue, telegrams and resolutions coming from various meetings of compatriots abroad, mainly from Damascus and Turkey.[151] Any reader ignorant of the strong ties of the CPSU with other countries, might find the content and style of these messages puzzling. They appear to have been composed and edited at some regional committee of the CPSU in the days before perestroika. By 1989 most reasonable people had already seen through the clichés of communist propaganda. Not, apparently, certain members of the Abkhaz community in Turkey:

'We, representatives of Abkhaz nationality, your fellow countrymen living in Turkey, are greatly concerned about the bloody events taking place in the Abkhazian ASSR owing to the anti-constitutional actions of unofficial extremist groups in Georgia, directed at the abolition of Abkhazian statehood and national self-determination...

We have complete solidarity with the demands of the Abkhaz people and are fully convinced that the Supreme Soviet of the USSR and the GSSR will take immediate steps to stabilize the situation and will satisfy the legitimate rights of the Abkhaz people, fighting for the preservation of their culture and their origins in the historical homeland of Abkhazia.

Long live Leninist national policy!

Long live the revolutionary policy of perestroika!

Long live the friendship of the peoples of the USSR!

Long live the Abkhazian people and let them prosper in the indivisible family of the peoples of the USSR!

The telegrams from Damascus that appeared in *Aidgylara* ran along similar lines. (See Appendix 4) These texts hardly need any comment.

Their readiness to blame Georgian extremism and to defend Soviet power in Abkhazia lays bare the political orientation of their fraternal solidarity. It was to such compatriots that Ardzinba opened the borders of Abkhazia and gave his hospitality.

As to the economic and social policy carried out by the new leadership in 1991-1992, it rested on three pillars. The first was to maintain the status quo with regard to all the gains of developed socialism. In other words, nothing changed. Collective farms and Soviet farms continued to be run and there was no private ownership of land. The distribution of miserly subsidies continued the economic stagnation. Communist reserves like the separately 'taken' sanatoria of the USSR Ministry of Health remained in place and the empty and tenantless state dachas were still patrolled by armed guards.

The second pillar involved the regime putting in place 'maximally favourable conditions' for mafiosi-controlled commercial structures, directly uniting the state system with them. These businesses, run by some very shady characters close to the leadership, could ensure that not only did the latter lead a fairly comfortable life, but that a wide arena was opened up for the purchase of arms, including the very latest in weapons and equipment. Also, under the cover of the local Soviets, there grew like mushrooms rather curious offices that busied themselves with leasing and selling real estate: dachas, plots of land and even public beaches were, without any legislative acts on land ownership, mysteriously bought and sold. Thus, for example, in Novy Afon in the spring of 1992, a three-storey building, a hotel belonging to the former district executive committee, was on sale. That same spring the board of the administration of the Slav Home was preoccupied not so much with the problems of the revival of Russian culture and communality as with the necessity of selling abroad, to Istanbul, packed cobalt, 50 kilos for 30,000 US dollars, red placer mercury, and other items of socialist property that were not too well guarded.[152]

Finally, the third pillar of this policy was the complete economic destabilisation of the situation in Abkhazia. To be sure, such destabilisation had deeper causes of its own within the general crisis of the former socialist economy and in the overall break-up of the disintegrating empire. But all the circumstances - the decline in production, the fall in revenue from tourism, the deficit of ready money, the price rises - were rendered more acute through the special efforts of those who were preparing for war.

From the early autumn of 1992 there were many cases of sabotage and criminal lawlessness which created a background of general despair and made it that much easier to unleash a civil war. If the leadership of Abkhazia had spent a hundredth part of the effort it put into fighting for independence from Georgia into trying to improve elementary living conditions, the timely baking and delivery of bread, the repair of ruined hotels, beaches and health resorts and the establishment of order, the developments in Abkhazia would have taken a different course. Trains travelling through Abkhazia were robbed by armed gangs unimpeded; hardly any transport at all ran in Sukhumi. There was little fuel and flats were not heated the whole winter. About three hundred people died of starvation during those months and cases of suicide due to poverty and hunger were recorded.[153] The leadership did not wish to calm, feed and warm the people of Abkhazia, but to drag it into a fratricidal war by driving them to despair. This seething current of mass indignation was directed by the politicians in Sukhumi against Tbilisi.

Until August 1991, the separatist leadership still cherished hopes of receiving help from the old Centre in transforming the Soviet Socialist Autonomy into a republic, a state equal among equals, reliable and loyal to the dear Communist Party. It would independently sign a Union treaty and break away from Georgia without a war - at least without a war waged by its own forces - relying on Moscow to suppress any Georgian reaction. Just a month before the August putsch, the central mass media[154] circulated a curious document, signed by the leadership of Soviet Abkhazia along with communist patriots of other trouble spots such as Estonia, Lithuania, Ossetia and Moldavia, appealing to the authority of the Supreme Soviet to solve their problems. (See Appendix 5) However, after the collapse of the State Committee on the Emergency Situation, there was no longer any hope of receiving help from Moscow, and in December the Soviet Union, within whose boundaries the leadership in Abkhazia so fervently wished to remain, ceased to exist.

Even so till the end of 1991 the Abkhazian leaders could still count on a secret collusion with the regime of Zviad Gamsakhurdia, though even without this they seemed to be able to act with impunity as no-one offered any effective resistance. Still, after the Tbilisi revolution and the flight of Gamsakhurdia from Georgia on 6 January 1992, the possibility existed that Georgia would fall apart of its own accord. Social and political upheavals would destroy its statehood and 'fighting Mingrelia', (the homeland of Gamsakhurdia) described by Yuri Voronov as 'this last hope of ours...this last flimsy shield', would do the bloody business for Abkhazia. This would ensure the de-facto inaccessibility of Abkhazia to Georgian law and give unrestricted freedom of action to the Abkhazian leadership in building an independent, national-communist state.

However, following the return of Eduard Shevardnadze to Georgia in March 1992, Ardzinba and his comrades could no longer look for help in this direction. By the summer of that year, the leadership in Abkhazia realised that the time had come for action.[155]

Chapter 6

The Summer of Menace 1992

Thus, at the beginning of 1992, Abkhazia was inevitably sliding into the abyss of national catastrophe. It was not the Abkhazian people that dragged their republic into this abyss: the people were not consulted. Their fate was decided by a cabal that had usurped power and they suffered most of all. With each day, as war approached, the great historical chance of a national revival within a renovated democratic Georgia slipped away. Nor is the multi-national Abkhazian intelligentsia to blame for all that happened in the summer of 1992. To the last they ignored the peremptory shouts and threats of court proceedings and resisted the onset of a new dictatorship. They formed opposition parties, blocs, factions of deputies (Democratic Abkhazia) protesting against the infringements of legality and of the constitution. No matter how strange it may seem, I shall venture to say that not even the leadership with all its ambitions (at present justly cursed by the people) was the main culprit.

Far more powerful forces acted here. Eduard Shevardnadze said afterwards: 'In Abkhazia the red-brown army of imperial revenge is waging a war with Georgia. This force is now threatening Russia with the removal of legal authority and the restoration of the totalitarian system.'[156] It was this army that began its manoeuvres in the summer of 1992 in Abkhazia.

While the South-Ossetian conflict blazed in Georgia, with its daily toll of human life, destroying peace, undermining the economic and political stability of the young independent republic, and inflicting irreparable damage to its international authority,[157] it was possible not to hurry. From time to time 'rehearsals', outbreaks of armed actions, were organised and public opinion was being gradually prepared for the future war.

The time to hurry came in the spring of 1992 - after Shevardnadze's return to Georgia. Whereas Gamsakhurdia, with his absurd short-sighted policy, led to a protracted crisis, Shevardnadze's coming to power opened absolutely different prospects. The communist reaction felt the real threat of losing Georgia not only de jure as an independent republic that refused to become a member of the CIS, but de facto as well, as a country that would finally take the road of free democratic development.

Shortly before his arrival in Georgia, during his visit to the USA in February 1992, Shevardnadze signed a contract with the company Brock Group Ltd on a strategy to revive the economy of Georgia. This was to include the reconstruction of the sea ports in Poti and Batumi, the expansion of the capacity of the international airport in Batumi, and also the expansion of the network of oil terminals, and so on. Shevardnadze's international authority as a politician of new thinking, one of the initiators and active directors of perestroika, Gorbachev's comrade-in-arms, defender of the White House in the dramatic August ordeal of 1991, on the one hand guaranteed Georgia success and recognition in the world arena but, on the other, greatly embittered the old guard and the forces of reaction at home.

These forces were ready to hold back the Abkhazian card, their trump card, while Gamsakhurdia was President of Georgia, for he was doing a fine job for them. Gamsakhurdia initiated the Law on the abolition of the South-Ossetian autonomous region and blessed the war in South Ossetia to the last Ossetian, which played into the hands of pro-communist reactionary forces profiting from this local war. An absolutely different course was taken by Shevardnadze. His concrete steps and initiatives, respectful attitude to the autonomies within Georgia, peaceful political settlement of conflicts, alliance with the new, democratic Russia, and the shaping of a political course that signified a real strengthening of Georgia, were intolerable for those who wanted to force the republic to its knees.

The complete settlement of the Ossetian problem soon came within sight and the fratricidal war practically ceased. A new stability developed in relations with Russia. Georgia established diplomatic relations with the Russian Federation and the Ukraine. In March 1992 Shevardnadze asked Yeltsin not to withdraw the troops of the CIS from the territory of Georgia, and practically all the arsenals and a considerable military contingent of the Transcaucasian Military District remained in Georgia.

On 24 June, 1992 a bilateral Russian-Georgian summit meeting was held in Dagomys, with the participation of representatives of North and South Ossetia. A decision was taken on a ceasefire and on the introduction of peace-keeping forces for the disengagement of the hostile sides. Understanding was also achieved on the lifting of Russia's economic sanctions against Georgia. The territorial integrity of the Georgian state was reaffirmed.

With the end of the war in South Ossetia, the time came for the Abkhazian separatists to act. And their first act in this reactionary rebellion took place on 24 June 1992, the day of the Dagomys meeting. Abkhazian insurgents on this day acted hand in hand with Zviadists, supporters of the ex-President of Georgia, who attempted to stage a coup in Tbilisi, where they stormed the building of the Television and Radio Stations. Concurrently, in Sukhumi Ardzinba ordered the battalion of the Abkhazian Guard under his command to attack the building of the Ministry of Internal Affairs of the autonomous republic. The purpose of the attack was to remove Givi Lominadze from the post of Minister of Internal Affairs.

A man of democratic convictions and loyal to law and duty, Georgian by nationality, Major-General Lominadze in no way suited the new leaders of Abkhazia. His persistent unwillingness to politicize the organs of internal affairs and turn local police offices into bases of national-separatism suited them even less. On Ardzinba's command the Supreme Soviet of Abkhazia had earlier (in May) decided to remove Lominadze and appoint Alexandr Ankvab (Abkhazian by nationality) as Acting Minister of Internal Affairs, a loyal adherent to the 'new course' and an activist of the PFA Aidgylara. However, according to the laws in force, removals and appointments of this kind had to be sanctioned by the Ministry of Internal Affairs of Georgia. A relevant sanction did not follow. On the contrary, on 22 June the Supreme Soviet of Abkhazia received a letter from Roman Gventsadze, Minister of Internal Affairs of Georgia, requesting the restoration of the status quo and observation of legality in the future. In Sukhumi on 24 June it was decided to act by force. A bandit attack was made on Lominadze; the blow he received nearly cost him his life; he was hospitalized and sent to Tbilisi for treatment. None of the attackers was brought to trial.

Later on, recalling the events of 24 June, Givi Lominadze said:

'That morning in the presence of Merab Gamzardia, Deputy Minister of Internal Affairs of Abkhazia, I was speaking on the town telephone. He saw through the window that the building of the Ministry of Internal Affairs was being surrounded by soldiers and an ATC... Within a few seconds a group of soldiers (about six to eight men) burst into the study. Later on the commander of the so-called Regiment of Internal Troops of Abkhazia - Viktor Kakalia - entered. I said to him: 'What have you done, you will have to pay dearly for this.' He answered that he was fulfilling an order, that all was 'agreed'.Then he phoned over the government telephone... I, naturally, did not obey the orders of the soldiers that burst into the study... I received a heavy blow, delivered without warning, in the area of the throat. I think that those who did this on the morning of June 24 believed the radio reports and decided that after the seizure of the TV Centre, there was no authority in Tbilisi ...I understand that the Abkhazian leadership wanted to take control of the MIA (Ministry of Internal Affairs) and unite all the military formations under its umbrella.'[158]

The attempted coup in Tbilisi, absolutely unsupported by the people, failed ignominiously. But the first warning of a possible war rang out and it could not be ignored. Later on, on 17 August 1992, a memorandum on the events in the Autonomous Republic of Abkhazia was circulated by the press corps of the State Council of Georgia. In particular, it said: 'All this was a natural result of the policy carried out by the leaders of Abkhazia, primarily by the Chairman of the Supreme Soviet of the Autonomous Republic, Vladislav Ardzinba. Taking advantage of the complex situation in which the authorities of Georgia found themselves, obliged, as they were, simultaneously to solve numerous problems connected with the settlement of the conflict in Tskhinvali region and the repulse of destructive forces, he planned to wrest Abkhazia from the integral Georgian state... Ardzinba enjoyed and still enjoys the support of those reactionary forces in Russia which try to halt the course of democratic reforms and to reverse the course of history. At the same time all the actions of the Speaker of the Abkhazian Parliament coincided with the activities of the ex-President's (Gamsakhurdia's) supporters... Having made up his mind to remove unlawfully from the post of the MIA of Abkhazia the minister, Givi Lominadze, Ardzinba ordered the battalion of the Abkhaz Guard under his command to attack the building of the

MIA. By a strange coincidence the assault was ordered on 24 June - the day on which the supporters of the ex-President attempted a coup...This step was evidently taken with the hope that the enemies of the new Georgian authorities would achieve the planned aim. The building of the MIA was taken by storm...the result was a sharply aggravated political situation in Abkhazia and around her, straining inter-ethnic relations to the utmost.'[159]

In spite of the comparatively short time (from June to August of 1992) the authorities of Abkhazia managed to derive maximum benefit from the situation that arose in the MIA of the republic after the removal of Lominadze and the transfer of powers to the Minister Alexandr Ankvab. The Ministry of Internal Affairs turned into a base for the preparations of war. The police, who on the eve of the war were the only legitimate armed force in the autonomous republic, (for all sorts of guard detachments, separate regiments, internal troops, and so on were essentially illegal), during the whole summer was being turned into a mono-ethnic structure, ready to fulfil implicitly the orders coming from the Presidium of the Supreme Soviet of Abkhazia. They were a hostile force with regard to the Georgian population, busy not with guarding public order but with its destabilization.

At the right moment the police were to ensure the start of hostilities throughout Abkhazia against the central Georgian authority: on a single order, all local police departments and posts of the State Traffic Inspectorate turned, from 14 August, into mobilization points for the assembly of the draftees and defence staffs. They became the regional headquarters for the war that was unleashed on the whole territory of Abkhazia. The first to use arms against regular troops of the State Council of Georgia in the Gali district were the detachments of the MIA of Abkhazia, transformed into the National Guard or 'detachments of self-defence'. Shevardnadze's opponents call these events a quasi-putsch, allegedly organised by Shevardnadze against himself to solve a 'triple task':

1. On the eve of the Dagomys meeting for the settlement of the Ossetian issue, to demonstrate to the Russian leadership the real threat to democracy in Georgia;
2. To persuade the world community to treat with understanding possible repressions against the Zviadists;

3. To stabilize the situation in Tbilisi with the aid of the *Mkhedrioni*
   forces (*Mkhedrioni = Horsemen;* Georgian paramilitary force, anti-
   Zviadist, led by Jaba Ioseliani. Played a central role in events;
   of mixed reputation).[160]

This is an absurd version of events. Over recent years I have often
come across conspiracy theories analogous to this on the pages of the
Russian Black-Hundred, pro-communist press: how Yeltsin organised attempts on his own life, how Gorbachev arrested himself in
Toros, how the democrats themselves organised the August putsch
to solve their problems and so on. The absurdity of such a version is
attested with fair eloquence by the second point of this fantastic triad:
that Shevardnadze organised these attacks against his own people to
justify in the eyes of the world community the programme of repression he wished to carry out against the Zviadists. But no repressions
followed after 24 June. Furthermore, outright criminals and active
participants of the putsch, attempting to stage a coup in Tbilisi, were
released within a few weeks of their arrest. A general political amnesty, timed for the Day of National Reconciliation, applied to all. It
seems beyond the wildest imaginings that Shevardnadze should have
ordered a quasi-putsch on the eve of the Dagomys meeting. After all,
in order to sit down at the negotiating table - as Russia was now
doing in her official relations with Georgia - it is always better to
have a strong partner that enjoys solid support and legitimate power
in his own house. The putsch on 24 June could only hinder the
Dagomys agreements, giving the Russians cause to doubt that the
State Council controlled the situation in Tbilisi.

And because the putsch, unsupported by the people of Georgia,
failed ignominiously, it became clear to Shevardnadze's opponents
that they could not do away with the new authority so easily and
simply. An Abkhaz war was needed. On 24 June this war was brought
another step nearer. From June 1992 the leadership of Abkhazia began to prepare for a decisive provocative move - official declaration
of 'the independence' of Abkhazia from Georgia.

On 13 June the republican newspaper *Abkhazia* published 'The
treaty principles of interrelations between the Republic of Abkhazia
and the Republic of Georgia (proposals for a draft)', signed by doctor
of law Shamba. The text essentially acquired the significance of an

official document, determining the policy of the Supreme Soviet of Abkhazia, ready unilaterally to establish relations with Georgia that would be absolutely different from those provided by the constitutions of both republics, which affirmed the status of the autonomous republic of Abkhazia within Georgia. Point Two of the draft treaty prepared by Shamba read: 'The sides recognize Georgia and Abkhazia as sovereign states and equal participants of international and for-eign-economic relations...the sides independently conclude treaties and agreements with other countries...'[161]

After this statement all the other points of the treaty, including the third, concerning 'voluntary unification' with the Republic of Georgia, only serve as a camouflage for the intended splitting of the country - the division of Georgia into 'sovereign states'. The treaty provided for 'the citizenship of the Republic of Abkhazia', the 'supremacy of the laws and the Constitution of Abkhazia on her territory', and the existence of an 'indivisible multi-national Abkhazian Guard with its subordination to the Supreme Soviet of Abkhazia.'

The notion of territorial integrity which both sides would decide to respect - meaning non-interference in each other's internal affairs - extended, according to this treaty, separately to Abkhazia and to Georgia; in fact, the former Georgian state with Abkhazia as part of it, would cease to exist. The very idea of concluding a special treaty with Georgia was brought forward by the Abkhaz politicians purely for propaganda, in the hope of concealing from world public opinion their true separatist aspirations. Referring to the text of the treaty (which by itself was no document at all - there were no signatories to it, except the signature of T. M. Shamba - the author of the Proposals on the draft). Ardzinba could subsequently claim that Abkhazia was not leaving Georgia but was uniting with her on the basis of the new treaty 'on the delimitation of powers'. He assiduously made such statements at many press-conferences, in interviews and at official meetings. It was supposed that this draft treaty would be discussed by the Supreme Soviet of Abkhazia (14 August was later claimed to have been the day of this discussion) and the treaty was offered to the State Council of Georgia 'as the basis for the negotiation process'. A working group of deputies to the Supreme Soviet of Abkhazia was set up headed by Zurab Achba, allegedly to work on the draft treaty. As a matter of fact, the Abkhazian leaders did not contemplate any treaty with Georgia. The beginning of the treaty process was to drag on indefinitely and the draft treaty itself would merely distract attention from the essence of the coup which Ardzinba and his entourage decided to stage on 23 July 1992, declaring the termination of the 1978 Constitution.

The choice of the last week of July to launch a decisive offensive was calculated with precision. By the end of July 1992 Russian diplomacy succeeded in settling two acute issues connected with chronic conflicts in South Ossetia and the Dniester Area. In both cases the settlement provided for the participation of Russian peace-keeping forces.

Two important conclusions followed from this for those forces that were preparing another coup. Firstly, part of the Russian forces was engaged in maintaining a fragile peace and order in South Ossetia and the Dniester Area. Russia might feel herself too stretched to get involved at this time in any other region and to introduce her troops into it - at any rate rapidly and operationally. Thus Abkhaz separatists would get a chance of free action for a period in August. Secondly, the choice of playing the Abkhazian card was prompted by the fact that other areas of strife (the Dniester Area and South Ossetia) were now bogged down in a big political game against new, democratic Russia. Also nothing had come of the adventure in the Crimea where from May to July there looked like a real possibility of civil war. The leaders of the Crimea rejected this provocative role, all but imposed on them. War really seemed possible if a referendum were held and a decision passed on their secession from the Ukraine and reunification with Russia. This would inevitably lead to a clash between Russia and the Ukraine. The Crimean leadership, however, declared a moratorium on holding a referendum, thereby gradually extinguishing the conflict that had already begun to flare up. The agreements reached by Boris Yeltsin and Leonid Kravchuk, in the course of their meeting on 3 August 1992 at Mukhalatka, about the fate of the Black Sea Fleet, removed the tension around this issue for the time being. Russia and her democratic leadership in the government of Yeltsin-Gaidar thus received a long-awaited respite from the bloody conflicts which threatened her frontiers.

So the time had come for a new strike at the fragile gains of the young democracy of the former Soviet Union. Events in the international arena further encouraged the putschists. On 30 July Yeltsin signed the order 'On measures, connected with the implementation of the UN Security Council resolution N757 of 30 May 1992', actually freezing Russia's relations with the Republic of Yugoslavia. It became clear that Russia would not be dragged into the Balkan war on the side of fraternal Serbia and so find herself opposed to the world community. Russian national-patriots, *derzhavniks*, and communists could not forgive Yeltsin for this 'betrayal', and were preparing their variant of the Balkan war in the Caucasus.

Meanwhile Georgia was preparing to join the UN (the day of official admission was 31 July), and this success for her new democratic leadership stuck in the craw of the reactionaries. In many respects this was a personal success for Eduard Shevardnadze, whose authority on the international scene played an important role in the adoption of the UN decision.

Within a short period more than thirty states recognised Georgia as an independent republic. The USA and Canada discussed the possibilities of granting Georgia large credits 'on condition of her observing the rights of national minorities' (USA) and 'on condition that free and honest elections would be held in Georgia' (Canada).

Nothing prevented the implementation of these conditions. The new Georgian leadership declared equal rights for all national groups. October 1992 was fixed for the parliamentary elections and the Chairman of the Supreme Council was to be elected not by Parliament but by a nationwide ballot which would serve as a true pledge of the legitimacy of the new authority and its leader.

According to a representative opinion poll conducted in August 1992 by the Institute of Sociology and Demography, 65% of the residents of Tbilisi expressed their support for the State Council, and 75% said that they pinned their hopes on Mr Shevardnadze.

Finally, real prospects appeared of overcoming the protracted conflict in Western Georgia and the resistance of the Zviadists, supporters of the ex-President, to the State Council. The Mingrelian fire belt to which from January to July 1992 the authority of the State Council of Georgia actually did not extend, served as a buffer zone as it were, beyond which Abkhazia considered herself inaccessible. The energetic measures of the State Council of Georgia for the elimination of the Mingrelian base of rebellion threatened Abkhazian separatists with the possibility of a head-on clash with Tbilisi.[162]

On 9 July 1992, Zviadists made a bandit attack in Mingrelia on the car of Georgia's Vice-Premier Alexandr Kavsadze and kidnapped him. On 23 July, Shevardnadze arrived in Mingrelia. That evening, speaking on TV, he said that the members of the State Council would make a number of important decisions, secure the release of the hostages, and establish order. 'I do not believe', he said, 'even one man can be found in Mingrelia who would try to raise his hand against the representatives of the authorities who had arrived on a peaceful and important mission'.[163]

On the same day, 23 July 1992, with Shevardnadze in Mingrelia and the Prime Minister, Tengiz Sigua, about to leave for Turkey, the regular session of the Supreme Soviet of Abkhazia passed a resolution 'On the Termination of the 1978 Constitution of the Abkhazian ASSR'. Pending the adoption of a new constitution, the session decided to restore the 1925 Constitution of the SSR of Abkhazia, according to which Abkhazia was considered an independent republic and, according to article 4, 'united with Georgia on the basis of a treaty.' In point of fact the Abkhaz leaders were returning their country to the Stalinist era of the mid-20s.

The resolution itself was, of course, passed in gross violation of the constitution, according to which (Article 162 of the 1978 Constitution) 'alteration of the Constitution of the Abkhazian ASSR is effected by a decision of the Supreme Soviet of the Abkhazian ASSR by a two thirds majority of the overall number of the deputies.' Nothing of this kind happened at the 23 July session. Two thirds of the qualified majority of the Supreme Soviet of Abkhazia, which consists of 65 deputies, is 43 votes. Even purged as it was, only 36 deputies voted for the resolution (the faction Democratic Abkhazia abstained).

By a simple majority, Parliament took a decision on the name of the state, defining it as the 'Republic of Abkhazia' (excluding any mention of autonomy or a republic within Georgia), and altered the national emblem and flag. The new flag of 'Independent Abkhazia' was on the same day hoisted over the building of the Supreme Soviet in Sukhumi.

On 23 July, the session of the Supreme Soviet of Abkhazia passed these decisions without any referendum or opinion poll, as already said, in gross violation of parliamentary procedure and in the absence of the necessary quorum for constitutional changes. The parliamentary faction Democratic Abkhazia, uniting not only Georgian deputies but all the anti-separatists, walked out in protest against the policy of the leadership of the Supreme Soviet of Abkhazia, and on the same day made a statement on the violation of the Constitution and on the attempt 'to reanimate the decomposed corpse of Socialism in Abkhazia.' On 24 July the Council of Abkhazian Unity, uniting 19 democratically oriented public organisations, declared that the Parliament of Abkhazia, by annulling the Constitution on the basis of which it was formed, had practically outlawed itself.

Shevardnadze cut short his visit to Western Georgia owing to the events in Abkhazia and immediately returned to Tbilisi. The State Council of Georgia, convened on 25 July, nullified the 23 July resolution of the Supreme Soviet of Abkhazia. On the basis of the resolution of an expert juridical commission, headed by Tedo Ninidze, the State Council decided: 'The decree of the Abkhazian Parliament cannot be considered valid in as much as it cannot express the interests and opinion of the majority of the population of the Autonomous Republic, for it was adopted in the absence of the quorum.'[164] At the meeting of the State Council it was noted that Ardzinba's reference to Article 4 of the 1925 Constitution and all his talk about Abkhazia not seceding from Georgia but uniting with her by concluding a new 'special treaty' - was false camouflage for his true intentions. Shevardnadze, fearing the worst, said at this meeting of the State Council: 'Something can happen in Abkhazia which by its character and consequences will be much worse than what happened in the Tskhinvali region.' (Ossetia).

The positions of the Abkhazian leaders turned out to be rather shaky. A 'private trip' to Turkey, urgently undertaken by Ardzinba (24-31 July), with visits to Ankara, Istanbul and the twin city of Sukhumi, Adalazari, yielded no results in terms of recognition of Abkhazia by a neighbouring Muslim power. Russia and the other CIS republics actually ignored the 23 July act of the Abkhazian Parliament; no official congratulations on the occasion of the new status of the republic were received by Abkhazia. Tbilisi (the State Council of Georgia) resolutely and categorically countermanded the resolution 'On the Termination of the 1978 Constitution of the Abkhazian SSR.'

Even in Sukhumi itself opposition to Ardzinba was growing. On 28-30 July the parliamentary faction Democratic Abkhazia held an enlarged session with the participation of the public. This meeting was declared a session of the Supreme Soviet of Abkhazia, a sort of counter-session to that which was held on 23 July, and this time a resolution was adopted in the name of the Supreme Soviet of Abkhazia declaring all the acts of 23 July null and void. The leader of Democratic Abkhazia, Tamaz Nadareishvili, (who was also first Vice-Chairman of the Supreme Soviet of Abkhazia) opposed Vladislav Ardzinba resolutely. The attempt to resuscitate the 1925 Constitution was denounced; the constitution had existed for several months only, was cancelled in 1926 and did not reflect any political reality in the history of Abkhazia. Even Nestor Lakoba called it 'constitutional stupidity.' The participants of the 28-30 July session had no illusions about the true intentions of the leadership of the Supreme Soviet of Abkhazia. Ardzinba needed the illusory Constitution of 1925 (with the article on the dictatorship of the proletariat in the text) in order to carry out his separatist plans. 'Ardzinba is playing into the hands of the forces that want to restore the monster named the USSR', said the deputy Jemal Gamakharia at the session.

This 28-30 July session of Democratic Abkhazia passed a resolution on renaming the Abkhazian SSR as the Abkhazian Autonomous Republic. The word autonomous was crucial here: the archaic 'Soviet' and 'Socialist' disappeared. They assumed power, reaffirming the declaration that the rest of the Supreme Soviet, the 36 deputies that adopted the act of 23 July had, in fact, outlawed itself.

Thus Ardzinba, who at the beginning of August returned empty-handed to Sukhumi from his trip to Turkey, had a choice: to abandon what he had started, or by force assert his right to 'independence' with all its attributes. Vladislav Ardzinba, surrounded by Russian advisers who promised him success, chose the second path.

While preparations for war were under way in Sukhumi, and while the purchase of arms was stepped up and emissaries were sent to Moscow to the atamans' Council of Russian Cossacks (7 August), celebrations were held in Tbilisi on the occasion of Georgia's admission to the UN. Ardzinba declined Shevardnadze's invitation (telephone conversation in the morning of 4 August) to fly to the capital, saying that he had not yet got his personal plane, and that he had already missed the Sukhumi-Tbilisi flight. The Abkhaz delegation did not participate in the celebrations in Georgia. These included a mass demonstration in Tbilisi, blessings of the Catholicos Ilia II read in the Square of the Republic on 4 August, and the *Manifesto on the Great Reconciliation*. This decided on the lifting throughout the country of the state of emergency and the curfew, on the return of all armed units to barracks, including the detachments of Mkhedrioni, on the withdrawal of forces from Western Georgia, and on granting an amnesty to all those arrested after 6 January 1992, including the members of Valter Shurgaia's group - participants in the attempt to capture the TV Centre and to stage a coup on 24 June. There was also a rally, a military air-display and fireworks.

The Georgian national festivities did not last long. A week later, an attack carried out on 11 August against the Traffic Inspection post at the village of Machara, a village south-east of Sukhumi in the Gulripsh district, led to an exchange of fire. The soldiers of the first mechanized battalion of the Georgian regular army participated in it. The theatre of war was approaching Abkhazia. Bandit attacks on trains in Western Georgia resumed on the same night (Zviadists and Abkhaz robbers operated together). Two freight trains bound for Sukhumi were robbed and the passengers of several fast trains were relieved of valuable articles and money.[165]

The State Council of Georgia discussed the question of declaring a state of emergency on the railway in Western Georgia (Mingrelia and Abkhazia). It decided that the tracks should be guarded by the Ministry of Defence of the Republic. It was intended to assign 1800 men to the task.

And yet the main blow that provoked the war was delivered on 11 August, not on the railways or the Machara post of the State Traffic Inspectorate, but on Zugdidi where talks between officials from Tbilisi and supporters of Zviad Gamsakhurdia were under way at that time. The mission of Shevardnadze, launched on 23 July, was carried on by his advisers, ministers and representatives, including the recently released Valter Shurgaia, who in the first place sought to free Alexandr Kavsadze (kidnapped and held hostage by a bandit group) and reach a compromise over other issues of stabilization in Western Georgia.

The participants of the talks were treacherously attacked by an armed detachment of approximately fifty men commanded by Gocha

Bakhia, the chief of Gamsakhurdia's bodyguards (the very person who subjected prisoners to torture in the presidential bunker until 6 January - the day of the ex- president's flight). Twelve men, representatives of the State Council of Georgia, were captured (of whom eleven were still detained after the speedy release of one of them) and taken to the village of Kokhori, Gali district, in the territory of Abkhazia. Among those kidnapped were Georgia's Minister of Internal Affairs Roman Gventsadze, National Security Adviser (and Shevardnadze's aide) David Salaridze, Deputy Minister of Internal Affairs Zibert Khazalia, Deputy Head of the Chief Board of the Administrative Police, Valerian Rogava - all officials of the highest rank.

At midnight (11-12 August) Eduard Shevardnadze made a nation-wide address on television, saying: 'I believed that evil had limits, but now I am convinced that it has no bounds. In the eyes of the entire world we have demonstrated magnanimity and pardoned all our enemies, but there will be no more forgiveness.' In his appeal to the nation Shevardnadze made it explicit that Georgia would no longer tolerate regular robbing of trains, blowing up of bridges, toying with human lives, taking officials as hostages, the trampling underfoot of the laws of the State by bandit groups. 'The loss that Georgia has suffered since the beginning of 1992 due to highway robberies and acts of terrorism alone amounts to ten million roubles. It is high time we took the most drastic measures to re-establish order in Mingrelia and throughout the territory of Georgia', Shevardnadze stressed.[166] An almost 100,000-strong rally, held on 12 August in Tbilisi, responded to Shevardnadze's appeal by an expression of popular support. Tbilisi presented the kidnappers who kept the hostages in Abkhazia with an ultimatum, demanding their immediate release. The deadline of the ultimatum expired on 13 August but the hostages were not set free. Georgia's Minister of Defence Tengiz Kitovani was then put in charge of the conduct of operations to eliminate criminal groups, guard the highway and free the hostages. The plan did not anticipate an occupation of Abkhazia or any armed invasion of Abkhazia for the solution of political issues. The deployment of troops with the object of establishing order really was an inevitable measure forced upon a state which could no longer tolerate such appalling anarchy and such severe losses.

It is important to underline that the so-called 'act of invasion' was neither clandestine nor a surprise. The plan of the operation, which was worked out at the headquarters of the Ministry of Defence of Georgia, became known to the public on 12 August.[167] Furthermore, as pointed out by the Georgian Prime Minister Sigua, the action was not of a punitive character and it was undertaken for the purpose of establishing order. Its scene of operation was not the whole of Abkhazia, but the territory (primarily covering Mingrelia, and also the Gali and Ochamchire districts of Abkhazia) where the situation was out of hand: hostages were held, bridges blown up, posts of the State Traffic Inspectorate fired at, and trains robbed. It was no secret that the Georgian army would set up its field headquarters in Senaki, and that in his telephone conversation with Ardzinba, Shevardnadze informed him of the impending operation of the Georgian armed forces in the Gali and Ochamchire districts.

Mutual understanding was reached on this issue and even joint operations of the Georgian units and Abkhazian police detachments were envisaged to annihilate bandit formations and free the hostages in the village of Kokhori, Gali district.

In the night of 13-14 August a railway bridge was blown up near the Ingiri station. The road bridge - the last that linked the coastline (Batumi, Poti, Sukhumi) with Tbilisi - was threatened. There could be no more delay. In the morning of 14 August Georgian armed units under the command of Tengiz Kitovani took control of the Inguri river crossing and entered Abkhazian territory.

Later, the story given out by the propagandists in Ardzinba's entourage, gave rise to the legend that the Georgian units had been 'armed to the teeth' with tanks and helicopter gunships, and even nuclear missiles! In reality the strength of the Georgian troops was sufficient to ensure their own security and fulfil the task of setting free the hostages and guarding the roads. By 14 August in Mingrelia and Abkhazia there were only 3,000 men under Kitovani's command.[168]

In Ochamchire district the Abkhazian 'guards' opened fire on the Georgian units, which came as a total surprise for the Georgian command, as it had no intention of fighting the Abkhazia Guard, but on the contrary had planned to act jointly with it.

This episode could still be regarded as a misunderstanding, but the war broke out at noon on 14 August, when Vladislav Ardzinba addressed the people of the republic (his address was simultaneously broadcast on radio and television and reported every 30 minutes during the day), calling on the people of Abkhazia for a 'patriotic war' against the 'enemy'. The Supreme Soviet of Abkhazia, meeting in Sukhumi from 10 to 11 a.m. under the chairmanship of Vladislav Ardzinba, qualified the manoeuvres of the Georgian troops as an 'aggression against the Abkhazian statehood on the part of a hostile state'. Units of the Abkhazian internal troops were ordered to offer armed resistance to the 'aggressor'.

'Armed units of the State Council of Georgia have invaded our land', said Ardzinba, 'including criminal elements who sow death and destruction on our soil... Our proposals to settle issues of mutual relations by peaceful means were responded to by tanks, planes, guns, murders and robberies. This bears witness to the true nature of Georgia's present leadership. At last it can no longer hide behind its characteristic hypocrisy. The terrible mask has fallen.'[169] Radio and television kept spreading this lie throughout Abkhazia, scaring the people with 'criminal elements', 'guns, murders and robberies.' (See Chronicle of Events.)

But by 12 p.m. when the recording of Ardzinba's speech began for television and radio broadcasting, nothing of the kind had taken place in Abkhazia. He blamed the State Council of Georgia for 'the blood of Georgians in Tbilisi and other regions - Mingrelians in Mingrelia, Ossetians in Ossetia, and now Abkhazians and the whole of the population of our long- suffering homeland are added to the list.'[170] Convinced of the support of the forces of communist reaction, Ardzinba assured his people that these forces (he vaguely referred to these as 'the world') were aware of developments and that their support was certain: 'I must say that the world knows in what situation Abkhazia has been placed.The world resolutely condemns this barbarous action.We are assured of its moral and material assistance.'[171] 'Naturally', he went on, 'it is not easy to speak about this now, when at this very moment your houses are possibly being plundered, people are being beaten up and human life itself is not guaranteed. But I am deeply convinced that we have the appropriate support.'[172]

Of course, everyone knew what this support was and his speech appeared, with extraordinary dispatch, the very next morning in the pages of the strongly pro-communist newspaper *Pravda* in Moscow.

The Decree of the Presidium of the Supreme Soviet of Abkhazia on the 'mobilization of the adult population and on the transfer of arms to the regiment of the Internal Troops of Abkhazia' had been prepared in advance and was signed on the morning of 14 August. This was immediately after the previously known plans of the Georgian leadership to free the hostages in Gali district were confirmed:

'In connection with the introduction of the armed formations of the State Council of Georgia onto the territory of the Republic of Abkhazia', the Decree read, 'and the real threat posed to the sovereignty of the Republic and to the lives of the population, the Presidium of the Supreme Soviet of the Republic of Abkhazia decrees:

1. The adult population within the age bracket of 18-40 years inclusive be mobilized and sent to the regiment of Internal Troops;
2. The Commander of the regiment of the Internal Troops form 5 battalions of 500 men each as the basis of the regiment.

V. Ardzinba
Chairman of the Supreme Soviet of Abkhazia
City of Sukhumi[173]

Following Ardzinba, the newly appointed Chief of the Republican Defence Staff, Sergei Shamba, issued a televised call to arms of the entire male population of Abkhazia from 18 to 45 years of age inclusive. Within 24 hours the mobilised men were to assemble at the defence posts set up in all the districts of the Republic on the basis of the local departments of the police and the State Traffic Inspectorate. Thousands of people had been given weapons and many crimes were committed overnight. A huge army was being created. Arms came from secret depots of illegally purchased and imported material and from pillaged armouries of Russian troops in Abkhazia. People were enlisted for service regardless of their wishes and attempts by some parents to hide their offspring from the compulsory mobilization were thwarted. Drunken 'defenders' and those under the influence of drugs were seen firing at random - at animals, traffic, gardens, sea, windows - any target that aroused them. There was neither strict military discipline nor any clear-cut task for these groups. Even where there were no Georgian units, weapons were used for robbery, intimidation, paying off old scores with neighbours, and to terrorize the local Georgian population. The latter was not subject to mobilization and was not issued with arms. The assault groups of 'Abkhazian self- defence' were formed strictly according to the ethnic principle. In an attempt to lay the sole responsibility for the outbreak of war on the State Council of Georgia, Ardzinba's followers later tried to make - believe that Georgia had committed an 'aggression' against Abkhazia without any grounds for the use of force. Thus, for instance, O. Vasilyeva writes: 'Characteristically enough, the operation under the slogan of combating terrorism and taking hostages was conducted not in Mingrelia, where such actions took place, but in Abkhazia which had just taken steps towards forming a federal system with Georgia.'[174]

This is outright disinformation. The State Council of Georgia did not intend to use force against any steps taken by Abkhazia toward forming a federal system with Georgia. It did not introduce any troops into Abkhazia after the 23 July declaration and no repression followed, nor was any pressure brought to bear on the part of the Supreme Soviet led by Ardzinba. Georgia was getting ready to join the UN, to celebrate her Great Day of Reconciliation and finally to hold democratic elections of a new parliament and its Chairman and did not declare any war against Abkhazia in connection with the steps taken on 23 July.

In his statement at a press-conference in Moscow on 28 September 1992, Shevardnadze clearly formulated the essence of the Abkhazian provocation, emphasising that 'Georgia did not intend to fight anyone'. The State Council of Georgia was obliged to resort to military force against bandit units in Western Georgia and part of the Abkhazian territory inevitably had to turn into a theatre of these military operations, for it was there, in the forests between Gali and Ochamchire, that the hostages - high-ranking officials of Georgia abducted in Zugdidi - were held.[175] It would have been ludicrous to conduct a military operation for their release on the territory they had already left. They were in Abkhazia and that was where the troops were to be introduced according to a preliminary understanding reached with the leadership of Abkhazia during a telephone conversation between Shevardnadze and Ardzinba on 11 August. (*There continues, of course, to be much discussion of the true nature of the 'invasion'. Some say it was absolutely necessary, others that it should have been avoided in the tense situation prevailing.One version has it that troops were sent in without Shevardnadze's knowledge and that he later had to acknowledge them de facto. Shevardnadze denies this. It is extremely difficult to be absolutely certain of the precise sequence of events at this time; Georgians and Abkhaz make accusations and counter accusations. The author herself was eye-witness to a part of this situation. More time is needed to give a greater perspective. See Chronology of Events page 157.)*

Concealing from the people of Abkhazia and from his own Parliament the fact of the agreement on the necessary military operation in the Gali district, Ardzinba used the re-deployment of State Council troops, about which he had been informed beforehand, as a pretext for the declaration of the patriotic war.

The limited contingent of troops of the State Council (about a thousand guards), which found themselves on the morning of 14 August on the territory of Abkhazia, threatened neither the Supreme Soviet of Abkhazia nor the Abkhazian people. This army contingent had a definite task: to free the hostages in Gali. They were moving in that direction without a single shot fired and were not creating any real threat to Abkhazia. A republic is not conquered with one thousand troops; this was the minimum that could guarantee the security of the servicemen and the success of the operation against the armed gangs of Zviadists that were acting with impunity on the territory of Abkhazia. In his appeal to the people on radio and TV before a single shot was fired from the Georgian side, Ardzinba declared these troops an 'adversary' and called on the people for a 'patriotic war'.

Thus he started his long-planned war on 14 August 1992. The swiftness with which fortifications and barricades were placed along the whole highway from Sukhumi to the Russian border on 14 August confirms that the war had been prepared in advance by the leadership of Abkhazia. The author witnessed the squads maintaining all-round defences at the check-point by the entrance to Novy Afon, near the bus stop of the village of Primorskoye, with not a single Georgian soldier to be seen within many kilometres. Armoured personnel carriers and cars without licence plates speeding along the highway, were delivering groups of armed people to the check-points. They were not coming from their villages in order 'to defend their homes' or 'to stand virtually barehanded to the last man', as Ardzinba later claimed in his speeches. They were being transported to points

marked out under a clear-cut military plan. Boxes with ammunition
and shells were unloaded from the APCs. All the armaments were
new, modern and in perfect technical condition. This army was well
equipped and well prepared.

Let us once again underline the fact that this performance took
place at noon (between 12 a.m. and 2 p.m.) on 14 August, when the
radio and TV had just started to broadcast a series of addresses by
Ardzinba and Shamba with the call for a patriotic war and general
mobilization. These armed squads, stationed along the highway and
concentrated in populated areas (their main bases were the local police stations, the former military registration and enlistment offices
and check-points) launched a criminal war against the civilians and
especially against the Georgian population which found itself subject to uncontrolled and unchecked terror. Armed boeviks grabbed
everything that they wanted from Georgian houses and apartments.
They took people away to unknown destinations, killing on the spot
anybody who tried to resist or defend his property and his dignity.
They showed no mercy either for Russians, Armenians, nor peoples
of other nationalities.

In their own villages or towns, these Russian, Armenian, and other
families still had the opportunity to survive if they declared their
hatred towards Georgia and their solidarity with 'fighting Abkhazia',
and sent their sons to MRE offices. Their chances of survival became
even greater if they participated in the looting of neighbouring Georgian houses and in the violence. But, to be caught by an armed patrol
on the highway was equal to death for anyone. They stopped,
searched and robbed people under the pretext of 'defence requirements' and at the slightest manifestation of discontent, rebellious-
ness or resistance, they were beaten, detained or taken to headquarters. The fate of people who disappeared in this way was very tragic.
The cruelty of the boeviks particularly increased on the night from 14
to 15 August: boxes full of wine and vodka - looted from shops and
booths - as well as drugs, were distributed to the enlistment offices
and check- points throughout the night, so that by the next morning
there was not a single sober 'defender' at the check-points of
Primorskoye and Novy Afon. They shot in the air and at animals,
and rotting corpses of dogs on the highway from Sukhumi to Gagra
was the most characteristic sight in the first days of the Abkhazian-

Georgian conflict. Neighbouring gardens, vineyards and houses were destroyed by bursts from automatic rifles. After the night spent at the enlisting office, the head of the rescue station in Novy Afon, who was completely drunk, shouting 'we shall not let any saboteur pass', took the motor boat into the sea and opened fire at the sea and the beach.

Since the 'defenders' were supplied with only spirits and drugs, and were not provided with any food or rations, they started mass looting from 15 August. People with automatic rifles took everything they wanted from neighbouring houses, private households, gardens and orchards, markets that were already being closed, and from shops and canteens that managed to survive by some miracle. This nightmare, a senseless war against civilians, arbitrary violence, plundering, and marauding was witnessed by the author herself in Primorskoye and Novy Afon on 14-16 August, and continued in the following weeks.

This is attested, in particular, by the story of an eye-witness from Alakhadzy, a suburb village of Gagra, published in the newspaper *Demokraticheskaya Abkhazia*: 'By 1-2 p.m. in August 1992', he says, 'barricades appeared in Pitsunda ... similar constructions were built at the Bzyb bridge, by the poultry farm.And interestingly enough, fully armed Abkhazian and Chechen boeviks appeared at these barricades...They started mass confiscation of private cars...From August 25 till September 12 (this is the day I managed to flee the village) there were many cases of car-stealing and burglary (the houses of Omar and Otar Tsuleiskiri, Arvashi Kharebava, Nugzar Shalia, and many others were looted). On August 19, Abkhazians and Chechens, armed with automatic rifles, broke into Alakhadzy secondary school N13, where the only telephone, connecting Alakhadzy with Gagra, was installed. The attackers cut the wire and headed for the post-office where they smashed the switch-board...The village was completely isolated from the outside world...By day and night, Abkhaz and Chechen bandits were committing outrages without any hindrance...In Akhali Sopeli,....the boeviks cut the throat of a former agronomist of the collective farm Razhden...Lobzhanidze and his wife...Here are some more facts from Gudauta: the savage murder of L. Petriashvili (as well as the director of the Sukhumi flour mill Ugrekhelidze, who was buried alive), the murder of the Gigineishvilis (mother and son) and...seizure of Georgian private houses by boeviks. People had not experienced the horrors of war since 1941-1945. And now the current leadership of the autonomous republic plunged our region into a fratricidal war...'[176]

If Abkhazia really had found herself the victim of a sudden aggression, as claimed by Ardzinba's propagandists (let us leave aside the argument that it is actually impossible for Georgia to commit aggression on her own territory against a part of her own state), it is probable that the actions taken by the Abkhazian leadership would have been absolutely different. In such a case, the mobilised squads and volunteers' detachments should have been sent to the front line, against the aggressors, and should not have been deployed along the roads and in settlements where they established terror and waged a real war against the Georgian population. They terrorized any Georgians they found and began, in fact, a deliberate process of ethnic cleansing.

If the Abkhazian leaders had been concerned with the organisation of resistance and problems of defence, they would have tried to normalize life in war conditions. They would have made attempts to achieve necessary labour discipline, order, efficient functioning of the communication system, and transportation, and would also have provided the population and army with food instead of allowing the total destabilization of the region and the complete economic breakdown that, in fact, came about. Regular transport routes were cancelled, telephone lines were cut off, post offices were closed down, local markets were dispersed, unpunished robbery, looting and violence became commonplace. The purpose was to destroy normal everyday life, unsettle the population, drive it to despair, and convince it that war was the only hope of survival.

Ardzinba was very much concerned with the creation of ideological cover for this war. A myth had to be created about imperialist Georgia violating tiny, unprotected Abkhazia whose only crime was allegedly to have briefly enjoyed freedom.

On 17 August Ardzinba signed an appeal to the 'Parliaments, Presidents and Nations of the World', which gives his official version of events: '...On August 14, 1992 troops of the State Council of Georgia broke into the territory of the Republic of Abkhazia with the objective of its occupation'.[177] When Ardzinba laments, in his appeal, the fact that 'dozens of innocent people, holiday-makers, women and children have died, houses, hotels, schools and hospitals are being fired at, the residents are being robbed, driven out of their houses, hundreds of people are taken hostage and being tortured...the economy is paralysed, there is a shortage of bread, medicines and fuel and an informational blockade is organised in Abkhazia,'[178] he deliberately distorts the truth for his own ends. There were not hundreds of hostages who were being tortured, the Abkhazian side was not running out of fuel, arms and medicines, for they had been stockpiled beforehand in preparation for hostilities, and there was no 'information blockade' - all the mass media outside Georgia were following these menacing events with great interest. Newspapers published everything they could find out during the first two days (from 14 to 17 when Ardzinba signed the appeal). It must also be mentioned that the 'patriotic', pro-communist, newspapers of Russia echoed the beginning of the war with a well-prepared, simultaneous burst of condemnation levelled at Shevardnadze and Yeltsin: let us recall the well-known refrain of the *Den* newspaper: 'Abkhazian blood is on the Kremlin.'[179]

As we have seen, the real victims during the first days of the war were the residents (mostly Georgian) who were robbed and driven out of their own houses in areas controlled by the Abkhazian separatists. Holiday-makers in the Sukhumi Air Defence sanatorium, women and children, were shot by snipers. These holiday-makers were mostly family members of the Russian military personnel. The purpose of this order was to provoke political reaction from official Russia and its Armed Forces. Accusing the troops of the State Council of Georgia of the perpetration of these atrocities, Ardzinba hoped for Russia's interference with the purpose of defending the interests of her compatriots.

The partially paralysed economy was the direct result of the actions taken by the Gudauta authorities who fled there from Sukhumi. They gave orders to close down markets, and policemen scattered and trampled on the vegetables and fruit brought to the markets by peasants. The population was not being supplied with bread because the necessary vehicles were commandeered by military forces for 'defence requirements.' On the entire territory controlled by Abkhazians, and especially along the Sukhumi-Gudauta- Gagra highway, houses, flats and cottages belonging mostly to Georgians but also to Armenians and Russians, were being looted. On orders from Gudauta, passenger and railway services were cancelled in Abkhazia (the last train bound for Moscow left Sukhumi on 14 August). All the motor pools on the territory controlled by the Supreme Soviet of Abkhazia were commandeered. There were looted and ransacked booths, shops, canteens, railway stations, filling stations and bus stations over the whole territory of Abkhazia. One may presume that some of the disorders and crimes were spontaneously committed by criminal elements, uncontrolled by the authorities, or by the scared people who fled leaving behind everything they had. Then why did the Supreme Soviet and the Council of Ministers not take steps to stabilize the situation? If, instead of publishing pathetic, heart-rending and false appeals to the 'Parliaments, Presidents and Nations of the World', the leadership of Abkhazia had adopted a single resolution concerning the functioning of bakeries and markets, bread distribution, traffic restoration, and some determination to put a stop to marauding, perhaps they would not have had to speak of the 'paralysed economy.'

I must also mention one more lie in the appeal to 'Parliaments, Presidents and Nations of the World'. Ardzinba writes: 'Abkhazians, Russians and representatives of other nationalities (Armenians, Greeks, Turks and Estonians) are defending their own houses, villages and towns practically barehanded.' But these people were not practically barehanded. They were called to the mobilization stations and armed with modern automatic rifles from the depots where they had been stored up with the expectation of a coming war. The weapons were taken from the armouries of the Armed Forces of the Russian Federation deployed in Abkhazia. Often these weapon transfers took the form of robberies by unarmed Abkhazians, but these robberies were actually badly staged performances (as, for example, at the base of the Bombora military airfield). Sometimes open deals were made for the transfer of weapons for arming Abkhaz boeviks. The Supreme Soviet of Abkhazia received not only containers of automatic rifles, hand grenades, etc., but was also supplied with modern equipment suitable for launching large-scale operations such as tanks, artillery, combat helicopters, fighters, tactical rocket launchers, fragmentation bombs of great destructive power, and all this was finally used by the leadership of Abkhazia to bombard and destroy its own capital, Sukhumi.

Russian armed units deployed at Sukhumi, Lower Eshera, and the Bombora airfield near Gudauta found themselves in a war zone. At all negotiations and in all of her statements Russia formally insisted that her troops exercised strict neutrality in the Abkhaz-Georgian conflict and were ready to use force only in the case of 'armed provocations directed against them, no matter from which side they came.'[180] But the real situation looked somewhat different on 15 August 1992. Abkhaz extremists 'attacked' the Russian armoury at the Bombora airfield and stole weapons from one of its depots. They met with no rebuff whatsoever. On the contrary, they were met with a highly benevolent attitude and much cordiality.

That was how the war declared by Vladislav Ardzinba on Georgia broke out. Of course, like any other war, this one was also fraught with reciprocally bitter cruelty, and when Georgian military units entered the villages and towns where Georgian houses had been burnt down and robbed, they did not display angelic gentleness. Robbery, pillage, violence, as well as the humiliation of the peaceful population became the norm of behaviour of both belligerents. However, the Abkhazian side bears responsibility for preparing, provoking and starting the military conflict, and for its escalation in drawing other peoples of the ex-Soviet Union into the war.

From the very beginning, monstrous provocation was used to draw Russia into this conflict. We have already spoken about one such provocation: snipers shooting at holiday-makers in an attempt to lay the blame on Georgian landing troops.[181] The shelling of the passenger ship *Kometa*, sailing from Batumi to Sochi on 27 August, was of a similar provocative character. A helicopter without any markings fired at the ship in the area of Gudauta, fully controlled by the Abkhazian side, where the helicopter was based. This did not prevent Abkhazian propaganda from blaming the Georgian 'vultures' for the tragedy (passengers were wounded and killed on board the ship).The Abkhazians even named the Georgian pilot - Jimi Maisuradze - who allegedly flew the helicopter and gave the order to fire at the Kometa. It was soon ascertained that on that very day and hour Maisuradze was carrying out another task and could not have acted in the Gudauta area.[182] However, such exposures do not embarrass the Abkhazians, for similar provocations immediately followed by lies, were of frequent occurrence. The cynicism of Ardzinba's entourage reached the point where his emissaries brought photos of corpses and the wounded, of burnt and destroyed houses from places where Abkhaz guards and North-Caucasian volunteers had run amok, to press conferences in Moscow and passed them off as casualties of Georgian aggression!

From the very beginning, Ardzinba sought the help and support of outside political forces and acted in several directions:

1. In Grozny, with Dzhokhar Dudayev (the Chechen President) and Zviad Gamsakhurdia (in exile), where he flew on 15 August;

2. In Gudauta, where he visited Russia's landing troops and detachments of *Omon* (special police units) quartered there (16 August); at their headquarters he sought their sympathy and aid;

3. With the official leaders of the North-Caucasian republics (the first to whom he appealed was the president of Kabardino-Balkaria Valeri Kokov; then the Chairman of the Supreme Soviet of the North-Ossetian ASSR Aslanbek Galazov) and other governmental bodies where the positions of the former communist party nomenclature and those politicians of communist orientation are still very strong;

4. With the atamans of the North-Caucasian Cossacks;

5. With the Confederation of the Mountain Peoples of the Caucasus;

6. With Russian national-patriots and chauvinists who, against the logic of their usual appeals for the unity of the Orthodox faith and the strengthening of the State, unanimously rose up in defence of the Muslim separatist Abkhazia and against Christian Georgia. As a matter of fact, there was nothing strange in this, for Orthodox Christian and *derzhava* (state) solidarity to these political forces was nothing but a camouflage for their plans to restore the communist regime. In as much as the Abkhazian war could assist in such restoration, Abkhazia immediately became their 'best beloved sister' like Serbia and the Moldavian Dniester SSR. The deputy Sergei Baburin, who at once flew to Abkhazia, stating that 'the blood of Abkhazia is on the Kremlin',[183] and the former KGB colonel Alexandr Sterligov, as well as Alexandr Nevzorov, TV journalist of the programme *600 seconds*, were immediately sympathetic to the Abkhazian separatist cause.

Not every attempt to find allies was successful. Despite the obvious help given to them already, they failed to harness properly the Russian army and use it against Shevardnadze; nor did they succeed in provoking Yeltsin into action since he took a tough stand on the inadmissibility of Russia's military involvement in the Transcaucasian conflict and supported the principle of the territorial integrity of Georgia.

Ardzinba did not benefit much from the generosity of North-Caucasian official authorities. Considerable restraint was also shown by the Cossacks who gave a more meagre and lukewarm support to Abkhazia than had been expected. But the Confederation of the Mountain Peoples of the Caucasus (CMPC) was real manna from heaven for belligerent Abkhazia. Already on 17 August, at its Parliamentary session in Grozny the CMPC had worked out a programme of solidarity with Abkhazia.

National organisations and movements of anti-Russian and anti-democratic orientation, such as the *International Circassian Organisation* (ICO) and *the Congress of the Kabardinian People* (CKP) joined the CMPC. At the same time the factor of ethnic solidarity of the Adyghe-Abkhaz peoples, the 'brothers', was brought into play. With the connivance of the authorities - composed of many former party and soviet functionaries - terrorist groups of so-called 'Confederates' (CMPC troops) were created in the regions and autonomous republics of the South of Russia, and openly or secretly transferred to Abkhazia along mountain paths and Caucasian passes. Ruslan Hajibekov, Deputy-Chairman of the Adyghe government, tried to justify himself and his actions by saying: 'We failed to keep them back. The Adyghe and the Kabardinians, the Circassians and the Abkhaz are fraternal peoples - very close in culture. The Abkhaz people already suffered a genocide in the 19th century and we shall not allow another to happen. The delay of Russian reaction may alienate the North-Caucasian peoples from Russia.'[184]

The forces of the Confederates were organised and simultaneously directed against Georgia as well as against democratic Russia. This is shown by documents revealing the real aims of the organisers of 'another August' - a provocation against the democratic forces in Georgia and Russia. The following is the resolution of the 'extraordinary enlarged session' of the CMPC Parliament: 'On the Situation in Abkhazia and the Repulse of the Aggressive Acts of the Troops of the State Council of Georgia':

'Having discussed the situation in Abkhazia and considering the treacherous character of Georgia's aggression and the violation by

her of the legitimate rights and interests of the sovereign Republic of
Abkhazia and its peoples, acts of genocide involving peaceful residents; actual collusion between the leadership of Georgia and the
Russian Federation aimed at overthrowing the legitimate constitutional bodies of power in Abkhazia, stating the indecision and lack of
a principled stand on the part of the leaderships of the North Caucasian republics; also taking into account the Treaty on Confederative
Alliance of the Mountain Peoples of the Caucasus as well as the appeal for help of the Abkhazian leadership and the Abkhazian People's Forum, the tenth extraordinary CMPC session resolves:

1. To file a protest against the policy of the Georgian State Council and Russian leadership in Abkhazia; to demand the withdrawal
of Georgian troops from the territory of sovereign Abkhazia before
August 21; and also compensation for the damage done to the Republic during the occupation.

2. In the case of continued occupation of Abkhazia to announce
the start of CMPC military actions.

3. To support the initiatives of the International Circassian Association and other national movements and parties in the region on
the formation of voluntary units for defending the 'just cause' of the
Abkhaz people, and to send CMPC voluntary units to Abkhazia.

4. To create permanent working groups for providing all-out support for CMPC troops (medical, food, organisational, technical, etc.).

5. In the given situation the leaders of the North Caucasian Republic must:

(a) resolutely dissociate themselves from the policy of the Russian
leadership in Abkhazia (in the region, in particular) and demand the
withdrawal of the landing force from Abkhazia.

(b) denounce the so-called Federation Treaty with Russia and adopt
a Joint Declaration on the Confederative Alliance of North Caucasian republics.

(c) provide for the effective actions of the CMPC in support of
Abkhazia.

In case of non-fulfilment of point 5, the leaders of those North Caucasian republics that betrayed the national interests will take full responsibility for the situation in the region and in Abkhazia. In its
turn, the CMPC reserves the right to act in defence of the rights and
interests of the Mountain Peoples of the Caucasus.

6. To call on the public movements and the peoples of the Caucasus to support the actions of protest against the co-ordinated policy of Georgia and Russia in the region.

7. To urge the deputies of the Russian Federation from the North Caucasian republics to raise the question on the collusion between the Russian Federation and the Georgian State Council, which has led to tragic consequences in Abkhazia and to a sharp aggravation of the situation in the Caucasus.To appeal to the people's deputies from other republics of the Russian Federation to back up this demand.

8. To propose to the Cossacks of the South of Russia to combine our efforts for a joint solution of all the aggravating problems in the region.

Adopted at the special (10th) enlarged session of the Parliament of the CMPC in the presence of 9 delegations (21 persons in all) and observers. City of Grozny. Chairman of the CMPC Parliament Yu. Soslambekov; President of the CMPC M. Shanibov.(185)

Even more monstrous was the document adopted on 22 August 1992 under the title: *'The Directive of the President of the Confederation of the Mountain Peoples of the Caucasus Musa Shanibov and the Chairman of the CMPC Parliament Yusup Soslambekov'*, which is, in fact, a declaration of open, all-out, war. It runs as follows:
'Considering that all peaceful measures directed towards compelling the Georgian occupational forces to leave the territory of sovereign Abkhazia have proved futile, and in order to meet the resolution of the 10th session of the CMPC Parliament, we order that:

1. All headquarters of the Confederation must ensure the transfer of volunteers to the territory of Abkhazia to fight the armed aggressors.

2. All the armed formations of the Confederation must engage any forces offering resistance and fight their way onto the territory of Abkhazia by any method.

3. The city of Tbilisi is to be declared a disaster area.Any methods to be used, including terrorist acts.

4. *All persons of Georgian nationality on the territory of the Confederation to be declared hostages.*

5. All types of freights bound for Georgia should be stopped, as well as all kinds of shipments.[186]

Indeed, this was another August. It was only a few days short of the exact anniversary of the first August putsch - the attempt at a reactionary coup in 1991. History repeats itself, first as tragedy, then as farce. In the present case it is difficult to say when there was more tragedy and when farce prevailed: in August 1991 or August 1992. True, the Kremlin conspirators in Moscow, holding key offices and heading the ministries of a great nuclear power are one thing, and a handful of politicians somewhere on the subtropical Black Sea coast, far from the main political arena, is another. But since we are well aware that great world wars often began with events in some remote, god-forsaken province (the shot in Sarajevo in 1914; the staged seizure of the radio station in Gliwitz, Poland at the end of August 1939), we should not be misled by the apparent provincial character of the Abkhazian events. For a mine laid in the tangerine groves of the southeastern Black Sea littoral of Western Georgia can have a charge powerful enough to disrupt the peace of the whole of Europe.

Chapter 7

And so there was war...

And so there was war and it might be too early now to write its complete history, for the war has not yet ended. The war itself will be discussed in other books, describing, perhaps, the hostilities and the provocations which frustrated all the attempts at a peaceful, political settlement of the conflict. They will tell us how the two antagonists entered into a difficult ceasefire agreement, with the help of the Russian leadership, on 3 September 1992, and how the agreement was wrecked by the Abkhazian separatists. They will tell us of the tragedy in Gagra - the town that was seized and turned into ashes by the Abkhaz guards and the Confederates on 1 October. They will write about the shellings of Sukhumi, and about the participation of Russian aircraft in the bombing of peaceful towns and villages. This book is not written about the war itself. It addresses the sources of the conflict and the causes of its outbreak.

In order to fully comprehend and objectively assess the Abkhazian tragedy, it is vital to consider the whole situation, and admit all the contradictions and paradoxes that are revealed on both sides. It would be naive to suppose that only the 'forces of evil' (criminal formations, bandits, political adventurers and the like) are acting on the Abkhazian side, whereas the Georgian side is represented only by angels in white garments. No black and white scenario can possibly describe and reflect the complicated, muddy spectrum of the real military and political situation in the Abkhazia of 1992. On the one hand, it cannot be denied that there are honest separatists who sincerely believe in the just struggle against Georgian imperialism. On the other hand - and this is especially regrettable - Georgia (particularly her armed forces which have been on the territory of Abkhazia since the August of 1992) does not at all look like an innocent defender of the great ideals of democracy and liberty in this conflict. It seems that a war is always a war - with terrible bloodshed, violence and killing. The Georgian side also has shown some brutality towards prisoners of war and the peaceful non-Georgian population. Robbery, marauding and vandalism, as well as numerous other cases of the violation of human rights have been recorded by some objective informants and proved to be an unpalatable reality.

It would be hopeless and ridiculous to justify all that has been done in Abkhazia, particularly in Sukhumi after it was taken on 18 August 1992 by Georgians. All levels come in for criticism: the war command, quasi-independent armed groups, the civil administration for permitting nationalistic extremism to filter into the mass media, and even ordinary citizens. There has been the usual sorry tale of abuses: in queues at the baker's for bread non-Georgians have been discriminated against. Olga Suprunenko, a deputy of the Moscow Soviet, witnessed cases of discrimination while distributing humanitarian aid among the local population in Sukhumi: 'Mingrelians were given a sack of flour and a kilogramme of sugar, whereas Russians were given only a kilogramme of flour and a glass of sugar.'[187] It would be absurd to deny all these facts even if there may be some exaggeration and bias, and of course, there are many rumours. So, I do not propose to defend or justify everything done by the Georgians, certainly not to prepare some kind of whitewash. I want to reveal the inner sources of the tragedy, to try to make out who has pulled the strings; who caused the chain reaction of mutual extermination and violence; who is to be blamed for what made Sukhumi, Gagra, Tkvarcheli, Eshera, Novy Afon, Gumista as well as many other towns and villages of Abkhazia turn into a real hell for peaceful residents of all nationalities.

The question has only one answer: the war in Abkhazia, the war against independent, democratic Georgia was planned, provoked and started by a group of politicians that have recently come to the leadership of the Supreme Soviet and governmental bodies of the Abkhazian ASSR. These new leaders were inspired by the Special Services of the State Security Committee of the former Soviet Union. From 1989 they have been carrying on purposeful work, establishing a network of their supporters throughout Abkhazia, promoting stooges of the Union 'Centre', forming a fifth column, all aimed at undermining Georgia, who had conceived and implemented her secession from the USSR.

The historical transformation of the Soviet State and the collapse of the USSR changed the political situation in Georgia. In the autumn of 1990, the bloc of parties of the Round Table triumphed in the elections, gaining the majority of seats in the Parliament of Georgia. Consequently, the radicals led by the former dissident, Zviad Gamsakhurdia, came to power. The deterioration of his regime into an extraordinary dictatorship finally resulted in a coup, the Tbilisi Revolution, which lasted from 22 December 1991 to 6 January 1992.

The arrival of Eduard Shevardnadze in Georgia in March 1992 to head the State Council altered nothing for the forces that had been preparing, since 1989, the anti-Georgian bridgehead in Abkhazia. There were those who were ready to wage a war against Georgia in any circumstances, under any alignment of political forces (the only exception being that Georgia should remain within the USSR, which was quite impossible after April 1989 and the more so after August 1991). For the final goals of this war were the restoration of the Communist regime, the Soviet political system and the imperial order either in the form of the old USSR or some modernised version, as well as the punishment of the disobedient colony and its reintroduction into the imperial fold.

From the very beginning, activation of the national factor was considered to be the most effective device in this war. Abkhazia was the first to be thrown into the voracious furnace of political provocation, then some other nationalities (the Russians, the Armenians, the Turks and the Adyghe-Kabardian people of the Northern Caucasus) were to be drawn into the conflict. In all these cases effective use was made of existing inter-ethnic contradictions. Feelings of national grievance, wounded national dignity, factors of ethnic or religious solidarity between the Abkhazians and peoples close to them were all exploited. All the circumstances were linked with the imperfect political structure of the former Georgian SSR with her curious autonomies, social upheavals and demographic changes; everything was added to the fire. Even before the war broke out, at a session of the Democratic Abkhazia faction, one of the deputies, Jemal Gamakharia, said: 'Ardzinba is playing into the hands of those forces that are eager to restore the monster which goes under the name of the USSR'.[188] Fortunately, it now seems impossible to restore that monster, but the scale of the crimes of those who started this terrible war and raised the Abkhazian rebellion to achieve this aim, must be understood by our contemporaries and by posterity.

On 22 June 1993, giving an interview to the journalist Andrei Karaulov on the TV programme *Moment Istiny*, Vladislav Ardzinba, who was noticeably nervous, began to talk about the monstrous atrocities on the part of the Georgian units that had taken Sukhumi: 'They burnt down the Theatre, destroyed the Institute of Language, Literature and History, the most valuable manuscripts, books, archives were destroyed as well...horrible! It was impossible to imagine in advance that human beings were able to commit such baseness.'

Indeed, this is terrible, but we need to make comparisons. That is why I decided to end the closing pages of this book with a small sketch made by a young journalist from Moscow, Dmitri Kholodov, who has no Georgian roots. The sketch depicts the situation in Sukhumi after it was taken by the Georgian guards, and against which the Supreme Soviet of Abkhazia and Vladislav Ardzinba personally have been conducting their declared war since August 1992. I shall reproduce some of it here. People need to know what has happened in Abkhazia.

'A terrible find has been made by the local residents of the mountains of Abkhazia, on the Black Sea littoral, near the spot where clashes with the sea-borne landing troops (attempting to cut the Ochamchire-Sukhumi highway) had taken place...Pieces of a human body were hanging on long wires from the tree...Those were the remains of two skinned men...It is not only soldiers that are killed. In the same woods, near one of the villages there was found a corpse of a pregnant women. She had been raped and disembowelled.'

'The wounded from that side are never sent to us', said the doctors from Sukhumi hospital, 'evidently, they are simply shot'...At the front line we were told how some of the prisoners of war had been taken to an open area. They were pricked with knife-points and were made to curse their own government. The poor souls were stabbed all over until being finally dispatched.' They had 'Columbian Ties'. It is an ordinary thing to be done - an incision of the throat is made, five centimeters below the chin, and the victims' tongues are pulled out through the hole'. The hatred of another nation has no bounds! A man has been walking the streets of the Abkhazian capital for several months now. Children are scared by his appearance - cut off ears, torn nostrils and missing finger nails. Beware of being taken prisoner!

... the Georgian guards told us that the enemy often left their corpses unburied, refusing an armistice in order to sort out the dead scattered about in the fire zone...After all, behind each killed person there was a family that had become convinced of the criminal senselessness of this war...Russians, too, are fighting there. We often heard from Georgian guards how Russian mercenaries were attacking. 'It's a blood-curdling sight - they have helmets and firm, bullet-proof jackets on, and their legs are armoured as well. They advance with their heads bent down, like robots. There is no use shooting at them. No tanks are needed, they are followed by Abkhazians. No city transport runs in Sukhumi, the trolley-bus lines have been torn down. Only one vehicle moves about the town, but let us not wish anybody to become its passenger. The schedule of the hearse and its routes coincides with the shelling schedule. It always goes straight to the shelling zone and there is always enough fuel for it.

The shelling of Sukhumi is the most disgusting thing in this war. All the residents of Sukhumi remember the first shelling. It took place on 2 December 1992. The first rocket fell on *Peace Street* (the name of the street is symbolic, isn't it?). They struck at crowded places. The next strategic 'target' was the town market which was hit with great precision. Eighteen people were killed that day. There were always lots of people in the market. They sold every trifle just to gain a few extra coupons. Besides, it was the only place where one could buy something. Since then, the market has become the most deserted spot in the town. It was split into several small branches in different parts of the town, some ten to fifteen persons selling their wares in each. Within half a year, the town has turned into a heap of ruins. The residents told us with indignation how many buildings, including the luxurious hotel Ritsa, and the Pushkin school built in 1870, were set on fire and looted by drunken guards. Then, the rocket-launcher *Grad* played havoc in the town; the sweet factory was destroyed by bombing, fine trees in the famous Sukhumi Botanical Garden were uprooted, the recently completed new housing district for 45,000 tenants was levelled to the ground. Nobody can live there now, it is dangerous.

Everyone who remained in the town saw death either in their own or in neighbouring families. 'At present, half of the wounded at hospitals are civilians', said the doctors sadly. Over the last two days 146 wounded were registered at only one of the medical distribution points. Most fearful are the shell-splinters. They fly 200 metres, destroying everything around. A whole block is covered - 40 missiles are launched simultaneously. One must not be in an open area at the moment of launching, otherwise one is sure to die...

Yesterday an agreement on ceasefire, reached not so much through negotiations but by the persuasion of Russian diplomats, came into force at 12 o'clock. The commanders-in-chief of both sides issued ceasefire orders. UN and Council for Security and Cooperation in Europe (CSCE) observers are now expected in Abkhazia. But if this agreement fails, Sukhumi cannot survive another winter, it will die out...'[189]

There is a measure of crime and a measure of responsibility. The hour of trial should and will come: let this book be the witness for the prosecution.

Moscow
1 August 1993

Chronicle of the Main Events
in the Political Life of Abkhazia
1917-1992

The present Chronicle embraces, basically, the period between 1989-1992, connected with the preparation and beginning of the Abkhazian war. The most important events outside Abkhazia, creating the historical background and context of the Abkhazian events, have been selected and included in the Chronicle. All the significant political acts of the past, primarily of the 1917-21 period, are briefly summarised, since they explain the movement of modern political thought, the peculiarities of the administrative-state system of the region, etc.

25-29 February 1917(10-13 March - Old Style)
The beginning of the February Democratic Revolution in Russia, the collapse of the Russian Autocratic Empire.

10 March 1917
The Committee on Social Security of Sukhumi District (a body of the provisional government of Russia), headed by Prince Shervashidze (Chachba) was formed.

20 October 1917
A delegation from Abkhazia (of the Committee on Social Security of Sukhumi District) participated in the signing in Vladikavkaz of a treaty on the establishment of a 'South-Eastern Union of Cossack troops, the Mountaineers of the Caucasus and the Free Peoples of the Steppes.'(which soon broke up).

7 November (25 October) 1917
The storming of the Winter Palace in Petrograd, overthrow of the Provisional Government, and seizure of power by Bolsheviks marked the beginning of the October Revolution.

8 November 1917
At the Congress of the Abkhazian people in Sukhumi the Abkhazian People's Soviet was formed. (Its composition and activities changed constantly and drastically between 1918-1921; nevertheless it played a leading part in the political life of Abkhazia. The Congress adopted a Declaration of the Congress of the Abkhazian People, which set the task of conducting further work towards self-determination of the Abkhazian people, as well as the Constitution of the Abkhazian People's Soviet.)

9 February 1918
In Tiflis (Tbilisi) an agreement on Abkhazia joining Georgia as an autonomy was reached between the representatives of the Abkhazian People's Soviet and the National Council of Georgia. Georgia was also to assist 'Abkhazia to re-establish its historical borders' (under the administrative system of the Russian Empire, Abkhazia was dismembered: Sukhumi district, formed in 1883, was a part of Kutaisi province, Gagra and its vicinity were subordinated to Sochi district of the Black Sea province).

10 February-25 May 1918
The Transcaucasian Sejm represents the interests of the Transcaucasian peoples in Tiflis (Tbilisi).

16-21 February 1918
The first attempt to establish the Bolshevik dictatorship (Soviet Power) in Abkhazia. A Military Revolutionary Committee (chaired by Ephrem Eshba) was set up in Sukhumi. The outrages committed by Bolshevik sailors of the Black Sea Fleet (from the cruiser Dakia, and the destroyer Derzki). Mass resistance to the Bolshevik usurpers of power was led by the Abkhazian People's Council. By 21 February the Military Revolutionary Committee was abolished.

8 April-17 May 1918
The second attempt to establish Soviet power in Abkhazia (it extended over the entire territory of the former Sukhumi district, excepting the Kodori (Ochamchire) area.

22 April 1918
The Transcaucasian Sejm declared the independence of the Transcaucasian Federal Democratic Republic from Soviet Russia(RSFSR).

17 May 1918
Liberation of Sukhumi and Sukhumi district from Bolsheviks by the troops of the Transcaucasian Federal Democratic Republic under the command of V. Jugeli.

26 May 1918
Georgia declared her independence. The process of the revival of Georgian statehood started. The Georgian Democratic Republic was created. Abkhazia, liberated from Soviet Power, also joined her.

8 June 1918
An agreement on providing internal and military support to Abkhazia was reached between the government of the Georgian Democratic Republic and the Abkhazian People's Council.

17-22 June 1918
Georgian troops under the command of General Mazniev (Mazniashvili) were introduced into Abkhazia. They were deployed along the coast from Tuapse to Sochi.

12-13 September 1918
A delegation of the Abkhazian People's Council appealed to the Command of the Russian Volunteer Army (General M.S. Alexeev, heading the Cossack formations of Kuban), with the request to liberate Abkhazia from the armed intervention of Georgia.

9-10 October 1918
The Georgian government dissolved the Abkhazian People's Soviet because of its attempted coup aimed at wresting Abkhazia from Georgia, arresting the conspirators who had established ties with the voluntary Army. Chkhikvishvili was appointed Extraordinary Commissar of Sukhumi District. Preparations for the elections to the Abkhazian People's Council started.

January 1919
General Denikin's Voluntary Army began to march on Sukhumi claiming Abkhazia from the Georgian government as a part 'of integral and indivisible Russia.' Georgian troops repulsed this aggression.

18-22 March 1919
The first session of the Abkhazian People's Soviet, re-elected on a democratic basis, adopted a resolution on Abkhazia joining the Democratic Republic of Georgia as an autonomous unit.

Spring 1920
Elections to the Constituent Assembly of Georgia (boycotted in several districts of Abkhazia).

26 April 1920
The address of the Chairman of the National Assembly of Turkey, Mustafa Kemal (Ataturk) to Vladimir Ilich Lenin, proposing to establish diplomatic relations between Soviet Russia and the Turkish Republic.

7 May 1920
An agreement was signed between the Democratic Republic of Georgia and Soviet Russia, providing for non-interference in the internal affairs and recognition of the Democratic Republic of Georgia by Soviet Russia as an independent state within the borders including Abkhazia.

Summer-Autumn 1920
In Moscow the Caucasian Bureau of the RCP (B) (Russian Communist Party - Bolsheviks) stepped up its activities towards sending Abkhazian militants (boeviks) and propagandists (Eshba, Lakoba, Inal-Ipa and others) to Turkey to conduct underground work and expand the influence of the Communist Party of Turkey (established in September 1920 in Baku) to strengthen links with the Abkhazian diaspora which was ready to render political assistance to Soviet Russia.

11-15 August 1920
The first Kuban-Black Sea Congress of the Working People of the Mountains in Ekaterinodar (Krasnodar) was held with the active participation of Abkhazian Bolsheviks (Eshba, Lakoba and others) in it.

End of February 1921
The 11th Red Army invaded Georgia in breach of the Agreement between the Democratic Republic of Georgia and Soviet Russia of 7 May 1920.

21 February 1921
The Constituent Assembly of Georgia adopted the Constitution of the Democratic Republic of Georgia and ratified the Provision on the recognition of Abkhazia as an autonomous part of Georgia.

25 February 1921
The units of the 11th Red Army occupied Tbilisi. In conditions of terror, following the dissolution of the Constituent Assembly and the overthrow of the legitimate government, an act on the re-establishment of the Soviet Socialist Republic of Georgia was adopted.

March 4, 1921
Establishment of Soviet Power (Bolshevik dictatorship) in Abkhazia.

6 March 1921
The Revolutionary Committee of Abkhazia (composed of Eshba, Lakoba and Akirtava) was formed. An Organisation Bureau of the RCP(B) was set up in Abkhazia.

16 March 1921
The Federal Republic of Russia and Turkey signed a Treaty in Moscow.

28-31 March 1921
The Batumi Conference, directed by the Caucasian Bureau of the Central Committee of the RCP(B) (Ordjonikidze), discussed the question of 'the framework of Soviet power' in Abkhazia, paving the way for the proclamation of the Abkhazian SSR.

31 March 1921
The Abkhazian SSR is officially proclaimed.

Summer-Autumn 1921
The changed policy of the Central Committee of the RCP(B) shows an orientation towards the 'autonomization' of Abkhazia within the Georgian SSR.

16 December 1921
Soviet Georgia and Soviet Abkhazia signed 'a special Union Treaty', actually unifying the territory of the Republics.

February 1922
The 1st Congress of the Soviets of Abkhazia endorses the unification of Abkhazia with the Georgian SSR.

12 March 1922
The Transcaucasian Soviet Federal Socialist Republic (TSFSR) is formed, unifying the three Transcaucasian republics into a single Federation: the Azerbaijanian, the Armenian and the Georgian SSR (Abkhazia is included in TSFSR as a part of the Georgian SSR).

30 December 1922
The USSR is formed - a 'Union' agreement providing for the union of the RSFSR, the Ukrainian and the Byelorussian SSR and the Transcaucasian Federation.

1925
The newly adopted Constitution of the Georgian SSR stipulates the entry of the Abkhazian SSR into the Georgian SSR under the treaty signed on 16 December 1921. Simultaneously the Constitution of the Abkhazian SSR is adopted.

April 1930
The 3rd Session of the Central Executive Committee adopts a resolution on the transformation of the 'treaty-based' Abkhazian SSR into an autonomous republic within the Georgian SSR.

11 February 1931
The 6th Congress of the Soviets of the Georgian SSR and the Abkhazian SSR adopts a resolution on the transformation of the 'treaty-based' Abkhazian SSR within the Georgian SSR into the Abkhazian Autonomous Soviet Socialist Republic within the Georgian SSR.

18-26 February 1931
A protest rally lasting for many days (a national assembly of the Abkhazian people) is held in the village of Duripsh against the resolution adopted by the 6th Congress of the Soviets, expressing non-confidence in the leadership of Abkhazia.

4 March 1936
Celebration of the 15th anniversary of Soviet Abkhazia. On its eve the Abkhazian SSR is awarded the Order of Lenin by a Decree of the Central Executive Committee of the USSR (1935).

25 November-5 December 1936
The 8th All-Union Extraordinary Congress of Soviets adopted a new Constitution of the USSR, following Joseph Stalin's report. According to this Constitution the TSFSR ceased to exist, the Georgian SSR directly joined the USSR as a 'Union' republic. The status of the Abkhazian ASSR within the Georgian SSR was endorsed.

28 December 1936
The Chairman of CEC of the Abkhazian SSR, Nestor Lakoba, died unexpectedly, during his sojourn in Tbilisi (he was presumably poisoned at supper at Lavrenti Beria's place).

31 December 1936
Lakoba's funeral in Sukhumi, attended by a huge crowd.

1937-1938
A wave of ruthless political reprisals in Abkhazia. Lakoba was posthumously declared an enemy of the people, all his relations and comrades-in-arms suffered arrests, tortures and liquidation. Alexei Agrba, Beria's protégé, took over the post of Chairman of the CEC of

Abkhazia (arrested on 18 September 1937 and shot on 21 April 1938). An open trial of fifteen 'Lakoba followers' took place in Sukhumi in autumn 1937. However, the reprisals continued even after the trial. According to incomplete data, 2186 people were affected, of which 748 were shot. The collectivization of the agriculture of Abkhazia, hampered earlier, was implemented compulsorily within a year.

22 June 1941-9 May 1945
The Great Patriotic War, in which the Abkhazian people, along with the other peoples of the USSR, took an active part both at the fronts and in the rear, sacrificing thousands of lives to the total victory over fascism.

August-September 1941
The remnants of Abkhazia's intellectuals were subjected to another wave of reprisals in 1937-1938. An action on the mass deportation-expatriation of Abkhazians from their historical homeland was being prepared (though not implemented).

May 1942
Expulsion of Greeks - foreign subjects - from the Black Sea Coast to the eastern regions of the USSR.

14-15 November 1944
Forcible deportation from Georgia to Central Asia and other eastern parts of the USSR of the Turks from Meskheti (over 115,000 people, as well as Kurds, Khemshils (Armenians of Muslim religion), and some Azerbaijanis).

13 March 1945
The Abkhazian Regional Committee (and following it - on 13 June the Central Committee(CC) of the CP of Georgia) adopts a resolution 'on the measures for the improvement of the quality of educational work at schools in the Abkhazian SSR', actually doing away with the Abkhazian national school, reducing to nil the teaching of Abkhazian, which provocatively set Abkhazian and Georgian cultures against each other.

June 1949
Deportation of the Pontic Greeks - citizens of the USSR - from Abkhazia and Ajaria to Kazakhstan and Kirghizia. The places of their residence were settled by Georgians.

5 March 1953
The death of Stalin.

14-25 February 1956
The 20th Congress of the CPSU exposed 'the cult of the personality' of Stalin and the criminal reprisals of his regime, qualified as a 'violation of socialist legality'. Work started towards the political rehabilitation of the former Party and Soviet leadership of Abkhazia (the followers of Lakoba).

1957
The first appeals of the Abkhazian intelligentsia to the central bodies of power for the solution to the question of the transfer of the Abkhazian ASSR to the jurisdiction of the RSFSR (with no consequences).

1967
The second appeal of the Abkhazian public to the CC of the CPSU and other departments, with the proposal on the secession of Abkhazia from the Georgian SSR.

1978
In connection with the adoption of a new constitution of the USSR, the question of the transfer of Abkhazia to the RSFSR and granting it the right of 'free secession from the Georgian SSR' is raised again.

April 1985
The April Plenum of the CC of the CPSU - the beginning of the new political course of perestroika, headed by Mikhail Sergeyevich Gorbachev.

20 February 1988
The Regional Soviet of the Autonomous Region of Nagorny-Karabakh

(ARNK), summarising the results of the Referendum on the Status of Nagorny-Karabakh, appealed to the Supreme Soviet of the USSR, the Azerbaijanian and the Armenian SSR with the request to sanction the secession of Nagorny-Karabakh from Azerbaijan and its incorporation into Armenia.

17 June 1988
The 'Abkhazian letter' was sent to the Presidium of the coming 19th All-Union Conference of the CPSU. Its authors (writer Alexei Gogua and other representatives of the Abkhazian intelligentsia) raised the issue of altering the status of Abkhazia and its transformation from an 'autonomous' republic within Georgia into a 'Union' one.

18 June 1988
In the section 'on the development of national relations' in Gorbachev's report to the 19th All-Union Party Conference, he formulated the task of careful consideration of national interests and renunciation of Stalin's chauvinistic policy.

1988
A national movement of the Ossetians in the South-Ossetian Autonomous Region, Adamon Nykhas, (People's Conversation) was launched, initially putting forward economic demands (an epidemic of typhoid in the region spurred the movement).

1988
The People's Forum of Abkhazia (Aidgylara, (Unity), is formed - originally as a national movement of the Abkhazian people).

12 July 1988
The session of the Regional Soviet of the Autonomous Region of Nagorny-Karabakh adopts a resolution on the secession of the Autonomous Region from Azerbaijan and its incorporation into Armenia.

18 July 1988
The Presidium of the Supreme Soviet of the USSR adopts a Decree on the preservation of the previous status for the Autonomous Region of Nagorny-Karabakh within the Azerbaijani SSR and the allocation

of additional funds for the social-economic development of the autonomous region.

August-September 1988
The 'Stone War' on the roads of the Autonomous Region of Nagorny-Karabakh. The beginning of a blockade.

November 1988
Pogroms of the Armenian population in Baku; rampage of violence. On 24-25 November introduction of troops and declaration of a state of emergency in Baku and Yerevan.

12 January 1989
A Committee on Special Rule of the Autonomous Region of Nagorny-Karabakh is set up.

18 March 1989
A 30-thousand-strong sanctioned rally (general assembly) of the Abkhazian people, called by the People's Forum Aidgylara in the village of Lykhny, Gudauta district (with the approval and partici-pation of the local party and soviet authorities), addressed Gorbachev with demands to grant Abkhazia the status of a Union republic and to introduce temporarily the regime of 'Special Rule' from the Centre (after the example of the Nagorny-Karabakh Autonomous Region).

20 March-8 April 1989
Mass rallies of protest against the decisions of the Lykhny Assembly swept all Georgia. From the cities and villages of Abkhazia (Sukhumi, Gali, Gagra, Leselidze) rallies spread to other regions of Georgia, reaching ultimate tension in early April at a continuous rally lasting for many days in Tbilisi. Unlike the Lykhny Assembly, the rally in defence of the integrity of Georgia was disapproved of by the local authorities, being considered unsanctioned. Also, unlike the Lykhny Assembly, the protest rally adopted not an address to the CC of the CPSU, or the Supreme Soviet of the USSR, or personally to Mikhail Gorbachev, but resolutions and declarations, expressing anti-communist and anti-Soviet sentiments of the masses, demanding the secession of Georgia from the USSR.

9 April 1989
Tragic events in Tbilisi, use of armed force against the peaceful population (operations of troops under the command of General
Rodionov). As a result of the punitive military action with the use of
sapper spades and poison gases, 21 people died, over 4,000 were
wounded, among them 3,000 with symptoms of poisoning. A curfew
was introduced in Tbilisi. The former first Secretary of the CC of the
CP of Georgia, J.I. Patiashvili, resigned.

10-13 May 1989
Mass assemblies and meetings of the Georgian population are held
in the villages of Kochara, Tsagera and in other districts of Abkhazia;
the Sukhumi section of the railway is paralysed. An 'open letter to
the Georgians of North-Western Georgia' is being circulated at the
meetings (the letter was compiled under the editorship of Zviad
Gamsakhurdia). It questioned the validity of the existence of the
Abkhazian autonomy.

14 May 1989
The Council of Ministers of the Georgian SSR issued an order on the
creation of a branch of Tbilisi State University in Sukhumi.

25 May 1989
The first Congress of the People's Deputies of the USSR. At the sug-
gestion of the deputy, V.F. Tolpezhnikov, the Congress paid its respects to the victims of the Bloody Sunday in Tbilisi with a minute's
silence.

30 May 1989
At the session of the Congress of the People's Deputies of the USSR,
the deputy, Th.V. Gamkrelidze, raised the question of condemning
the annexation of the Independent Georgian Democratic Republic in
February 1921 as a result of a gross violation of the Treaty between
Russia and Georgia of 7 May 1920. At the evening session the same
day, the Congress discussed the events in Tbilisi.

Colonel-General Rodionov, justifying his actions, called the actions
of 'the extremist groups' of Georgia hostile, describing the rally in Tbilisi
as an 'anti-Soviet Sabbath lasting for many days'. The Congress set up a

commission of deputies for the investigation and assessment of the events in Tbilisi.

7 June 1989
Organised mass pogroms of Meskhetian Turks in Fergana valley, Uzbekistan.

25 June 1989
Escalation of inter-ethnic relations and clashes between Georgians and Azerbaijanis in Eastern Georgia, holding rallies under slogans demanding the setting up of a Borchalo Azerbaijani Autonomy in Georgia and expulsion of Georgians (Svans, settled here earlier from the disaster areas).

25 June 1989
The first founding Congress of the Popular Front of Georgia in Tbilisi adopts an appeal to the Georgian and the Abkhazian peoples, calling upon them to consolidate and avoid violence.

8 July 1989
The People's Forum of Abkhazia, Aidgylara, makes public its appeal to the Chairman of the Supreme Soviet of the USSR on the immediate introduction of a special form of rule in Abkhazia, with direct subordination to the Centre.

14 July 1989
At night, unidentified persons destroyed the stand in the centre of Sukhumi with the photos of the victims of 9 April in Tbilisi.

15-18 July 1989
Inter-ethnic clashes in Sukhumi and in other districts of Abkhazia, incited by the boeviks of the Abkhazian People's Forum Aidgylara. As a result, 17 persons (11 Georgians, 3 Abkhazians, 1 Greek) died, and 448 were wounded. On 18 July 'a special regime of the conduct of citizens' was introduced in Sukhumi.

August 1989
Start of tension in the districts with predominantly Armenian population

in the South of Georgia. Armenian rallies in Akhalkalaki and Bog-danovka demanding the setting up of an Armenian Autonomy.

25-26 August 1989
The first Congress of the Peoples of the Caucasus was held in Sukhumi, with the participation of the representatives of unofficial public organisations (of national movements) of the Abkhazians, the Abazins, the Adyghe, the Ingush, the Kabardians, the Circassians and the Chechens. The decision to set up an Assembly of the Mountain Peoples of the Caucasus was adopted. The Assembly aimed at the re-establishment of the Caucasian Mountain State with Sukhumi as the capital. The Congress adopted 'an appeal to the Abkhazian and the Georgian peoples', expressing regret at the bloody July events in Abkhazia.

14 September 1989
The People's Forum made an attempt to organise a strike at the vital enterprises of the Republic. It was accompanied by a hunger strike by 20 persons, protesting against the suppression of the national rights of the Abkhazian people in Georgia.

21 September 1989
A general meeting of the Kabardian National movement Adygha Khase in Nalchik appealed to the Supreme Departments of the USSR and the Georgian SSR, demanding the status of 'special rule' for Abkhazia, similar to that in Nagorny-Karabakh.

4 November 1989
The 3rd session of the Assembly of the Mountain Peoples of the Caucasus in Nalchik demanded that the Supreme Soviet of the USSR and the Georgian SSR take immediate measures for the protection of the constitutional rights of the Abkhazian people.

10 November 1989
The Regional Soviet of the South-Ossetian Autonomous Region adopted a decision on the transformation of the South-Ossetian Autonomous Region into an Autonomous Republic within the Georgian SSR. The Supreme Soviet of the Georgian SSR annulled the decision. Many thousands of representatives of unofficial public

organisations left for Tskhinvali to hold a rally in support of the Georgian population of the Autonomous Region.

23 November 1989
Another 50-thousand-strong Georgian march was stopped by the armed Ossetian population. Clashes and hostilities lasted from November 1989 till January 1990.

November 1989
The 2nd Congress of the People's Deputies of the USSR endorsed the findings of the commission of deputies on the investigation of the 'Tbilisi events' (the Commission was chaired by Anatoly Sobchak). It condemned the use of force against the peaceful population. The Resolution of the Supreme Soviet of the Georgian SSR of 18 November 1989 was the first step on the road to Georgia's obtaining independence and her secession from the USSR.

11 March 1990
Proclamation of independence by the Supreme Soviet of Lithuania, the beginning of the collapse of the USSR. By the decision of 8 March and 20 June the Supreme Soviet of Georgia recognised the illegal annexation of Georgia by the Russian Army in February 1921 and restored the 1921 Constitution of the Democratic Republic of Georgia.

31 May 1990
A 30-thousand-strong rally of the representatives of the Mountain Peoples of the Caucasus in Sukhumi demanded the secession of Abkhazia from Georgia.

August 1990
An attempt of the Vaadat movement of Meskhetian Turks to organise a march from Russia to Meskheti and Javakheti through the territory of Abkhazia.

25 August 1990
The Supreme Soviet of the Abkhazian SSR adopted a Declaration on the state sovereignty of the Abkhazian Soviet Socialist Republic and a resolution on the legal guarantees of the defence of the statehood of Abkhazia.

26 August 1990
The Presidium of the Supreme Soviet of the Georgian SSR adopted a Resolution, declaring the acts adopted by the Supreme Soviet of Abkhazia on 25 August null and void and noted that they violated the territorial integrity of Georgia and contravened her Constitution.

October 1990
The victory of the bloc of left-wing parties Round Table-Free Georgia at the election to the Supreme Council of Georgia marked the beginning of the movement towards the independence of Georgia and her legal secession from the USSR. Zviad Gamsakhurdia was elected President of the Republic of Georgia.

4 December 1990
The resumed 10th session of the Supreme Soviet of the Abkhazian ASSR elected Vladislav Ardzinba Chairman of the Supreme Soviet.

17 March 1991
At the All-Union Referendum, the majority of the Abkhazian population voted in favour of a Union of Soviet Socialist Republics on the basis of a renewed Treaty.

19-21 May 1991
The 1st World Circassian Congress in Nalchik with the participation of an Abkhazian delegation.

9 July 1991
A new electoral law is adopted in Abkhazia. The elections to the Supreme Soviet, held on its basis, ensured the Abkhazian minority population (17%) 28 seats in the parliament (with 65 members).

19-21 August 1991
A reactionary coup attempt in the USSR. Power is taken over by a State Committee for the Emergency Situation (GKChP). A powerful popular resistance toppled the GKChP, leading to the August revolution in Russia.

6 September 1991
Chechnia, led by president Dzhokhar Dudayev, declares its independence.

1-3 November 1991
The 3rd Congress of the Assembly of the Mountain Peoples of the Caucasus in Sukhumi.

1 December 1991
The elections to the Supreme Soviet of Abkhazia are summed up (the first round of the elections was held in October); the separatist leadership of the Supreme Soviet (Ardzinba and his supporters) was enabled to rely on a parliamentary majority.

1 December 1991
The Referendum on the Independence of the Ukraine delivered the last stroke to the USSR.

8 December 1991
The USSR ceased to exist as a result of the agreements concluded in Belovezhskaya Pushcha by the leaders of the Russian Federation, Ukraine and Byelorussia, and the USSR. The foundation was laid for the CIS, soon joined by Kazakhstan, the republics of Central Asia and some others. Georgia refused to join the CIS.

22 December 1991-6 January 1992
The Tbilisi Revolution. Former president Zviad Gamsakhurdia fled from Tbilisi (first to America, then to Chechnia, where he was granted political asylum). A military council took over in Georgia.Soon it was transformed into the State Council of Georgia. The new leadership was headed by Kitovani, Ioseliani, Sigua (the latter was first acting prime minister,   later, the prime minister of the republic).

January-March 1992
The first military campaign of the troops of the State Council to Western Georgia (Mingrelia), where the armed supporters of the ex-president (Zviadists) offered resistance to the new authorities. On 18 March an agreement was signed between the State Council of Georgia and the 'resistance campaign' in Zugdidi, under which the Zviadist formations

were to merge into the National Guard and the Tbilisi units of the National Guard were to withdraw from the conflict area.

February 1992
In South-Ossetia a Referendum was held on joining Russia. In response to separatism, units of the National Guard besieged Tskhinvali; the armed conflict escalated.

21 February 1992
The State Council of Georgia abolished the existing Constitution of the Georgian SSR and restored the Constitution of 1921.

March 1992
Eduard Shevardnadze returned to Georgia to head the State Council of the Republic. The elections of the Supreme Council of Georgia were fixed for October 1992.

21 April 1992
The State Council of Georgia and the Regional Soviet of Krasnodar Region of the Russian Federation adopted a conceptual plan for the repatriation of the Meskhetian Turks to their homeland.

24 June 1992
An abortive coup attempt in Tbilisi, seizure of the TV station. The rebels were arrested. On the same day, in Sukhumi, the Minister of Internal Affairs of Abkhazia, Givi Lominadze, became the target of a bandit attack.

24 June 1992
The Dagomys summit meeting of the leaders of Russia (Boris Yeltsin) and Georgia (Eduard Shevardnadze) marked the beginning of the settlement of the South-Ossetian conflict and an end to bloodshed.

June 1992
An attempt by Zviadists to assassinate Ioseliani, Chairman of the Council of Defence of Georgia. Several people were killed.

End of June 1992
Zviadists stepped up their activities in Mingrelia. An attempt by the Committee of National Disobedience to organise a general strike in Zugdidi. A military campaign of detachments of Mkhedrioni to Western Georgia in order to stabilise the situation.

9 July 1992
Hostages were taken by Zviadists in Chkhorotsqu district (Megrelia), including Alexandr Kavsadze, Vice-Premier of Georgia.

23 July 1992
With a simple majority of votes (36 out of 65) the Supreme Soviet of Abkhazia adopted a Resolution on the abrogation of the Constitution of the Abkhazian ASSR of 1978 and restoration of the 1925 Constitution. It underlined the tendency towards secession from Georgia and preservation of the Soviet Socialist system in Abkhazia.

25 July 1992
The State Council of the Republic of Georgia adopted a Resolution, declaring the given act null and void.

4 August 1992
A National holiday in Georgia in connection with her joining the UN (July 31). Manifesto on the Great Reconciliation was made public in Tbilisi. All the participants of the putsch of 24 June were granted amnesties, as well as all the supporters of Zviad Gamsakhurdia, arrested after the Tbilisi Revolution.

11 August 1992
Capture of hostages (11 responsible officials of the Ministry of Internal Affairs of Georgia) in Zugdidi and their transfer to Abkhazia. The Vice-Premier, Alexandr Kavsadze, captured earlier, was also taken there. Telephone conversation between Shevardnadze and Ardzinba in which the Chairman of the State Council informed the leadership of Abkhazia on the necessity of conducting a military operation to free the hostages on the territory of Abkhazia. An agreement was reached on co-operation.

14 August 1992

The agreed introduction of troops of the State Council of Georgia onto the territory of Abkhazia was used by the leadership of Abkhazia as an excuse to declare a general mobilisation and war against Georgia. The Chronicle of hostilities, attempts at ceasefire, and all political developments beginning with 14 August 1992 is intended for a separate publication, dealing with the political history of Abkhazia from August 1992 to August 1993.

Chronicle of Events

August 1992 - March 1994

In order to bring the reader up to date, we have added our own Chronicle of Events from August 1993 to April 1994. Our information was gathered from various sources, particularly from The Georgian Chronicle edited by P.J. Hillery. We have tried to verify the details as far as is possible and are confident that our information is as accurate as can be in the present fluctuating situation. Time will lend a greater perspective to these events.

13 August
Deadline for the release of hostages expires. Georgia sends 3000 troops to west, heading towards Zugdidi.

14 August
12.00 - Abkhaz irregulars open fire on Georgians near Ilovi. Fighting continues over 50 kms to Sukhumi.
15.00 - Georgians stop at Sukhumi railway station. Abkhaz withdraw to Sukhumi new town. Fighting in Sukhumi. All but three hostages released by Zviadists.

15 August
Talks in Sukhumi between Georgians and Abkhaz separatists. Proposals for joint units to protect railways and trains from banditry. Situation tense. Ceasefire agreed but clashes occur. Abkhaz formations capture equipment from CIS army unit. Telegram from Ardzinba to Dudayev, President of Chechen Republic, requesting help for Abkhaz separatists.

17 August
Georgian troops withdraw from Sukhumi but clashes continue in the city. Criminal elements on the rampage, looting, highjacking and terrorizing. Chechen President orders preparations for military operations against Georgia.

18 August
Georgian troops take over Sukhumi. Ardzinba and separatist Parliament leave Sukhumi for Gudauta.

19 August
Dudayev refuses to issue weapons to volunteers of the Confederation of Mountain Peoples who are making their way into Abkhazia.

20 August
Russian troops in Sukhumi come under fire. Believed to be an attempt by separatists to draw Russia into open conflict. Skirmish between forces of ex-President Gamsakhurdia and Georgian National Guard near Zugdidi.

21 August
Evacuation of people from Abkhazia. Black Sea fleet helps. Nearly 12,000 evacuees, mostly Russian tourists and families of servicemen.

22 August
Shevardnadze says opportunities for peaceful resolution to conflict in Abkhazia almost exhausted.

24 August
Large groups of volunteers from North Caucasus take up positions outside Gagra.

25 August
Musa Shanibov, president of self-styled Confederation of Mountain Peoples of the Caucasus (CMPC) issues decree of intent to step up hostilities against Georgia.

26 August
Yeltsin appeals for cessation of military action. Representatives of International Red Cross Society (IRCS) attacked near Zugdidi.

27 August
Russian deputies on peace-keeping mission to Tbilisi. Jaba Ioseliani and units of the Mkhedrioni arrive in Sukhumi. Sukhumi returning to normal life.

29 August
Meeting of delegates from Russia, Georgia and Abkhazia meet in Sochi. Sides refuse to talk at same table though protocol is signed. Agreement to cease hostilities from 31 August.

30 August
Clashes between separatists and Georgian troops outside Gagra. Georgian troops shelled from ship at sea. Russian Navy denies involvement. Armenian delegation arrives in Sukhumi and supports territorial integrity of Georgia.

3 September
Successful Moscow talks lead to document on cessation of hostilities. Commission appointed to oversee cease-fire. Georgian integrity assured; exchange of prisoners; humanitarian aid to be provided; transport routes unhindered; human rights; neutrality of Russians etc.

7 September
Hostilities continue. Each side accuses the other of cease-fire violations.

11 September
Russian peacemakers state that warring parties in Abkhazia now withdrawn to other side of Gumista river.

12 September
Abkhazian fighters and mercenaries attack Georgian guards near Ochamchire. Confrontations also continue in Ossetia. Georgian government declares call-up. All those aged 18-25 are liable for conscription.

More than 80% of all liable for conscription in the spring failed to report at call-up stations for various reasons.

13 September
Reports of CMPC forces attacking Georgian families at Eshera. Looting. In Sukhumi, too, marauding beyond control. Relative peace along Gumista, but hostilities around Gagra and Ochamchire.

17 September
UN mission to Abkhazia. UN office to open in Tbilisi.

20 September
Trilateral Commission of Georgians, Abkhaz and Russians in Gudauta, checking on violations of human rights in conflict zone.

28 September
Boris Yeltsin and Eduard Shevardnadze meet in Kremlin. Agree on further meetings.

3 October
Abkhaz take Gagra.

11 October
Shevardnadze elected Parliamentary Chairman with 96% of vote. Seats in Parliament divided between 26 parties.

19 November
Georgians, Abkhaz and Russians negotiate temporary cease-fire. In this month Russian Central Bank refuses to supply Georgia with banknotes.

2 December
Abkhaz bomb and shell Sukhumi and Ochamchire. Georgians shell Akhali Athoni and Eshera.

14 December
Russians accuse Georgians of shooting down helicopter on humanitarian aid flight. 58 passengers (mostly women and children) and

three pilots die. Georgians deny responsibility. Shevardnadze accuses Russian hardliners of helping Abkhaz.

21 January 1993
Abkhaz guerillas take hostage 700 civilians in Georgian village of Kutoli.

7 February
Eight government tanks captured by pro-Gamsakhurdia group, led by Loti Kobalia near Zugdidi.

20 February
Russian warplane assault on Sukhumi. Russian, Georgian talks suspended.

2 March
Abkhaz seize village of Labra.

6 March
North Ossetian Republic (in Russian Federation) recognises self-proclaimed South Ossetian Republic in Georgia. Its territory remains beyond the control of Tbilisi.

9 March
Fourth round of negotiations with Russia begins. Atmosphere tense due to Russia's growing involvement in Abkhazia. Shevardnadze stresses hope that Yeltsin is unaware of the activities of his military.

11 and 13 March
SU 35s bomb Tsagera and Sukhumi.

16 March
Bloodiest military action so far. Separatists attack Sukhumi unsuccessfully. Hundreds killed and wounded. Russians at first admit to their planes bombing Sukhumi, but then Grachev says on Moscow TV that Georgians had repainted their own planes and bombed Sukhumi in order to blame it on the Russians. At the same time the Abkhaz leader and Russian commander in Gudauta say the planes were Abkhaz planes!

19 March
Georgians shoot down Russian SU 27.

25 March
CSCE delegation visits Tbilisi. Lord Bethel says he had 'no doubt the conflict in Abkhazia was a result of a conspiracy of reactionary forces in Russia and the old and new KGB networks...'

5 April
Near Armenian border, gas pipeline blown up for fifth time this year.

6 April
Georgian/Russian delegation works on draft treaty in Sochi. Georgian coupon introduced in April. Both sides in conflict retain positions across Gumista river and shell each other. Russian army continues to shell Georgian positions, saying this is in retaliation for Georgian shelling of laboratory at Eshera.

6 and 14 April
Pro-Gamsakhurdia rallies dispersed in Tbilisi.

2 May
Russians shoot down Georgian plane over Abkhazia.

6 May
Russians bomb Sukhumi; Russian/Abkhaz consultations in Maikop.

7 May
Local Svan conflict in Bolnisi.

12 May
Conflict between Mkhedrioni and Russian army unit in Kutaisi. Six Mkhedrioni dead and ten wounded. Mutual accusations. Most observers regard incident as outcome of broken deal on illegal arms trade.

14 May
Russian/Georgian summit in Moscow.

20 May

Cease-fire agreement in Abkhazia comes into effect.

27 May

Agreement on humanitarian action for Sukhumi, Tkvarcheli. Also this month Kitovani and Ioseliani resign; Kakarashvili appointed Minister of Defence.

3 June

Russian Foreign Minister Kozyrev visits Sukhumi, Tbilisi, Gudauta. IMF turn down appeal for emergency aid.

16-18 June

As a result of cease-fire, delivery of humanitarian aid to Sukhumi and Tkvarcheli. Implemented by Russia under supervision of UN. Great number of population evacuated. Estimated that in eleven months of war Georgians so far lost 1175 dead and 3446 wounded.

19 June

Fighting resumes.

23 June

Shevardnadze visits NATO Headquarters.

2 July

Abkhaz attack Sukhumi. Shelling by Grad rocket-launchers and artillery in the morning, kills 39; 175 wounded. Separatist commandos land from three warships near Tamish. Shevardnadze given additional powers.

5 July

Rally in Gudauta in support of negotiations with Tbilisi.

6 July

Tbilisi declares martial law in Abkhazia.

7 July
Shevardnadze appeals to G7 Summit in Tokyo. Georgian-Russian-Abkhaz talks deadlocked with Abkhaz insisting on withdrawal of all Georgian troops and Georgians refusing.

10 July
Georgians break Abkhaz encirclement of Sukhumi. Georgian forces had been joined by pro-Gamsakhurdia militia led by Kobalia. After heavy fighting, separatist commandos almost wiped out. However, well armed groups continue to arrive from North Caucasus, including ethnic Russians. Georgian resources rapidly becoming exhausted.

27 July
Georgia, Russia and Abkhazia sign cease-fire agreement in Sochi. Some Georgian politicians call this capitulation.

14 August
Withdrawal of forces from conflict zone commences. Fortifications blown up, mines cleared.

26 August
Withdrawal of heavy equipment along Gumista almost complete.

29 August
Zviadist forces under Kobalia (supporters of ex-President Zviad Gamsakhurdia) take Senaki, later Abasha and Khobi.

30 August
Ioseliani leaves Tbilisi for western Georgia promising to 'blow out the brains of all destructive forces.'

13 September
Russian fleet removes last items of Georgian heavy equipment from conflict zone. 80% of government forces now removed. Georgians complain of violations of agreement by Abkhaz and vice versa.

14 September
Shevardnadze announces his resignation, later relents.

15 September
Zviadists attack government forces west of Samtredia.

16 September
Abkhaz separatists launch attack on Sukhumi. Beginning of offensive clearly tied to withdrawal of Georgians. Renewed attacks from Zviadists in west.

17 September
Shevardnadze meets Russian Defence Minister Grachev in Sochi. No tangible results despite Russia as guarantor of peace process. Georgian intelligence reports of trucks with fighters and equipment entering Abkhazia across the Russian border. Separatist detachments composed of Abkhaz, North Caucasians and ethnic Russians. Western reporters say that most of separatist field commanders are Russians.

20 September
Abashidze brokers temporary truce between Zviadists and government.

24 September
Gamsakhurdia returns to Mingrelia.

27 September
Sukhumi falls to Abkhaz forces. Shevardnadze sends telegram to Yeltsin in which he talks of 'Georgia's prostration' and says assault was planned by General Staff of Russian army.

30 September
Zviadists seize Ochamchire and Gali.

By the beginning of October the separatists have suppressed almost all Georgian government troops. Almost the entire remaining ethnic Georgian population, some 200,000, flee, either across the Inguri river or through Svaneti. Half the refugees take the former route without too many problems; the other half try to cross the mountains of

Svaneti. Terrible hardship ensues with exposure to freezing cold, exhaustion and starvation. After international assistance arrives, the situation improves. Armenia, Ukraine, the International Red Cross, Medecins sans Frontieres - all help. After losing Abkhazia, Georgia is plunged into civil war.

2 October
Zviadists seize Poti and begin advance to east. Mingrelia and most of Guria under their control. Russian government condemns Abkhaz violation of 27 July agreement and accuses them of genocide of Georgian population.

8 October
Shevardnadze decides to join CIS. Military and economic aid needed to solve problems in Georgia. Many in Georgian Parliament strongly disapprove of this decision, especially Opposition parties.

14 October
Russian seaborne force lands at Poti.

22 October
Government troops begin offensive in western Georgia. By end of month only Zugdidi, Tsalenjikha and Chkhorotsku still under control of Kobalia's (Zviadist) militia.

25 October
Warrants issued for arrest of Gamsakhurdia and his military commander, Kobalia. Pardon promised by Shevardnadze for all those who handed in weapons.

28 October
Russian military detachments, in co-operation with Georgian army, begin patrolling railway line between Poti and Samtredia.

6 November
Government forces occupy Zugdidi with no resistance. Insurgents disperse. Government troops take all key towns in Mingrelia. Success of Government forces owes much to intimidating effect of Russian

military presence, though took no part in fighting. During hostilities North Caucasians and Abkhaz captured, fighting alongside Zviadists.

9 November
Shevardnadze elected chairman of new party: the Union of Citizens of Georgia - a union of previous parties and factions broadly in support of Shevardnadze's policies.

15 November
State-controlled price of bread increased tenfold. Bread queues continue. Inflation rampant. Criminal elements continue to hijack, kidnap and loot.

23 November
Separatists continue hostilities especially against 'Abkhazian Svaneti' mountainous region populated by ethnic Georgians. 2000 separatists attack villages here. Many casualties.

30 November
Georgian/Abkhaz negotiations take place in Geneva under aegis of UN with Russia as facilitator. Both parties pledge to refrain from use of force during negotiations. However, more clashes. Some refugees from Gunmukhuri begin to return home and are well received. By the end of December, they are forced to flee once more after attacks by armed separatists.

4 December
CMPC mark 'glorious victory over Shevardnadze's fascist clique.' Only clouded by refusal of world community to recognise its results.

10 December
Mafia group - Sviri brotherhood - disarmed. Struggle against criminal groups intensifies but State of Emergency and curfew in Tbilisi ineffectual. Mysterious string of assassinations of criminal figures; also members of Mkhedrioni.

19 December
POWs exchanged.

21 December
Consultations on future status of Abkhazia end in Moscow. No sign of agreement.

28 December
One US dollar costs 108,300 coupons. Inflation at 100%.

31 December
Reported suicide of ex-President Zviad Gamsakhurdia. Many rumours about his death. Visit by vice-President of Chechenia confirms death. Supporters gather daily in front of his house in Tbilisi.

9 January 1994
Speaker of Georgian Parliament calls for Georgia to join 'rouble zone'.

11 January
Second round of Geneva talks begin. Withdrawal of troops from Inguri river envisaged, return of 20,000 refugees, introduction of peace-keeping forces. Both sides consent to Russian troops among peace-keepers.

15 January
Zviadists try to hold rally in Tbilisi. Police prevent them.

24 January
Zviadists hold sit-down protest in front of Parliament in Tbilisi. Demand no autopsy on body of ex-President in compliance with his widow's wishes.

28 January
Shurgaia and Kobalia, former pro-Gamsakhurdia leaders, captured. Supporters still hiding in woods. Uneasy calm in Mingrelia.Temur Talakhadze, commander of Rustavi branch of Mkhedrioni, killed in explosion in barber's shop. Several other Mkhedrioni also assassinated.

3 February
Yeltsin in Tbilisi. Unprecedented security. Russia and Georgia pledge respect for mutual sovereignty, lifting of barriers to trade and co-op-

eration in economic and military fields. Russia to have three bases in Georgia: at Tbilisi, Batumi, and Akhalkalaki. Georgian border with Turkey to be guarded by Russian frontier troops. Georgia to be granted credit of 20 billion roubles. Opposition criticises agreements but Shevardnadze says that Russia is best guarantor of Georgia's independence.

10 February
Return of refugees should have begun. However, hostilities renewed. Abkhaz accuse Georgians of firing at positions on Inguri river and start 'punitive operations' which last for ten days. In Tbilisi crowds protest over lack of water and power.

14 February
President Ter-Petrosyan of Armenia visits Tbilisi to discuss economic co-operation and safe passage of Armenian goods through Georgia.

24 February
Gamsakhurdia reburied in Grozny, Chechenia.

1 March
Debate to ratify joining of CIS brings tensions in Georgian Parliament to boiling point. Shevardnadze stresses that the decision to join had saved the country from civil war in western Georgia. After stormy session, ratification: 125 for, 69 against, 4 abstain.

7 March
Shevardnadze meets President Clinton in Washington. Americans promise $70 million in humanitarian aid. Georgian/Abkhaz negotiations in New York fail to bring results.

10 March
Leaders of separatists at a rally in Sukhumi say that 'unchecked crime raises doubts about the possibility of building a civilised and law-abiding society in Abkhazia'. Refugees still continue to make their way into Georgia. The Georgian State Committee for Refugees reports that 188,970 officially registered.15,000 more had been forced to leave Gali district in February. Citizens of Syria, Jordan and Yemen

having Abkhaz-Adyghe origin, settle in homes vacated by refugees. Explosion at Mkhedrioni HQ. Two killed, several injured. Anzor Sharmaidze, 21, found guilty of shooting American diplomat Fred Woodruff. Sentenced to 15 years.

18 - 20 March
First Congress of Union of Citizens of Georgia (UCG). Addressed by former US Secretary of State, James Baker.

24 March
Separatist forces take village of Lata. Renewed assaults on villages of Abkhazian Svaneti.

31 March
Tbilisi Chief of Police, David Zeijidze, bursts into Parliament with 300 armed policemen in protest at appointment of Minister of Internal Affairs, Givi Kviraia. After meeting with Shevardnadze, Zeikidze withdraws. Later dismissed from his post.

4 April
Emergency office created in Mestia, capital of Svaneti, to cope with renewed flow of refugees. Abkhaz separatists continue to attack villages in Kodori gorge (Abkhazian Svaneti) throughout April.

8-9 April
Meeting in Sochi on return of refugees. UN delegation to travel to Gali.

13 April
Georgian and Abkhaz meet in Geneva to discuss role of peace-keeping forces.

20-22 April
Consultations on political status of Abkhazia held in Geneva. Abkhaz say that Georgia and Abkhazia are now two separate states.

Postscript

The Policy of Genocide in Action

Professor Levan Alexidze

Professor of International Law; Senior Human Rights Officer of the Department of Human Rights at UN Secretariat in New York and Geneva 1970-77. Chief Adviser to the Head of State, Eduard Shevardnadze, on matters of international law. At present participating in the negotiations on Abkhazia.

On 27th July 1993 yet another ceasefire agreement was signed in the war between Abkhazia and Georgia, obliging the sides to withdraw tanks and artillery from the conflict zone. The Georgian side fulfilled its obligation and refugees returned to Sukhumi. Calm reigned briefly in the city. Ostensibly the Abkhazians too carried out a withdrawal. But on 16th October Abkhazian units and mercenaries launched an attack against Ochamchire and Sukhumi, using 'concealed' artillery and tanks. Georgian homes were again in flames. International observers - primarily Russian - were obliged to return to the Georgian side the breach blocks of the tanks and artillery removed at the disarming.

Bloody battles lasted for a fortnight. Eduard Shevardnadze flew immediately to the front line, joining the defenders of Sukhumi. However, Sukhumi fell to the separatists on 27th September. Escaping death by a miracle, Shevardnadze and some of his associates managed to break out. Others, with tens of thousands of peaceful residents, fled and made their way through mountain passes and paths, called 'the paths of death', for they were strewn with corpses of old men, women and children, frozen or dying through exhaustion.

In *Izvestya* (19 October 1993) Yuri Dyakov, representative of Russia's State Committee for Emergency Situations, said: 'Genocide reigns in the republic. Dozens of corpses in the sea... Disembowelled women.

Severed heads on the beaches...Georgians have been wiped out in Abkhazia.'

Beginning with the capture of Gagra, early in October 1992, and taking advantage of temporary armistices, the Abkhazian separatists methodically 'cleansed' the districts they had seized of Georgians. Thousands - over 200,000 - the entire Georgian population of Abkhazia in fact, became forcibly displaced refugees. They have filled nearly all the districts of Georgia, some are stranded in Moscow, in Sochi, and other cities. Their homes have been taken by mercenaries and boeviks from North Caucasia, by Cossacks, and by terrorists from countries of the Middle East, as has been recorded in the *Report of the UN Secretary General's Fact-Finding Mission to Investigate Human Rights Violations in Abkhazia, Republic of Georgia* (Doc. S/26795, 24 September 1993).

This policy of forcibly changing the demographic structure of Abkhazia, was condemned by the UN Security Council (Res.896, 31 January 1993). Here the real face of aggressive separatism has been revealed and the conflict in Abkhazia has threatened to develop into a major war throughout the entire Caucasus.

In an attempt to avert this, the government of Georgia appealed to the UN and the CSCE for help to settle the conflict. The UN Secretary General, the Security Council, and the CSCE repeatedly stressed the inviolability of the sovereignty and territorial integrity of the Republic of Georgia. They called for the return of the refugees and the determination of the status of Abkhazia within the borders of the Republic of Georgia with due account to be taken of the interests of the entire multi-national population of Abkhazia.

In order to ensure the safety of the refugees, Georgia asked the UN to send its peace-keeping forces to the region. However, the report of the UN General Secretary (Doc.S/1994/253, 3 March 1994) states: 'By not acceding to the Council's demand that all concerned recognise the territorial integrity of Georgia, the Abkhazian side is in effect preventing the United Nations from responding to a call for assistance from Member States and blocking the orderly return of refugees.'

Today over 300,000 people, three fourths of the entire population of the region, are beyond its borders. This means that the policy of genocide and the war have scorched not only the Georgians, but also the Russians, Armenians, Greeks, Estonians, and the Abkhaz themselves. Many thousands of them have left their homeland refusing to recognise the fascist diktat of the group entrenched in Gudauta.

The coming time will show how events will unfold. However, one thing is obvious: nothing can justify Ardzinba's regime for the policy which has brought so much death and destruction to Abkhazia.

Appendix 1

The Presidium of the Supreme Soviet of Abkhazia decrees:

1. Military units, offices, border and internal troops and the naval forces are deployed on the territory of Abkhazia in accordance with the will of the people and the Constitution of Abkhazia.Their further presence in Abkhazia fully refers to the competence of the Supreme Soviet of Abkhazia and will be decided by political agreements and legal norms.Any legal acts, irrespective of who they come from, contradicting this provision and aimed at undermining the defence capability of the republic, destabilizing the military-political situation in the region and contradicting the presently effective Constitution of the republic have no juridical force.

2. Taking into consideration the impending transfer to the jurisdiction of the republic of the bodies of local military control (military registration and enlistment offices, civil defence, military technical societies), as well as military units 5482, 3697, their property, equipment and armament, as well as buildings, military installations, etc., according to article 11 of the Constitution of Abkhazia are declared the property of Abkhazia.At the present time, the staff and office schedule of the indicated military structures is not subject to change on the part of Abkhazia, and, pending the final settlement of the question on the basis of intergovernmental agreements, are regulated according to the established rules.

3. Officials of military commissariats, of the staff of civil defence, and military-technical societies of Abkhazia are no longer permitted to give away or destroy - according to the rules established earlier - their property, equipment and armament without an appropriate order of the Council of Ministers of Abkhazia.

4. The Council of Ministers of Abkhazia is to determine the order of the execution of points 2 and 3 of the present decree.

5. The Military commissar, Chief of staff of civil defence, chairman of the military-technical society (voluntary society) for assisting the army, air force and navy are requested to submit to the Supreme Soviet of Abkhazia proposals on the organizational and staff structure of the subordinate military offices till 15 January 1992.

6. The present Decree comes into force from the moment of its adoption.

Chairman of the Supreme Soviet of Abkhazia
V. Ardzinba
Sukhumi
29 December 1991' [143]

At the same time the Decree of the Presidium of the Supreme Soviet of Abkhazia on the setting up under the Chairman of the Supreme Soviet of Abkhazia of a Provisional Council for the coordination of the activity and transfer of subordination of military and police units, stationed on the territory of Abkhazia was adopted.

The Decree says:
'In connection with the ceasing of existence of the Union SSR and abolition of union structures, including military units of the MIA, guided by the interests of the multi-national population of Abkhazia a Provisional Council be set up for the coordination of the activity and transfer of subordination of military and police units stationed on the territory of Abkhazia. Its composition to be:
Chairman of the Council, Ardzinba V.G., Chairman of the Supreme Soviet of Abkhazia.
First Vice-Chairman of the Council, Arshba A.I., colonel, first Deputy Minister of Internal Affairs of Abkhazia.
Vice-Chairman, Godzhian L.P., lieutenant-colonel.
Members of the Council:
Chkadua T.N., colonel, military commissar of Abkhazia.

Dbar S.P., colonel, military commissar of Sukhumi.
Mirvelov B.G., colonel, military commissar of Gagra.
Klimov A.B., police major, commander of the military unit 5482.
Dyakonov G.P., commander of the military unit 3697.
Agrba G.K., lieutenant colonel.
The Provisional Council for the coordination of activity and transfer
of military and police units is to be guided in its daily activities by
appropriately approved Regulations.

Chairman of the Supreme Soviet of Abkhazia
V Ardzinba
Sukhumi
29 December 1991[147]

Appendix 2

The Presidium decrees:

1. To call up in April-June of the current year to active military service in the regiment of the Internal Troops of Abkhazia citizens who are 18 by the day of call-up and have no right of deferment.

2. To form Republican call-up committees for the direction of district call-up committees and for controlling their activities under the chairmanship of the chief of the Sukhumi joint military-mobilization board.

3. To determine that call-up to active military service beyond the borders of Abkhazia be carried out in accordance with the arrangements and on the basis of the call-up warrant sanctioned by the chairman of the temporary council for the coordination of military units.

4. The Ministry of Internal Affairs and Prosecutor's Office of Abkhazia, in co-operation with the executive bodies and military-mobilization office, are to ensure absolute observation of the order of call-up for active service. To make answerable persons avoiding call-up, according to the legislation in force.

5. Directors of secondary, special secondary and higher schools and colleges are to submit lists of pupils and students of call-up age according to the established form to the military-mobilization board.

6. Military-mobilization departments and boards attached to the executive committees of the Soviets of people's deputies are to prepare the data on persons of call-up age before May 1 of the current year.

7. Permanent commissions of the Supreme Soviet of Abkhazia (on human rights, ethnic relations and legal questions) are to prepare a law for consideration by the Supreme Soviet of Abkhazia 'On active military duties' and a law 'On alternative military service'.

8. The decree enters into force from the very moment of its adoption.

Chairman of the Supreme Soviet of the Republic of Abkhazia
V. Ardzinba
Sukhumi
31 March 1992[150]

Appendix 3

The given law establishes subordination of some bodies of the state administration of the Republic of Abkhazia:

Article 1: In connection with the re-organization of the Security Committee of the Republic of Abkhazia it be withdrawn from the structure of the Council of Ministers of the Republic of Abkhazia and subordinated to the Supreme Soviet.

Article 2: In order to ensure normal conditions for carrying out the nationalization and privatization in the Republic, the management of state property and privatization be withdrawn from the structure of the Council of Ministers of Abkhazia and subordinated to the Supreme Soviet of Abkhazia.

Article 3: Taking into consideration the tendency to deterioration of the ecological situation and the necessity of taking radical measures for its improvement and preservation of the recreational resources of the Republic, the State Committee for environmental protection be withdrawn from the structure of the bodies of the Council of Ministers of Abkhazia and subordinated to the Supreme Soviet of Abkhazia.

Article 4: The permanent committees of the Supreme Soviet of Abkhazia to work out and submit for consideration to the Session of the Supreme Soviet of Abkhazia drafts of regulations for the Security Committee of the Republic of Abkhazia, the State Committee for the management of state property and privatization, and the State Committee for environmental protection.

Chairman of the Supreme Soviet of the Republic of Abkhazia
V. Ardzinba
Sukhumi
5 March 1992[151]

Appendix 4

'The telegrams from Damascus', published in the Aidgylara (N2), April 1990, read:

Moscow, the Kremlin
Mr. M.S. Gorbachev:

On behalf of those assembled at the Soviet Cultural Centre in Damascus in connection with the Day of the establishment of Soviet power in Abkhazia - traditionally marked by us - we, representatives of the mountain peoples of the Caucasus in Syria, are sending you our best wishes...Realizing the complexity of the problems you have shouldered, we are convinced that you are closely following and will continue to follow the Abkhazian question and will not allow a handful of extremists from Georgia, blinded with nationalism, to destroy the historical relations established between the people of Georgia and the peoples of the Northern and North-Western Caucasus.

At the same time, we hope that at this historic point the Soviet Union will give its attention to the condition of all Circassian peoples of the Caucasus, the bulk of whom was exiled abroad as a result of the colonial policy of Tsarism and the Sultan's Empire, and will meet the desire of many of us to return to our homeland in accordance with international conventions and the Declaration on Human Rights.

We wish you, Mr Gorbachev, good health, prosperity to the Soviet people, as well as successes in the implementation of the programme of revolutionary Perestroika.

Another telegram:

Tbilisi, Central Committee of the Communist Party of Georgia.

We, representatives of the mountain peoples of the Caucasus in Syria, assembled at the Soviet Cultural Centre in Damascus, on the occasion of the 69th anniversary of the establishment of Soviet power in Abkhazia, are sending you warm congratulations and expressions of our kindly feelings to your people...Today, however, we cannot con-

ceal our profound anxiety about the dramatic developments of violence in Abkhazia and South Ossetia. It is hard to believe that this
can occur between fraternal civilized peoples.But familiarity with the
chauvinistic views of some nationalistically disposed representatives
of the Georgian people prompts us to declare our solidarity with our
blood-relatives in the Caucasus ...

And finally, a still more eloquent message:

The Abkhazian ASSR, Sukhumi

To the Government of Abkhazia, To the leaders of the Communist
Party of Abkhazia, To the people of Abkhazia, our brothers who, remaining in their homeland, have shed their blood in its defence, To
the Assembly of the Mountain Peoples of the Caucasus.
We, your brothers abroad, the part that was severed from you 125
years ago by the conquerors of peoples of the last century - that of
colonialism and exploitation - wish to tell you that we are not only
alive but are also not oblivious of our roots. That is why we, here in
Syria, for the 8th year running have been marking our common national holiday - the Day of the creation of Soviet Abkhazia - at the
Cultural Centre of Damascus. On the occasion of this event, dear to
our hearts, we are sending our cordial sentiments and wishes of prosperity of our republic. We, also, express our full support to you. Be
assured that we are bleeding for every wound in your life. At the
same time, we are convinced that a bright future awaits you notwithstanding all the difficulties.
Damascus[157]

Appendix 5

Appeal to the Supreme Soviet of the USSR:

We, representatives of the regions whose population in the course of the All-Union Referendum (and local polls) unambiguously expressed its will to remain within the renewed Union SSR, having discussed the present situation, note: These results have been obtained notwithstanding the counter-action of the republican authorities who did everthing possible to hamper the work on the new Union Treaty, banned holding the referendum, and declared themselves outside of the Union in defiance of the procedure provided for by the law 'On the Order of the Secession of Republics from the USSR'. To suppress the people's will the republican authorities resorted to various methods of moral and physical terror. The new draft of the Union Treaty declares the right of joining the Union of newly created state entities. The same rule is confirmed also by the provision of the law 'On the Order of the Secession of Republics of the USSR', as well as by the Decree of the Supreme Soviet of the USSR adopted on the results of the All-Union Referendum of 17 March 1991. Correct application of these provisions allows effectively and on legitimate grounds to solve the most acute questions of inter-ethnic and inter-republican contradictions and to overcome the difficulties on the way of creating a renewed Union.

However, these declarations were not strengthened by an appropriate mechanism for their realization, which is fraught with a threat to civil peace and inter-ethnic accord not only in our regions but in many others as well.

Considering the cited circumstances, we insist on:

1. The recognition of the will of the people, expressed at the Referendum, as a sufficient basis for admitting the delegations of our entities to the signing of the Union Treaty.

2. The setting up of a committee at the Supreme Soviet of the SSR, empowered to consider and solve the questions provided for by the above legislative acts.

On behalf of:
The Dniester Moldavian SSR - Marakutsa G.S.
The Gagauz Republic - Kendighelian M.B.
The Abkhazian Autonomous Republic - Shamba T.M.
The South Ossetian Autonomous Republic - Checkhoev A.G.
The Inter-Regional Council of the Estonian SSR - Kogan E.V.
Shalchininkai District of the Lithuanian SSR - Bilans K.I.[160]

Notes

1.   It was in Sukhumi that in 1988 the last but one 'All-Union session on the results of field ethnographic and anthropologic investigations in 1986-1987' was held. It was organised by the N.N. Miklukho-Maklai Institute of Ethnography (now of Ethnology and Ethnic Anthropology). The Abkhazian People's Forum Aidgylara, forming at that time, was met with sympathy and support by Moscow scholars who saw in the Aidgylara the mouthpiece of the national interests of the Abkhazian people. M.Yu. Chumalov's work on gathering documents and analysis of civic movements in Abkhazia - later named the Abkhazian Knot - was included in the plan of the Centre for the study of inter-ethnic relations under the direction of M.N. Guboglo, which was set up as a leading subsection of the Institute in 1989.

2.   In 1992 M.N. Guboglo and I completed and published our two-volume study 'The Crimean Tatar National Movement'. We discovered such deep humanistic values and civic virtues there that our admiration for them was involuntarily extrapolated to other national movements of the former Peoples of the USSR. We wanted, and it seemed to us feasible, to find here, in Abkhazia, in Aidgylara and the Slav Home - similar democratic ideals, the same examples of civic valour and courage as in the Crimean Tatar national movement that had challenged the totalitarian Communist regime.

3.   This chapter is written on the basis of the literature given in the bibliography. The author expresses her sincere gratitude to the reviewer of the manuscript, historian Zaliko Kikodze whose observations, particularly valuable in view of the historical retrospect of the Abkhaz-Georgian relations are taken into consideration in the present chapter.

4.   This idea was elaborated by M. Kvirilidze at the meeting with the academic staff of *Novosibirsk Akademgorodok* in 1989. 'The Abkhazian question is forced.The Abkhazians as well as the Kakhetians, Imeretians, Gurians, Svans, Megrelians, etc., are all Georgians and together they make up the Georgian nation...' *(Aidgylara) (Unity)*, 1990, N3, page 5.

5.   The number of the population and some of the socio-demographic characteristics of the nationalities of the Russian Federation. Moscow, 1992, page 7. According to the data published in the Abkhazian People's Forum *Aidgylara*, the number of Abkhazians in the Abkhazian SSR is a little more than 95,494 while Georgians, according to the official statistics, are not more than 239,872, but fewer than 233,049. *(Aidgylara)* 1990, N4, page 1.

6.   Views differ in the historical literature as to the date of the 'christening' of the Abkhazians. S. Lakoba writes: 'Under the Byzantine Emperor Justinian (527-565) the Abasgoi and the Apsili officially adopted Christianity (Christianity spread in Abkhazia from the first centuries). As far back as the 4th century there was a Greek Christian Cathedral in Pitsunda'.Stanislav Lakoba: *Essays on the Political History of Abkhazia*. Sukhumi: 1990, N4.

7.   S. Lakoba: *Essays on the Political History of Abkhazia*. Sukhumi, 1990, pages 4-5.

8.   *Peoples of the World. Historico-ethnographical reference book*. Moscow: 1988, page 35.

9.   Only shortly before the outbreak of war did the leaders of the Abkhazian national movement make a feeble attempt to open a mosque for the religious Muslims in Sukhumi. This was initiated and financed by their 'fellow-countrymen' in Turkey. The city executive council had no time to implement the undertaking.

10.   The idea of Abkhazian paganism has been cultivated with particular care and enthusiasm among national literary and artistic circles. Thus, in the paintings of Tariel Ampara, the mythologems based

on ancient layers of Abkhazian-Adyghe folklore correspond to his subjective notions and reflections on 'paganism in the Abkhazian blood and national consciousness'. However, this manifests a certain romanticism, the pagan spirit of the nation rather than a genuine national mass mentality. It would be as absurd to talk seriously of pagan traits in contemporary Abkhazian ethnic culture as to view the Abkhazian people as representatives of Islamic fundamentalism or Christian humbleness. Of course the notion of the ancient pantheon of gods, including the supreme god Antsea, the god of fire and lightning Afa, and the god of the smithy, 'the golden sovereign' Shyashva, has been preserved not only in mythology but to a certain extent in the religious consciousness of the Abkhazians as well, as testified by the results of the field ethnographic studies of 1991-92. These results are summed up in the paper of M. M. Bartsits: *On the Image of God - Protector of the Smithy Shyashva in the Religious Beliefs of the Abkhazians;* In: *On New Approaches to Native Ethnology.*Grozny, 1992, pages 55-56. But any exceptional religiousness of the Abkhazians either along Muslim or pagan lines is out of the question.

11.   S. Lakoba: *Essays on the Political History of Abkhazia*, Sukhumi, 1990, page 7.

12.   Yu. N. Voronov: *The Russian Diaspora in Abkhazia: The Past and the Present*. In: *Russia and the East: Problems of Interaction*. Abstracts of papers of an international scientific and practical conference. Moscow, 1992, page 12.

13.   Zurab Achba: *Time to Realise that Abkhazia is Russia. (Den)* 29 November-5 December 1992, N48, page 2.

14.   See: *The Abkhazians. Ethnopolis (Ethnopolitical Herald of Russia)*, 1992, N1, page 123.

15.   A. Avtorkhanov: *The Kremlin Empire*. Moscow, 1991, page 48.

16.   Andreas Kappeler: Russland als Vielvoelkerreich. Entstehung.Geschichte. Zerfall. Muenchen: 1993, S.146, 149, 153, 354.

17.   Quoted from Stanislav Lakoba.*Essays on the Political History of Abkhazia*. Sukhumi, 1990, pages 39, 42.

18.   Ibidem, page 23.

19.   In this connection, Z. Kikodze drew my attention to an interesting point. 'Abkhazian culture', he says, 'or if you will, Abkhazian civilisation in the Middle Ages is represented by Georgian monuments of cult architecture which in the history of Georgian art are referred to as the Abkhazian school...Not only the alphabet is Georgian, but also the language of epigraphic and other monuments of writing. As it were, only Georgians are recorded in space and time in Abkhazia.At the same time frequent mention is made of the Abkhazians in the Georgian sources (the people, dynasty, etc.)...The Abkhazian nobility, aristocracy and Christian clergy spoke and used the Georgian language and writing...' (from the review of the manuscript of this book).

The inward conviction in the unity of the historical fates of the Abkhazian and Georgian peoples, living from ancient times side by side on the same land and regarding it as their home, and the impossibility of even speculatively demarcating it according to the ethnic principle, let alone giving it to one of the two native peoples and depriving the other of the right to consider this land as its own, has deeply penetrated into the scholarly thinking and consciousness of the progressive, democratically-minded public of Abkhazia. 'Our two peoples', wrote the historian B. Sichinava expressing this idea, 'have together passed a long historical road. Since hoary antiquity they have lived side by side; sharing sorrow and joy; their fates are closely interwoven. Nobody has ever the right to forget this (Viktor Sichinava: *The Destiny of Abkhazia and Georgia is One. Demokraticheskaya Abkhazia*.30 September 1992, page 2).

An appeal of the State Council of the Republic of Georgia to the 'Abkhazian brothers and sisters' runs as follows: We, Georgians and Abkhazians, are brothers by blood. Our home was and is single, single is our history, culture and our existence comes from a single source...' (Dear Abkhazian Brothers and Sisters: Utsqebani.Records.21 August 1992, page 2). 'No one can sow discord between us', says Arkadi Khashba. 'We are destined to live together and build a single country on the land of our forefathers.The historical joint past of the Abkhazians and Georgians has not yet been passed.' Arkadi Khashba: *No One Can Sow Discord Between Us. Svobodnaya Gruzia*, 18 February 1993, page 2.

20.   See: Yu.N. Voronov: *The Russian Diaspora in Abkhazia: Its History and the Present*.In: *Russia and the East: Problems of Interaction*. Moscow 1992, page 12.

21.   On the eve of summoning the Sejm, on 9 February a special agreement was concluded between the delegations of Georgia and the People's Council of Abkhazia, ensuring the representation of Abkhazia in the Transcaucasian Sejm as a constituent part of Georgia. In addition, the borders were fixed and the autonomy of Abkhazia was guaranteed.

22.   Quoted from: S. Lakoba: *Essays on the Political History of Abkhazia*. Sukhumi, 1990, page 65.

23.   From December 1918 Efrem Eshba was one of Stalin's assistants at the People's Commissariat for the Nationalities of the RSFSR, and became a member of the Central Bureau of the communist organisations of the peoples of the East under the CC of the RCP. Moscow trained with care the cadre of the future leaders of Red Abkhazia for underground party work and terrorist activity in Baku, Batumi, and Trabizon. Abkhazian communists tried - not unsuccessfully - to win over the national military units, specifically the Abkhazian squad Kiaraz, formed at the end of 1917, which jointly with the 9th Red Army units 'liberated' Abkhazia, inspiring terror among the local population.

24.   N. Vorobyev: *On the Groundlessness of Georgia's Claims to the Sukhumi District* (Abkhazia). Rostov-on-Don, 1919.

25.   The Act on the Autonomy of Abkhazia published on 21 March 1919 ran as follows: The first People's Council of Abkhazia, elected on the basis of general, direct, equal and secret suffrage, at its meeting of 20 March 1919, passed the following resolution on behalf of the peoples of Abkhazia:

1. Abkhazia is part of the Democratic Republic of Georgia as her autonomous unit.

2. For the purpose of drawing up the Constitution of Autonomous Abkhazia and determining the interrelations between the central and autonomous authorities a joint committee is elected with an equal number of members from the Constituent Assembly of Georgia and the People's Council of Abkhazia. *(Nashe Slovo)* 21 March 1919; *(Literaturnaya Gruziya)* 1989, N11, pages 155-156.

26.   The 12th Congress of the Communist Party of Russia. *Shorthand Report*. Moscow 1923, page 472.

27.   The Cyrillic alphabet was used for Abkhazian writing already in tsarist Russia - from the 19th century. In 1926 Abkhazia switched to a new, Latin alphabet, and in 1937 to Georgian letters. The Cyrillic alphabet was restored after 1953.

(The sequence of events seems to have been as follows:

1862 - Pyotr Uslar devised first alphabet for Abkhaz.

1926 - Abkhazian government introduces Latin-based orthography devised by Nikolay Marr.

1929 - New Latin-based alphabet introduced devised by N.Yakovlev.

1938 - Introduction of Georgian-based system devised by the founding father of Abkhazian literature, Dmitri Gulia, with assistance of Georgians Simon Janashia and Akaki Shanidze.

1954 - Cyrillic-based system in use (includes 14 non-Cyrillic characters).

(As one specialist of the Abkhaz language, B.G.Hewitt, noted 'the Georgian alphabet is undoubtedly the most suitable candidate to meet the needs of any Caucasian language requiring an orthography.')

28.   Thus, in tsarist Russia according to the data on the census of the population in 1897, the number of Abkhazians within the bounds of the present Abkhazian ASSR totalled 55% of the population (58,697), and Georgian - 24% (25,640) (See: *The First General Census of the Population of the Russian Empire, 1897. The Province of Kutaisi*. St. Petersburg, 1905, page 32). By the start of the revolution the percentage of the Georgian population exceeded 42%, and toward the end of the 1980s

it reached 45.7%. The share of the Abkhazian ethnos in the population of the republic dropped to 17.8% (according to some estimations to 17.4%).

29.   *Aidgylara*. 1990, N3, page 3.

30.   The most dramatic events of 1978 in Abkhazia must have formed an exception, when disturbances involved rather broad sections of the public, even the troops were placed on alert to establish order. However it did not come to bloodshed, and the 'stern measures' were restricted to the June decision of the CC of the CPG pointing out the ideological errors in historiography. As was the custom in the Brezhnev years, an impervious information blockade was imposed on these events and the Soviet public knew nothing about them.

31.   Debate at the Plenary Meeting of the CPSU Central Committee, *(Pravda)* 1989, September 21, page 4.

32.   Details of this campaign are highlighted in the newspaper *Aidgylara*, 1990, N5.

33.   Foreign press as well as the press of the neighbouring (former Union) independent republics is not considered here, it was impossible to cover such immense material. Newspapers studied include: *Izvestya, Argumenty i Fakty, Nezavisimaya Gazeta, Express-Khronika, Rossiya, Den* and selectively - newspapers of various social associations and republics of the Northern Caucasus such as *Severnyi Kavkaz* (The Northern Caucasus), *Kavkazskii Dom* (Caucasian Home), *Nart* (founder of the latter: International Circassian Association), *Yuige Igilik* (The Karachai newspaper Peace to Your Home), *Ir* (Northern Ossetia), *Golos Chechnskoi Respubliki* (Voice of the Chechen Republic), *Lezgi Khabarar* (Lezgian Herald) and finally, an independent political newspaper *Pod Nebom Gruzii* (Under the Sky of Georgia) published since the February of 1992 in Grozny by the supporters of the deposed ex-president Zviad Gamsakhurdia.

34.   *Under the Sky of Georgia*, 1992, N39.

35.   *Yuige Igilik*, 1993, N16.

36.   Darrell Slider: *Crisis and Response in Soviet Nationality Policy: the Case of Abkhazia - Central Asian Survey*. 1985, Volume 4, N4.

37.   See, e.g. S.Z. Lakoba, S.M. Shamba: *Who are the Abkhazians? Sovetskaya Abkhazia*, 8 July, 1989; B.E. Sagharia. *Education through History (Bzyb)* 21, 23, 25, 28 June 1988.

38.   Alexei Gogua: *Our Concern (Druzhba Narodov)* 1989, N5, page 158.

39.   Marika Lordkipanidze: *Incompetence - in the Rank of Truth? (Zarya Vostoka)* 21 July 1989, page 3.

40.   Viktor Sichinava: *The Fates of Abkhazia and Georgia are the Same. Historical evidence of Abkhaz-Georgian relations. (Demokraticheskaya Abkhazia)* 30 September 1989, N7, page 2.

41.   Zurab Papaskiri: *Some Reflections on the Past of Abkhazia and Georgian-Abkhazian Relations. (Demokraticheskaya Abkhazia)* 12 November 1992, N13, page 2.

42.   Quotation from the publication in the newspaper *Demokraticheskaya Abkhazia*, 30 September 1992, N7, page 3.

43.   Avtandil Mentshashvili: *Georgian-Abkhazian Relations* and *Experts from the State Committee of the Nationalities. Svobodnaya Gruziya*, 20 November 1992; *(Demokraticheskaya Abkhazia)* 2 December 1992, N17, pages 2-3.

44.   The publication of such elaborations is included in the book by B. Stepankov, E. Lisov: *The Kremlin Plot. Version of the investigation*. Moscow, 1992.

45.   O. Vasilyeva writes: 'During the talks in Moscow Shevardnadze demonstrated the skill of a politician of world calibre. In highly unfavourable circumstances for him, as a representative of an illegitimate

government body, Shevardnadze managed to use the desire of the North Caucasian leaders (reference is to the party leaders of the former autonomous republics and regions) to suppress the national movements in these regions, whose victory is highly probable in the coming elections. Having no political experience, Ardzinba gave in and signed a document legalising the presence of Georgian troops in Abkhazia and making no mention of a federal system for Georgia. As a matter of fact, this last circumstance is very important for the leaders of the Northern Caucasus in their relations with the Russian President, as well as for further continuation of military operations on Georgian territory.

Shevardnadze managed to gain a local victory which, however, will lead to the radicalization of national movements in Abkhazia and the Northern Caucasus, continuation of hostilities in Abkhazia, with gradual involvement in it of not only representatives of the South of Russia, but the foreign Adyghe diaspora as well...For Russia this treaty meant not only the continuation of war close to her borders with all the resulting consequences (regular shady inflow of arms, efficient units in the administrative entities of the South, etc.), but future problems with the autonomies whose trust in the federal treaty will be undermined'. - O. Vasilyeva. *Georgia as a Model of Post-Communist Transformation*. Moscow., 1993, pages 36-37.

46.   See *Komsomolskaya Pravda*, 1992, 19 December.

47.   Such is for instance, an article by L. Orazaeva *No Way Back (Nart*, September 1992, N3 , pages 3-4. 'Young fellows who fight in Abkhazia' the journalist writes 'Russians, Armenians, Karachai, Adyghe, Chechens and many others deserve the kindest words and deep respect...While there is even a single armed Georgian in Abkhazia we shall not go away...'

A lengthy anonymous historical reference *My Pain, Abkhazia!* opens ostentatiously with a quotation from a statement by Andrei Sakharov and ends thus: 'So the small empire decided to occupy Abkhazia. The doctrine of the fascist marauders in the republic is clearly expressed by the words of the commander of the Georgian troops in Sukhumi, Karkarashvili: 'I shall let 100,000 Georgians die, but I shall solve the Abkhazian problem for ever, I shall exterminate 97,000 Abkhazians...' *Nart*, 2 September 1992, page 2.

The outright exaggeration of Karkarashvili's statement, which is easily revealed if this text is compared with what he actually said on TV, does not seem to confuse the editors in the least.

48.   *Under the Sky of Georgia*, 28 August 1992, page 1.

49.   Emil Pain: *The Russian Echo of the Caucasian War. (Izvestya)* 9 October 1992, page 3; *(Democraticheskaya Abkhazia)* 14 October, page 2.

50.   Ibidem.

51.   Viktor Kuvaldin: *The Caucasian Outcome for Georgia and Russia. (Moscow News)* 25 October 1992, N43, page 8; *(Svobodnaya Gruzya)* 6 November 1992.

52.   Ibidem.

53.   *Moskovskaya Pravda*, 3 October 1992.

54.   In *Den* Sergei Baburin wrote that 'Georgia was conducting this war with the Abkhazians with the latest and at the same time most barbarous arms...All this was transferred to the military formations of the illegitimate State Council of Georgia, that came to power as a result of a coup...what is happening in Abkhazia is in the interests of the present Russian leadership ...' - Sergei Baburin: *The blood of Abkhazia is on the Kremlin. Den*, 30 August-5 September 1992, N35, page 1. This is followed by A. Sterligov's article. He goes as far as saying that 'Russia, in the person of the citizen, E.A. Shevardnadze, is conducting an undeclared war against the peoples of Abkhazia'.

55.   O. Suprunenko: *The Russians in Sukhumi. (Express-Khronika)* 19-26 April 1993, N17, page 3.

56.   Owing to his striking photogenicity and nervous-artistic manner of behaviour in front of the cameras, Vladislav Ardzinba can probably evoke a certain effect of admiration, among the women's audience in particular.

57. I am aware of cases when Russian publicists are paid from the funds of 'warring Abkhazia', and their writings are published with 'Ardzinba's money'.

58. *This is How it Was. National Repressions in the USSR.1919-1952. The Repressed Peoples Today* (compiler, editor, author of the preface and afterword, comments and notes: S. Alieva). Moscow 1993, volume 3, page 328.

59. Sergei Labanov. *The Georgian-Abkhazian Conflict: Prologue - Russia,* 1992 (Quoted from the *Demokraticheskaya Abkhazia* newspaper, 13 December 1992, N19, page 4).

60. Zurav Achba: *Time to realise that Abkhazia is Russia (Den)* 29 November-5 December 1992, N48, page 2.

61. See: *Civil movements in Latvia - 1989.* Moscow 1990, pages 155-156.

62. Vadim Bakatin: *Getting Rid of the KGB.* Moscow 1992, page 49.

63. Quotation from the book by O. Vasilyeva. *Georgia as a Model of Post-Communist Transformation.* Moscow 1993, page 59.

64. O. Vasilyeva publishes a fragment of the interview given to her by Irakli Tsereteli, leader of the National Independence Party of Georgia, in September 1989, who allegedly said: 'As a matter of fact, those whom we today call the Abkhazians are not Abkhazians. The Abkhazians were a Georgian tribe that inhabited Georgia, as well as the Svans and Mingrelians. During the conquest of the Caucasus by Russia the Abkhazians - Muslims - left for Turkey and the Kabardinians and Balkars came to Abkhazia in the middle of the 19th century, and the greatest part of the present Abkhazians are their descendants. I believe that a people must have its autonomy if it constitutes an autochthonous population - neither the Abkhazians nor the Ossetians are such'. From: *Georgia as a Model of Post-Communist Transformation.* Moscow 1993, page 62.

65.   This was in particular discussed by Tariel Kvanchilashvili long before the bloody events in South Ossetia and Abkhazia, in his article _What is going to happen next?_, published in _Literary Georgia_ (_Literaturuli Sakartvelo_) on 30 September, 1988. Statements of this kind are characteristic of different political figures, and though in reproducing them serious misinterpretations and distortions are possible (e.g. 'according to the information of the press-service of the Supreme Soviet of Abkhazia, the Minister of Defence, Tengiz Kitovani, said that there would be no autonomies in Georgia', NEGA, 23 August, 1992, does not mean that Kitovani really made such a statement). However, it is obvious that extreme subjectivism is creeping into the Georgian press and into Georgian politics, on pre-election platforms, and in the programmes of a number of parties. There is also sometimes a scornful, haughty attitude to national minorities and crude nihilism as far as the future of the territorial and national-cultural autonomies is concerned. Such facts are indisputable, and the reader, acquainted with the Georgian press or the statements of Georgian national parties, can easily find a great number of flagrant examples confirming this.

66.   The Abkhazian Letter was not published in full. The quotations from it are cited in _Aidgylara_ 1990, N4, page 2.

67.   Comparing the situation in Abkhazia and Nagorny Karabakh one fundamental distinction should be stressed: both manifestations of separatism - striving for a change of the status of the autonomy, taking it out of the Soviet Republic - are similar in form but in essence they are absolutely different movements. Karabakh, a democratic radical movement directed against the communist leadership of Azerbaijan and the Centre, was supported by the progressive forces of Russia (A.D. Sakharov, G.V. Starovoitova, and others. Abkhazian separatism, on the contrary, was orientated to the communist Centre.

68.   See: Shamba, T.M., Koveshnikov, E.M.: _The Political System of Developed Socialism_, Moscow, 1977; Shamba, T.M., Muramets, O.F.: _Law and Order in Developed Socialist Society_, Moscow, 1979; Shamba, T.M.: _Party Guidance of Bodies of Protection of Socialist Law and Order_, Moscow, 1979. In 1985 T.M. Shamba defended his Doctor of Law Thesis

at the Academy of Social Sciences attached to the Central Committee of the CPSU on the topic: Democratism of Soviet Law and Order (Theory and Practice).

69.   Tsushba, I.N.: *The Tasks of the Party for the Perfection of Inter-Ethnic Relations under Conditions of Perestroika (As exemplified by the Abkhazian SSR)* in *What is to Be Done? In Search of Ideas for the Perfection of Inter-Ethnic Relations in the USSR*, Moscow, 1989, pages 218-230.

70.   Ibidem, page 219.

71.   Ibidem, page 224.

72.   It will be recalled that in 1923 Stalin made an ideological attack against the Georgian national *uklonism* (deviation) drawing Abkhazians, Ajarians and Ossetians into provocative intrigues against Tbilisi.

73.   Ibidem, pages 229-230.

74.   *Aidgylara*, 1990, N4, page 2.

75.   *Aidgylara*, 1990, N4, page 2.

76.   *Aidgylara*, 1990, N4, page 3.

77.   Quoted from Anatoly Sobchak, *Entry into Power*, Moscow, 1991, page 104.

78.   Ibidem, page 93.

79.   Ibidem, page 93.

80.   '... I do not rule out', Sobchak wrote later, 'that the Tbilisi tragedy was the result of unconscious, instinctive self-preservation of the System. On the eve of its political collapse, but after totalitarianism was defeated at the elections of People's Deputies, the convulsion of

April 9th was predetermined'. Anatoli Sobchak. *Entry into Power*, Moscow, 1991, page 93.

81.   *Aidgylara*, 1990, N4, page 3.

82.   First published in the newspaper *Demokraticheskaya Abkhazia*, 13 December 1992, page 4.

83.   From the 'Information' about some results of the investigation of the events in Sukhumi and other towns of the Abkhazian ASSR on 15-16 July 1989, marked Strictly Confidential. The full xerox-copy of the text, sent to the Procurator's Office of the USSR from the Supreme Soviet of Abkhazia, is at the author's disposal. Some parts of this Information, including the quoted phrase, were published in the newspaper *Aidgylara*, 1990, N4, pages 2-5.

84.   Ibidem. Published in *Demokraticheskaya Abkhazia*, 13 December 1992, page 4.

85.   S. Labanov: *The Georgian-Abkhazian Conflict; Prologue.* *(Demokraticheskaya Abkhazia)* 13 December 1922, page 4.

86.   All this is listed in: *The information about some results of the investigation of the events in Sukhumi and others towns of the Abkhazian ASSR on 15-16 July, 1989.*

87.   O.Vasilyeva: *Georgia as a Model of Post-Communist Transformation*, Moscow, 1993, page 60. 17 persons (11 Georgians, 5 Abkhazians, 1 Greek) died, 448 were wounded (Ibidem, page 32).

88.   *Zarya Vostoka* (Dawn of the East) 23 July, 1989.

89.   Discussion at the Plenary Session of the CPSU Central Committee, *(Pravda)* 21 September 1989, page 4.

90.   S. Labanov: *The Georgian-Abkhazian Conflict; Prologue.* *(Demokraticheskaya Abkhazia)* 13 December 1992, page 4.

91.   The admission made by O. Vasilyeva in her booklet *Georgia as a Model of Post-Communist Transformation*, the obvious instigation of which by the Secret Services of the former USSR was referred to here, is characteristic. Citing some statistical data characterising a somewhat lower standard of living in the South Ossetian Autonomous Region as compared to the rest of Georgia, the author refers to the report *Economic Aspects of Inter-Ethnic Problems*, which was 'prepared in response to the author's inquiry in August 1989 by Kabisova Dzirasa Grigoryevna, research worker of the South Ossetian Scientific Research Institute' (SOSRI) (O. Vasilyeva: *Georgia as a Model of Post-Communist Transformation*, Moscow, 1993, page 61).

One very interesting detail: Why did the author (obviously backed by the Analytical Services of the KGB of the USSR) need to send inquiries of this kind to the SOSRI in the August of 1989 - three months ahead of the tragic events in Tskhinvali? Who wanted to think over or supply the explosive information in time, resulting from a comparison of the salaries and budgetary expenditure per capita in Georgia and South Ossetia?

92.   Yu.N. Voronov: *Russian Diaspora in Abkhazia: the History and the Present, in Russia and the East: Problems of Interaction*, Moscow, 1992, page 15.

93.   S. Shamba: *Abkhazia - for a sovereign federation of mountain peoples within the USSR. (Aidgylara)* 1991, N3, pages 6-7.

94.   Musa Shanibov: *To Serve the Revival.(Kavkaz)*, 1 October 1990, N1.

95.   Yusup Soslambekov: *A Protracted Walk on the Brink of an Abyss.Towards the History of one Annexation.(Kavkaz)*, 1 October 1990, N1.

96.   The address to the Abkhazian and Georgian Peoples was adopted in Sukhumi on 26 August, 1989. A xerox-copy is at the author's disposal.

97.   *Who's Who* in Georgian politics was rather vaguely conceived in Grozny and the names of the Secretary of the National-Democratic Party, G. Chanturia, and the Head of the Helsinki Union, Z. Gamsakhurdia, were obviously mixed up.

98.   As we can see, the historical knowledge of the authors of the statement was not very profound.

99.   This digression is very significant. At first sight the Jewish autonomous region has nothing to do with this but the militant anti-semitism of those Black-Hundred obscurantist forces shows clearly. Later on the zealous search for a 'Jewish-masonic' plot will go arm-in-arm with curses addressed to Menshevik Georgia and the destroyers of the USSR.

100.   The statement of the Popular Front of the Chechen-Ingush ASSR for the Promotion of Perestroika in connection with the tragic events in Abkhazia. NIISO (Grozny). 1989, N7-8, page 1. A xerox-copy is at the disposal of the author.

101.   The telegram signed by the vice-chairman of Adygha Khase, A.V. Khatazhukov, was published in *Aidgylara*, 1989, N2.

102.   The address dated 4 November 1989 was published in *Aidgylara*, 1989, N2.

103.   'On July 20', reported the newspaper *Zarya Vostoka*, 'after a five-day stand in Sukhumi area under the defence of the police and the forces of the Ministry of Internal Affairs of the USSR, the passenger train N184 Yerevan-Rostov broke through in the direction of Adler. With the exception of this only train, all others are still at the platforms of Sukhumi and the nearest stations. Many engine-drivers simply refuse to drive them because of the fear of being fired at by nationalistically-inclined hooligan elements'.(*Zarya Vostoka*), 21 July 1989, page 2.

104.   *Aidgylara*, 1990, N1, page 1.

105. Ibidem.

106. Stanislav Lakoba: *Essays on the Political History of Abkhazia.* Sukhumi, 1990, page 79.

107. Bajur Sagharia: *Georgian Oprichniks in Abkhazia. (Aidgylara)*, 1992, N1(022), pages 2-3.

108. Yu.N. Voronov: *Svano-Colchians, Ashcharotsuits and the Murdered Apostles. A reply to Assistant Professor T. Mibchuani. (Aidgylara)*, 1990, N3, page 6.

109. Alexi Papaskiri: *Only those with Equal Rights can be Friends. (Aidgylara)*, 1990, N3, pages 4-5.

110. The author had heard many times in Sukhumi, Novy Afon, Gudauta, etc. from the personnel of state dachas and sanatoriums: 'Before Gorbachev we used to live in Paradise. The damned democrats deprived us of everything'.

111. It must be noted that the persecution of Eduard Shevardnadze in the Abkhazian nationalistic press began long before the events of 1982. Thus, under the title *Political Portraits*, the newspaper *Aidgylara* in December 1990 reprinted from the Grozny newspaper NIISO a vicious anti-Shevardnadze lampoon (Superintendent of Stagnation or Architect of Perestroika? *Aidgylara*, 1990, N6, pages 2-4). It called him 'tyrant' and ascribed to him craving for absolute power' (ibid. page 5). It emphasised his party past, 'unmasked' his closeness to Brezhnev and his policy of the 1970s (see: Ivan Donelyuk: *Women and the Minister. Aidgylara*, 1990, N5, page 7). All these exposures merged into one reactionary chorus, inspired by a craving for revenge against Gorbachev's comrade-in-arms in Perestroika, the Minister of Foreign Affairs of the USSR who destroyed the Iron curtain. In this chorus the voices of some obscurantists could be heard from the Association of the Mountain Peoples of the Caucasus. Thus, Yusup Soslambekov wrote furiously about the Georgian 'unofficials' who 'follow the instructions of their *kunak* (loyal friend) and now Kremlin voyager - Shevardnadze' (Yu. Soslambekov: *A Protracted Walk on the Brink of an Abyss.* 1990, N1, October 1).

112.   The programme of the People's Forum of Abkhazia - Aidgylara, 1992, N1(022), page 4.

113.   Ibidem, page 1.

114.   Ibidem, pages 1-5.

115.   A xerox-copy of the document is at the disposal of the author. Reference N7-83 (28 April 1993) of the Supreme Soviet of Abkhazia in Gudauta.

116.   One should not be astonished by the fact that the addressee of V.A. Loginov in the given case is R. G. Abdulatipov, whose name together with the names of Yuri Skokov and Vladimir Lysenko are connected with the working out of the draft of the Conception of the Russian Federation in the Northern Caucasus (published in the Karachaevsk newspaper *Yuige Igilik*, (Peace to Your Home), 1993, N16, page 2.

I had an occasion to write in a comment on this disgraceful document: 'The main purpose of the authors of the 'conception' is the Russification of the Northern Caucasus. They bluntly demand from the state 'not to allow the critical fall of the ethnic status of the population, representing the ethnic core of the Russian Federation'. This sly wording is not difficult to decipher: 'Ethnic status' is a majority or at least dominance among the population of the area; 'the main ethnic core of the Russian Federation' are Russians, and Russians, according to the authors' imagination, are not only a nation enjoying equal rights along with others, freedom of choice in residence, and equal rights to enjoy the opportunity to live and work, but they represent a particular 'core' striving for statehood (*derzhavnost*). The number of Russians must be of special concern - it must not fall beyond the critical level. Hence the aim is the following - the assurance of Russian colonisation of the Northern Caucasus and the establishment of an actually Russian North-Caucasian Republic or gubernia on this basis: 'the Russian speaking population' should be the rulers of this land. This objective is formulated directly: 'Initiating the formation of a self-governed North-Caucasian region with maximum inclusion in it of the Russian speaking population, including the

Cossacks, and locking the ethnic and confessional contradictions of the region within it.' This could be understood thus: the Cossacks themselves will take care of everything and introduce proper order in this region, without disturbing the supreme authority' (Svetlana Chervonnaya: *The Conception of the Colonisation of the Northern Caucasus.(Yuige Igilik)*, 1993, N16, page 3).

The interests of Russian *derzhavniks*, patriots, the old Party elite and the new Soviet nomenclature agree on the main point, what Loginov tactfully called 'the rebirth of Russian communities on the territories of near, far and internal abroad'.

117. The author had an opportunity to become convinced from personal experience of the censorship functions of the Slav Home leadership with regard to the Abkhazian press. Winding up the press conference arranged in connection with my arrival in Sukhumi on 12 August, V.A. Loginov, addressing the journalists, said: 'So everything positive that was said here by our guest about Shevardnadze, about the policy of Tbilisi, about the possibility of Abkhaz-Georgian dialogue must be struck out.The materials prepared for printing must be shown to me and nothing be printed without my sanction'.

118. From the record of a conversation of the author with V.A.Loginov in Sukhumi on 13 August 1992.

119. In August 1992 the author had a chance to get acquainted at the Slav Home with the cited calculations as well as with the text of the Charter of the Association of Cossacks of Abkhazia and the protocol of the meeting of *Krug* on 14 June 1992.

120. See V. Savichev: *The Cossack region - a troubled region.(Argumenty i Fakty)*, 1992, N37.

121. Gregory Mosikyan: *I appeal to everyone for peace. (Demokraticheskaya Abkhazia)*, 7 October 1992, page 2.
The author heard similar statements from Armenians, Russians and other inhabitants of Abkhazia during her stay there, both before and after the start of the war.

122. See: Vakhtang Janashia: *There is no problem of weapons here!* (The President of the Confederation of Mountain Peoples of the Caucasus about the CMPC and himself). *(Nezavisimaya Gazeta)*, 2 September 1992, page 3. (The interview was given by Musa Shanibov in July, 1992).

123. Ibidem.

124. Musa Shanibov: *To serve the Revival.(Kavkaz)*, 1990, N1 (October).

125. The final 'agreement on the principles of co-operation and mutual assistance between the Confederation of the Peoples of the Caucasus and the Cossacks of the South of Russia' was signed by the elected representatives of the Chechen and Ingush Republics, Kabardia, Balkaria, Circassia, Karachai, Adyghe, Abkhazia and Cossacks of the southern regions in Stavropol on 28 April, 1993, when the war was in full swing.

126. The President of the Confederation of the Mountain Peoples of the Caucasus about the CMPC and himself. *(Nezavisimaya Gazeta)*, 2 September 1992, page 3. It should be noted in this connection that the foreign press of Muslim countries pays attention to the non-Muslim character of the entire movement of the mountain peoples of the Caucasus led by the Confederation, as well as Abkhazian attacks against Georgia.The Turkish politologist Osman Nuri Merjan in the magazine *Gercek*, published in Ankara (1992, N10), stressed:
    'Most of the Georgians and Abkhazians living in Georgia are of Christian religion. Hence all the views and speculations on the religious character of the conflict in Abkhazia, allegedly caused by the antagonism of Christians and Muslims, are false'(quoted from the abstract review: *Gercek on Abkhazia. (Demokraticheskaya Abkhazia)*, February 1993, (Moscow issue), page 3.

127. *Nezavisimaya Gazeta*, 2 September 1992, page 3.

128. Yusup Soslambekov: *A Protracted Walk on the Brink of anAbyss. (Kavkaz)*, 1 October 1990.

129. In this connection some historical parallels are not devoid of interest. The terror of the Bolshevik communist Centre towards the Georgian intelligentsia in the past - in the 1920s, at the peak of Stalin's 'national policy' - combined with subtle intrigues, in which the national minorities of Georgia, primarily Abkhazians, were involved. Under the pretext of caring for their infringed interests, Stalin launched the most merciless campaigns against Georgian 'nationalism', 'uklonism', etc., but in fact they were directed against the people of Georgia, against all attempts to defend the independence of Georgia. Facts of this kind are adduced by Abdurakhman Avtorkhanov in his study *The Empire of the Kremlin*, recalling that at the 12th Congress of the RCP(B) in April 1923 Stalin launched an attack against Georgian 'national-uklonism', equating it with Russian great-power chauvinism and asserting 'not only in the face of facts but also against commonsense that these national-uklonists wanted to establish their dominance over the entire Transcaucasia'. (A. Avtorkhanov: *The Empire of the Kremlin*. Minsk-Moscow :1991, page 21) Budu Mdivani - pronounced the leader of Georgian national-uklonists - found courage in himself to tell the Congress what intrigues were hatched in Georgia under the order of Stalin himself who attempted to draw Georgian national minorities - Ajarians, Abkhazians and South Ossetians into the struggle against persons in the Tbilisi leadership, disliked by Stalin (Ibidem, page 22).

It appears that the leaders of the Party structures and Soviet power-based offices of the 1989-1991 models have learned the lessons and tactics of the 'Father of Peoples' (Stalin) from their youth. They hardly remembered the details of the sad fate of B. Mdivani, Lenin's comrade-in-arms, destroyed by Stalin, but they sought to wipe out their ideological opponents in present-day Tbilisi who dared, like Mdivani, to think about the independence of Georgia and speak about the sovereignty of the Union republics.

130. See Vadim Bakatin: *Getting Rid of the KGB*. Moscow, 1992, page 49.

131. *For a Union of Equal States. (Kavkaz)*, 1 October 1990, N1

132.   It should be noted that the system of double cover in Abkhazia was so deeply rooted that even in the days when it was already possible to act openly without feeling shy, many organisers of the putsch did not venture to part with the facade screening their activities. Already on 15-16 August account departments and cash-desks of different cultural offices of Sukhumi gave out the last wages to the cultural workers who were hurrying, fully armed, to their command mobilisation points. To the very last moment of the hasty evacuation, the sign-board 'Committee on Human Rights' still remained on the door of Yu. V. Voronov's study in the building of the Supreme Soviet of Abkhazia, though it is hard to imagine anything more contradicting human rights than the war orders given at this moment behind the door.

133.   Vladislav Grigorievich Ardzinba, Abkhazian by nationality, was born in 1945. He graduated from the Teachers' Training Institute in Sukhumi. In 1966 he entered the post-graduate course of the Institute of Oriental Studies of the Academy of Sciences of the USSR. In 1967 he became a member of the CPSU. In 1971 he gained his candidate's thesis on: 'Hattic Sources of the social organisation of Ancient Hittite Society. The functions of officials with titles of Hattic origin'. Staying in Moscow for work at the same Institute of Oriental Studies for 20 years, he passed through all the stages from post-graduate to junior research worker to head of department, to which he was appointed in 1987. During this time he wrote a solid monograph on *Rituals and Myths of Old Anatolia*, published in 1982. Ardzinba had trouble with his doctoral thesis in Moscow, but the hospitable Tbilisi State University opened its door to the promising seeker of the degree, and here in Tbilisi in 1985 Ardzinba received the sought after degree of Doctor of Historical Sciences. Ardzinba's last contribution to historical science seems to have been his paper: *Towards the history of the cult of iron and blacksmith's craft (worship of the smithy among the Abkhazians, in the collection Drevnii Vostok: ethno-cultural relations* (Moscow, 1988). From this time Vladislav Grigorievich had no time for ancient cults: a different cult, that of his own power, became his major concern. In 1988 Ardzinba became the director of the Abkhazian D. Gulia Institute of Language, Literature and History, and in a couple of months (hardly having time to move from Moscow, he decided that by

his energetic measures on rallying national personnel at the Institute and involving the humanities in political debates, he had acquired enough popularity among his countrymen to run for people's deputy of the USSR. In May 1989, as a member of the group of Abkhazian deputies, he went to Moscow to take part in the 1st Congress. There it soon became clear that he might not return to Sukhumi for, as one of the four representatives (V.G. Ardzinba, R.A. Arshba, R.G. Salukvadze, K.S. Cholokyan of Abkhazia, he was elected for permanent work at the Supreme Soviet of the USSR with an appropriate salary, a flat in Moscow, and all the other amenities due to a member of the Supreme Soviet. He was appointed chairman of the sub-committee for the state and legal status of the autonomous republics, autonomous regions and districts. He could have worked here in full agreement with his superiors (Anatoly Lukyanov showed great respect for him and often did him honour by receiving him, listening to him and giving him advice) to the very end of the life of the Supreme Soviet. In Autumn 1990, senior comrades 'conferred and decided' that it was high time for Ardzinba to head the Supreme Soviet of Abkhazia. And the more unpredictable and uncontrollable the situation in Georgia seemed from Moscow - for she clearly did not intend to sign a union treaty - the greater the hopes that were pinned on Vladislav Ardzinba. He fully justified these hopes.

134.   The results of politological research are of interest (see A.Ya. Shainevich: *The Space of People's Deputies of the USSR - Analysis of voting by name at the Second and Third Congresses of People's Deputies. (Istoriya SSSR)*, N1, pages 4-40). Ardzinba held an average place in the table of tentative quantitative characteristics (sic!) of the activities of people's deputies (page 22). His opposition to the old regime is characterised by the score 100 (as compared with Gdlyan - 200), conservatism - 20, radicalism - 0, concern with the rights of republics - 40. Average oppositionist, careful populist, non-radical, sluggish conservative, he did not seem to represent any extreme force and it was precisely his averageness that made his candidature easily passable at various elections, including the elections to the post of Chairman of the Supreme Soviet of the Abkhazian SSR in December, 1990. He did not seem to be a dangerous or odious figure to anyone.

135.   Shevardnadze's address to the session of the Parliament of the Republic of Georgia. *(Demokraticheskaya Abkhazia)* 25 November 1992, page 2.

136.   The Tskhum-Abkhazian branch of the Ilia Chavchavadze Society, Tskhum-Abkhazian Bureau of the National-Democratic Party of Georgia (group 4), the Tskhum-Abkhazian Board of the Monarchist Party, the Abkhazian regional organisation of the Rustaveli Society and the Abkhazian Branch of Mkhedrioni.

137.   In December the 'Declaration' was distributed in manuscript form and xerox copies. Published in Georgia, *(Demokraticheskaya Abkhazia)* 21 October, 1992.

138.   Ibidem.

139.   A note by Ardzinba's assistant to the procurator E. Bartsits, written on the instruction of the leadership, requesting 'to decide on instituting criminal proceedings' published in *Demokraticheskaya Abkhazia*, 21 October, 1992, page 3.

140.   *How Vladislav Grigorievich and Albert Gasparovich became angry.* *(Demokraticheskaya Abkhazia)*, 27 October 1992, page 3.

141.   Shevardnadze's address to the Parliamentary Session of the Republic of Georgia, 25 November 1992, page 2.

142.   United Nations Organisation. Security Council. Preliminary shorthand account of the 3169 session (New York, 29 January 1993), pages 9-10.

143.   A xerox-copy of the decree is at the author's disposal.

144.   A xerox-copy of the letter signed by Ardzinba (reference number N15-73, 21 May 1993) is at the author's disposal.

145.   A xerox-copy of the report with a resolution in V.G. Ardzinba's hand and the appended list-calculation of 34 items of foodstuffs are at the author's disposal.

146. A xerox-copy of the decree of the Presidium of the Supreme Soviet of the Republic of Abkhazia, 31 March 1992 is at the author's disposal.

147. A xerox-copy of the document is at the author's disposal.

148. For ethical considerations these lists are not published in as much as they concern persons of different fates, their families, children, and so on.

149. A detailed study of this process is to be found in G.A. Dzidzaria's book *The Mahajir Movement and Problems of the History of Abkhazia of the 19th century*.Sukhumi, 1975.

150. This question is common to all national movements. For the sake of comparison, it may be said that the Russian democratic movement is forced to weigh carefully the reliability of allies from within the different circles, movements and waves of post-revolutionary emigration, and which phenomena of Russian emigration (E. Limonov, A. Zinovyev and like protégés) they should resolutely break with; thus leaving the Red and Brown 'patriots' from Den and Pamyat to fold them in their arms.The Crimean Tatar national movement (OKND, the Majilis of the Crimean Tatar People) must dissociate itself from the attempts of fascist, Turkic groups (like the Grey Wolves organisation) in Europe and Turkey to bring this movement under its control, etc.

151. All texts are quoted from the publications in the newspaper *Aidgylara*, 1990, N2.

152. The xerox-copy of proposals on trade deals are at the author's disposal.

153. These figures were passed on to the author by Yu.N. Voronov, Chairman of the Committee on Human Rights of the Supreme Soviet of Abkhazia, adding the conclusion: 'Such is the economic policy of Georgia in Abkhazia'. To my question: What did Georgia have to do with it as the supply of food to the population had always been within Abkhazia's competence, no answer was given.

154.   *Izvestya*, 17 July 1991, page 2.

155.   Hard times are awaiting us, says Zurab Achba, deputy of the Supreme Soviet of Abkhazia, vice-chairman of the Presidium of the People's Forum of Abkhazia Aidgylara. *(Tsbezha: Spectrum)*, 21-27 May 1992. Z. Achba knew the instability of the Abkhazian leadership. They had no support from the people nor even from the majority in parliament in which the strong Georgian democratic opposition could stop the course of the leadership towards secession from Georgia. 'The situation in parliament is a time-bomb', he said. Any attempts by the Abkhazian part of the parliament to fill the declaration on sovereignty with real content, were perceived by the Georgian deputies as a manifestation of separatism (Ibid.).

156.   Shevardnadze's address to the session of the Parliament of the Republic of Georgia. *(Demokraticheskaya Abkhazia)* 25 November 1992, page 2.

157.   Up to 15 January 1992 the Ministry of Foreign Affairs of Georgia has not received any official document about the recognition of Georgia as an independent state by the world community.

158.   Givi Lominadze. *We have Nothing to Avenge each other.* *(Svobodnaya Gruziya)*, 20 August 1992, page 2.

159.   Memorandum on events in the Abkhaz Autonomous Republic. *(Svobodnaya Gruziya)*, 20 August 1992, page 1.

160.   See O. Vasilyeva: *Georgia as a Model of Post-Communist Transformation.* Moscow 1993, page 12.

161.   T.M. Shamba: *Treaty on the principles of interrelations between the Republic of Abkhazia and the Republic of Georgia (proposals for the draft).* Abkhazia, 13 June 1992, page 1.Published also in the book: *Abkhazia. Chronicle of the Undeclared War.* Moscow 1992, page 24.

162.   'So far we are saved only by the Mingrelian cushion', Yu.N. Voronov used to say (from a record of the author's conversation with Yu.N. Voronov on 13 August 1992).

163. A record of Shevardnadze's Radio Address on 22 July 1992.

164. A xerox copy of a translation into Russian is at the author's disposal.

165. According to the Russian News Agency NEGA: Trains are still being robbed. (*Nezavisimaya Gazeta*) 12 August 1992, page 1. Ibidem. Galina Lapidus. *Georgians fire at Georgians. Extraordinary happenings on the railways.*

166. The intolerable situation obtaining in Western Georgia, which could be remedied only through the use of military force, is admitted even by outspoken opponents of Shevardnadze who accuse him of starting the war in order to put down independent Abkhazia. Thus, O. Vasilyeva quotes the following facts characterising the situation in Western Georgia on the eve of the introduction of the troops of the State Council: 'practically daily robbing of trains in which whole villages take part, attacks on the Mkhedrioni and the National Guard, the kidnapping of the Deputy Prime Minister Alexandr Kavsadze in Chkhorotsqu district on 9 July, and so on'. - O.Vasilyeva: *Georgia as a Model of Post-Communist Transformation*, Moscow, 1993, page 57.

167. See Besik Urigashvili: *Western Georgia: and permanent action?!* (*Izvestya*), 13 August 1992, page 2.

168. *Izvestiya*, 13 August 1992.

169. Quoted from the book: *Abkhazia.Chronicle of an Undeclared War.* Moscow, 1992, page 29.

170. Ibidem.

171. Ibidem.

172. Ibidem, pages 29-30.

173. A xerox-copy of the resolution is at the author's disposal.

174. O. Vasilyeva: *Georgia as a Model of Post-Communist Transformation*, Moscow, 1993, page 12.

175. Kavsadze himself, released on 19 August, told about his 40-day captivity: 'Of these 40 days I spent 37 on the territory of Abkhazia. I was openly taken from place to place... On the territory of Abkhazia terrorists moved about freely, without hiding, day and night.' *The UNO Security Council. Preliminary shorthand account of the 3169th meeting*. 29 January 1993, pages 8, 11.

176. P. Japaridze. 14 August. A clear sky over Abkhazia (an eye-witness story). (*Demokraticheskaya Abkhazia*), 26 October 1992, page 2.

177. Here and further on the document is quoted from a xerox-copy at the author's disposal. The appeal was published also in the book: *It Was So...*(compiled by S. Alieva, volume 3, Moscow, 1993, page 323).

178. Ibidem.

179. *Den*, 1992, N35, page 1.

180. See *Izvestya*, 7 April 1993, page 2.

181. The author had to leave Abkhazia on 16 August on board a military transport aircraft from the Gudauta military airfield, together with refugees from Sukhumi. She saw with her own eyes the wounded and dead who had fallen victim to Sukhumi snipers.

182. See: *Maisuradze did not fire at the 'Kometa'. (Nezavisimaya Gazeta)*, 19 September 1992, page 3.

183. Sergei Baburin: *The blood of Abkhazia is on the Kremlin.(Den)*, 30 August-5 September 1992, N35.

184. *Nezavisimaya Gazeta*, 21 August 1992, page 3.

185. A xerox-copy of the resolution is at the author's disposal.

186.   A xerox-copy of the decree is at the author's disposal.

187.   O. Suprunenko: *Russians in Sukhumi.* From a report on a trip to Georgia from 13 March to 1 April 1993. (Express-Khronika), 19-26 April 1993, N17, page 3.

188.   *Nezavisimaya Gazeta*, 30 July 1992, page 1.

189.   Dmitri Kholodov: *No one wanted to give in. (Moskovski Komsomolets)*, 29 July 1993, page 4.

Bibliography

The present list does not include the numerous newspaper articles that preceded and attended the 1992 war in Abkhazia.

1.   Abkhazia: Historical Reference, Moscow, 1992.
2.   Abkhazia: Chronicle of an undeclared war, Part I: 14 August-14 September 1992 (compiled by G. Ankvab and T. Illarionova), Moscow 1992.
3.   Avtorkhanov, Abdurrakhman: The Empire of the Kremlin, Minsk-Moscow, 1991.
4.   Anchabadze, Z.V.: On the History of Mediaeval Abkhazia, Sukhumi 1959.
5.   Anchabadze, Z.V.: The History and Culture of Ancient A bkhazia, Moscow 1964.
6.   Anchabadze, Z.V.: An Essay on the Ethnic History of the Abkhazian People, Sukhumi 1976.
7.   Anchabadze, Yu.D. Volkova, N.G.: The Peoples of the Caucasus.Book 1: The 16th-19th Century Ethnic History of the Northern Caucasus, Moscow 1993.
8.   The White Paper of Abkhazia (1992-93), Moscow 1993.
9.   Vasilyeva, Olga: Georgia as a Model of Post-Communist Transformation, Moscow 1993.
10.   Vorobyev, N.O.: On the Untenability of the Claims of the Georgians to Sukhumi District (Abkhazia), Rostov-on-Don 1919.
11.   Voronov, L.: Abkhazia is not Georgia, 1907.
12.   Voronov, Yu.N.: The Russian Diaspora in Abkhazia: History and the Present. In: Russia and the East. Problems of Interaction, Moscow 1992.
13.   Danilov, S.: The Tragedy of the Abkhazian People. In: Herald of the Institute for the Study of the History and Culture in the USSR (Munich) 1951, N1.

14.   Gulia, D.I.: A History of Abkhazia, Tbilisi 1925.

15.   Gogua, Alexei: Our Concern. In: Druzhba Narodov, N5, 1989.

16.   Javakhishvili, I. Janashia, S. Berdzenishvili: A History of Georgia, Tbilisi 1946.

17.   Dzidzaria, G.A.: Essays on the History of Abkhazia (1910-1921), Tbilisi 1963.

18.   Inal-Ipa, Sh. D.: The Abkhazians: Historico-Ethnographic Essays, Sukhumi 1965.

19.   Inal-Ipa, Sh. D.: Questions of the Ethnocultural History of the Abkhazians, Sukhumi 1965.

20.   A History of Abkhazia (textbook), Sukhumi 1992.

21.   Towards the National Composition of the Republic of Georgia (Information Material), Tbilisi 1993.

22.   Bloody Separatism.What happened in Abkhazia, Tbilisi 1993.

23.   Lezhava, G.P.: Change of the Class and National Structure of the Population of Abkhazia (End of 19th century to the 1970s), Sukhumi 1989.

24.   Lordkipanidze, M.: Abkhazia and the Abkhazians, Tbilisi 1990.

25.   Melikishvili, G.A.: The Political Unification of Feudal Georgia and Some Questions of the Development of Feudal Relations in Georgia, Tbilisi 1973.

26.   Menteshashvili, A.: On the History of the Interrelations of the Georgian, Abkhazian and Ossetian Peoples (1918-1921), Tbilisi 1990.

27.   Menteshashvili, A. and Surguladze, A.: Only Facts and Documents, Literaturnaya Gruziya, 1989, N11.

28   Miminoshvili, Roman and Panjikidze, Curam: The Truth about Abkhazia, Tbilisi 1990.

29.   Lakoba, Stanislav: Essays on the Political History of Abkhazia, Sukhumi 1990.

30.   Essays on the History of the Abkhazian SSR, Part I, Sukhumi 1960.

31.   Popov, Arkadi: Who will stop the 'Party of War'? - A Year after August. Bitterness and Choice. Collected papers and interviews, Moscow 1992.

32.   Sagharia, B.E: The National-State Construction in Abkhazia (1921-1931), Sukhumi 1970.

33.   Smirnova, Ya. S: The Abkhazians.In: The Peoples of the World, Historico-Ethnographic Reference, Moscow 1988.

34.   Fedorov, Ya. A: Historical Ethnography of the Northern Caucasus, Moscow 1983.

35.   Khoshtaria-Brosset, E.V.: Interethnic Relations in Georgia (the causes of conflicts and ways of overcoming them), Tbilisi 1993.

36.   What is to be Done? In Search of Ideas for the Perfection of Inter-ethnic Relations, Moscow 1989.

37.   The Ethnocontact Zones in the European Part of the USSR (geography, dynamics, methods of study), Moscow 1983.

38.   Akiner Shirin: Islamic Peoples of the Soviet Union, London 1983.

39.   Bennigsen, Alexandre: Les Musulmans Oubliés. L'Islam en Union Sovietique, Paris 1981.

40.   Darell Slider: Crisis and Response in Soviet Nationality Policy: the Case of Abkhazia, Central Asian Survey, 1985 N4.

41.   Die Muslime in der Sowjetunion und in Jugoslawien. Identitat, Politik, Widerstand, Kîln 1989.

42.   Hallbach Uve: Die Bergvîlker (gorcy) als Gegner und Opfer: der Kaukasus in der Wahrnehmung Russlands (Ende des 18 Jahrhunderts bis 1864) - Kleine Volker in der Geschichte Osteuropas, Stuttgart 1991.

43.   Kappeler, Andreas: Russland als Vielvolkerreich. Entstehung. Geschichte.Zerfall, Munchen 1993.

44.   Lakoba, S.Z.: On the Political Problems of Abkhazia - Central Asia and Caucasus Chronicle, 1990, Volume 4, N4.

45.   Lang, David Marshall: A Modern History of Georgia, London 1962.

46.   Menteshashvili, Avtandil: Some National and Ethnic Problems in Georgia, Tbilisi 1992.

47.   Nahaylo, Bohdan Swoboda, Victor: Soviet Disunion. A History of the Nationality Problem in the USSR, London 1990.

48.   Rhinelander, Laurens Hamilton: The Incorporation of the Caucasus into the Russian Empire: the case of Georgia, 1801 - 1854, Columbia University 1975.

49.   Salia, Kalistrat: History of the Georgian Nation, Paris 1983.

50.   Simon, Gerhard: Nationalismus und Nationalitenpolitik in der Sowjetunion.

51.   Labakhia, Z.A.: The Georgian Abkhaz War. Documents and Letters 1992-3. Moscow 1994.
52.   Ed.Kavsadze A., compiled by Putkharadze D., Beridse D.: Bloody Separatism.What happened in Abkhazia, Tbilisi 1980.
53.   Khashtaria - Brosse, E.V.: Inter-Ethnic Relations in Georgia, Tbilisi 1993.
54.   Menteshashvili, A: From the History of the Interrelations of the Georgians, Abkhaz and Ossetian people, Tbilisi 1990.

Note: The titles from 1 to 37 are in Russian.

Index